AUSTRALIA'S & NEW ZEALAND'S

Seafood Down under

A FISHING, COOKING & PICTORIAL BOOK
TO EVERYONE'S TASTE

HARPER MACRAE
AUSTRALIA Pty Limited
(A.C.N. 051 298 769)
PUBLISHERS

Big red Crayfish. These magnificent specimens come from the Half Moon Reef. Abrolhos Archipelago, W.A.

Published by:
HARPER MACRAE AUSTRALIA
PTY LIMITED
Unit 3, 181 McCredie Rd Guildford NSW 2161 Australia
Telephone: (02) 892 3122 Facsimile: (02) 892 3126

CONCEPT:	Mark Swadling
CREATIVE DIRECTION of Art, Photography and Production:	Jon Terpstra
ART AND ASSEMBLY:	Jon Puckridge
FOOD WRITERS:	Cheryl Goodman (Deasey)
	Tess Mallos
HOME ECONOMISTS:	Tess Mallos
	Sue Forster-Wright
	Kathryn Munro
FOOD EDITOR:	Tess Mallos
PHOTOGRAPHY (Food):	Howard Jones
INTRODUCTIONS AND SPECIES:	Mark Swadling
STYLIST AND PROPS:	Sue Forster-Wright
	Kathryn Munro
PRODUCTION:	Gas Graphics TGC
	Pty Limited
	Kay Osborne
COLOUR SEPARATION:	Prestige Colour Overseas Graphic Sdn. Bhd.
	27, Jln Kampong Pasir, Jln. Klang,
	Kuala Lumpur, 58200 Malaysia.
	Tel: 03-7919906 Fax: 603-7916529
PRINTING:	Globe Press Pty. Ltd.
	50 Weston Street, Brunswick,Vic. 3056, Australia.

National Library of Australia
Cataloguing-In-Publication Data
"Australia and New Zealand's Seafood Down Under
A Fishing, Cooking and Pictorial Book To Everyone's Taste"
Includes Index
ISBN 0 9588122 3 3.
1. Fishing — Australia. 2. Fishing — New Zealand.
3. Cookery (Seafood). 4. Cookery (Fish).
5. Cookery (Shellfish).

Rusty, beached boat. Fraser Island, Qld.

Foreword

Following the worldwide success of "The Australian Heritage Cookbook" it was only natural that the special qualities of that book should be applied to a seafood project. After all, the seafood found "Downunder" ranks with the best in the world.

"Australia and New Zealand's Seafood Downunder" is truly a pictorial cookbook to *everyone's* taste. The waters of Australia and New Zealand carry an incredibly diverse array of fish species and this book provides an invaluable guide to a broad selection of these, as well as presenting an outstanding collection of ravishing recipes to please the most difficult palate.

Of all nature's great bounties, perhaps it is the food we may so easily obtain from the world's oceans, lakes and rivers that is the greatest of all. In seafood we have an enormous diversity of flavour, colour and texture, providing one of the most interesting culinary groupings. More importantly, perhaps, we have in seafood a tremendous source of protein, vitamins and minerals, which is low in fats and calories. In short, we have what we've always been taught is impossible: something that tastes good and is good for us as well!

It's not without good reason that seafood is so popular — just as popular, we're sure, as "Seafood Downunder" will prove to be in your kitchen.

Good reading, fine cooking!

R & K Osborne
for the Publishers

A Shark is a match for this fisherman.

AUSTRALIA'S & NEW ZEALAND'S

Seafood Downunder

A FISHING, COOKING & PICTORIAL BOOK TO EVERYONE'S TASTE

HARPER MACRAE
AUSTRALIA Pty Limited
(A.C.N. 051 298 769)
PUBLISHERS

Diver admiring spectacular Fan Coral.

A salt water Crocodile settles down to dinner. Prince Regent River, W.A.

Contents

Contents

Sailing on the beautiful waters of Perth, W.A.

Rustic autumn colours surrounding Lake Hayes, Queenstown, New Zealand.

Introduction

The world's vast and mysterious oceans, seas, rivers and lakes together make an astonishing kitchen touched by magic. No other food supply meeting the daily needs of this planet automatically regenerates almost totally without human assistance. Indeed this amazing submerged basket of nutrients replaces itself despite the often irresponsible and indulgent way we dip into it with anything from a single hook to devastating 50km-long nets.

In many parts of our so-called civilised world we take food supply so much for granted that we are beginning to regard the whole subject of food as an inconvenience, a daily chore. How far removed we are from our hunter/gatherer ancestry

This book is designed to give the reader much more than mere instruction on how to create a seafood meal. It gives a rare insight into the underwater source itself.

On Page 20, for example, is an introduction entitled "About Fish", a guide to more than 150 edible marine species illustrated by truly brilliant living colour photographs. The guide is a lesson in the learning and has been thoughtfully cross-referenced with the recipes to help the enthusiast cook apply new knowledge and understanding to the creation of magnificent seafood meals.

Page 122 marks the beginning of the recipes. This section has been divided into 12 chapters, all representative of a particular style or zone of seafood. You will find the recipes all quick and easy to prepare, yet extremely tasty and exciting. However, it is recognised that, while a seafood dish is planned for a meal, you might prefer a non-seafood starter, and for certain you'll want a dessert! Such recipes are also included in each chapter. All the recipes have been thoroughly tested and the tantalising food photography captures some of the results "in-the-flesh".

The skills of our talented Art Director have been utilised to their fullest in producing a very modern, easy to follow format for the recipe layout — which is also very easy on the eyes — a great plus for the busy cook on the go!

As well as being both a brilliant cookbook and a comprehensive guide to fish species, "Australia and New Zealand's Seafood Downunder" may also be used as a standard reference for many other related topics.

Turn to page 312 and you will come to the beginning of an extremely instructive and detailed Food Preparation and Storage Guide. The extent and scope of this book is truly astounding!

The scenic photographs throughout these pages are not only stunning, they also provide another valuable source of information. From them we are able to see exactly what type of environment, both from above and below, the fish inhabit, and so appreciate that underneath the "postcard prettiness" of each shot there exists the intricate web of nature's plan — a plan that includes us all, a plan which, hopefully, we will all learn to respect.

Tess Mallos
AND
Sue Forster-Wright
Home Economists

One of the many lovable Seals at Seal Bay, Kangaroo Island.

The world famous Dolphins of Monkey Mia, W.A.

"About the Fish"

"About the Fish" is an interesting and informative directory to 47 listings of fish and shellfish which covers over 150 species.

In compiling this section, emphasis was placed on presenting the information in an easy to follow format. The names are presented in tabular form and the information under the headings: "Description", "Habitat", "Underwater Behaviour" and "Table Qualities" is presented in note form for ease of reading.

Fish nomenclature is often a confusing business — the variation in names within Australia alone is enormous — so comparing the names used in three countries presented quite a challenge.

The use of Scientific Names is limited to giving the Family name, except in some cases where the Species name is mentioned in the Comments. These names are only listed for reference and it is not anticipated that too much attention would need to be given to them. More important are the common names for each country, which are quite often very different as, for example, "Snapper" is a name which, in the US, describes an entirely different fish to that described in Australia and New Zealand.

There are several Australian species which are not found in the US or NZ. In such cases, the nearest equivalent fish is given, so that it may be substituted in the relevant recipes. In a few cases there is no near equivalent and "not found" is written.

You will notice that each species has been cross-referenced to the recipe section so that once you have learnt a little about the fish you can immediately find some fantastic recipe to cook it!

The photography in this section is nothing short of superb — the underwater shots allowing us a rare and clear glimpse of the fish in their natural habitat. The scenic shots "complete the picture" in presenting the total environment in spectacular form.

Over the page there is a handy reference section showing relevant parts of a fish and how they are described.

This diver explores a magnificent reef.

An explosion of sealife colours.

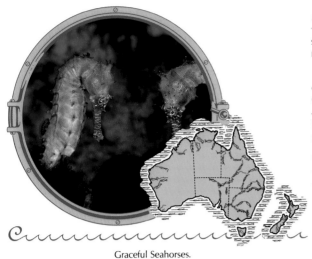

Graceful Seahorses.

What is a Fish?

A fish is a cold-blooded vertebrate that lives in the water and breathes with gills. It has fins rather than legs.

There are three major classes of fish: Jawless Fish (lampreys and hagfishes); Cartilaginous Fish (sharks, skates and rays) and Bony Fish. About 20,000 species are known to exist worldwide and 97% of them are Bony Fish.

Mouths & Snouts

superior mouth
eg GOLDEN PERCH

inferior mouth
eg ANCHOVY

terminal mouth
eg CORAL TROUT

subterminal mouth
eg LUDERICK

pointed snout
eg GROPER

sword-like snout
eg SWORDFISH

Bodies

ovate
eg DORY

fusiform
eg ATLANTIC SALMON

elongate
eg TAILOR

eel-like
eg EEL

depressed
eg SKATE

hemispherical
eg GROPER

compressed
eg TAILOR

Caudal Fins

forked caudal fin
eg TAILOR

lunate caudal fin
eg COBIA

emarginate caudal fin
eg ATLANTIC SALMON

truncate caudal fin
eg CATFISH

rounded caudal fin
eg LING

pointed tail
eg EEL

Parts of a Fish
Lateral View

spiny rays of dorsal fin
opercle
nape
eye
nostril
snout
lower lip
lower jaw
cheek
gill membrane
pelvic fin
pectoral fin

dorsal fin

branched ray
soft rays of dorsal fin
lateral line
adipose fin
caudal fin
anal fin

Anchovy
Engraulidae

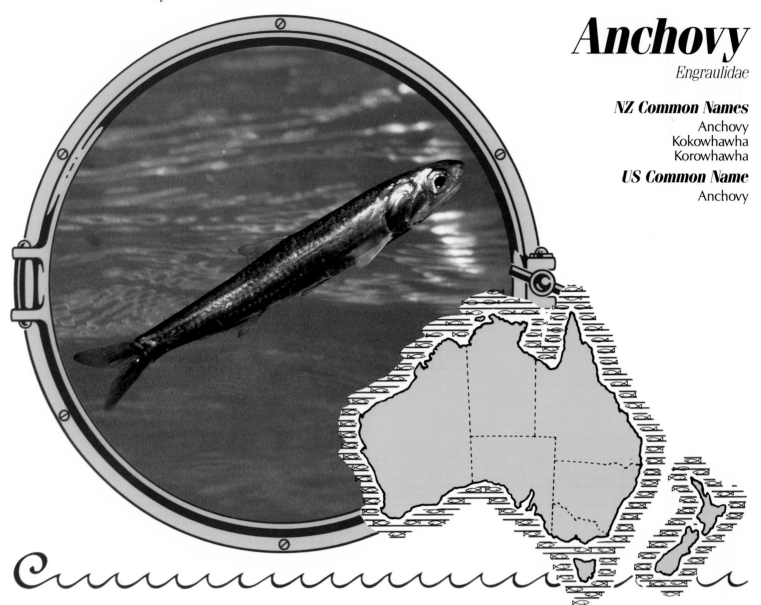

NZ Common Names
Anchovy
Kokowhawha
Korowhawha

US Common Name
Anchovy

Description

Conical snout, inferior mouth. Large mouth which extends beyond the large eye. Colouration almost entirely silver, with brighter silver mid-lateral band. Maximum length 15cm (6 inches).

Habitat

Almost entirely saltwater; some species may enter freshwater. More numerous in warmer climates. Found in large estuaries and shallow coastal waters to a depth of 64m (210 feet).

Underwater Behaviour

Extremely gregarious. Occurring in very large, tightly packed shoals. Plankton feeders, they are a prime source of food for many larger fish such as Mackerels.

Table Qualities

Traditionally Anchovies are processed as an essence or paste, or preserved in oil or salt, for various culinary purposes. However, use of the fresh fish is increasing as its distinct, rather strong flavour gains wider acceptance. The flesh is dark, soft and oily and cooks quickly. Fry, grill, barbecue or bake.

Recipes
Entrée/Appetizer:
pages 140, 287
Main: page 145

Comments

Not to be confused with Pilchards (US Sardines) or Herrings which are from different families.

Moray Eel, Hennand Island, New Zealand.

The Lion Fish, sometimes called Butterfly Scorpion Fish, is a pretty sight. But never try to pet him. His spines are highly venomous.

Barramundi
Percidae

Other Common Names
Giant Perch

NZ Common Name
Not Found

US Equivalent
Snook

Description

Large mouth with projecting lower jaw. Pointed snout. Long, compressed body. Colouration mainly silver with dark and yellow markings across midriff and on fins. Up to 1.5m (5 feet) in length.

Habitat

Shallow coastal waters, estuaries. Also upstream, generally in brackish or fresh water within tidal influence. Found almost exclusively in tropical waters.

Underwater Behaviour

Highly active foragers, feeding on fish and crustaceans. At the top of the food chain in their natural habitat, they generally feed alone.

Table Qualities

Highly sought-after table fish, the white, moist flesh is subtly flavoured and has a large flake. Use whole or in fillets. Skin fillets before cooking and score if very thick. Fry, grill, barbecue, bake, poach or steam.

Recipes
Entrée/Appetizer: page 140
Main: pages 144, 145, 291

Comments

Not to be confused with the unrelated "Dawson River" Barramundi otherwise known as Saratoga. The US Snook is unrelated but occupies a similar habitat and is similar in appearance and behaviour.

A Feather Star, Great Barrier Reef, Qld.

Sunrise on the yellow waters of Kakadu National Park, N.T.

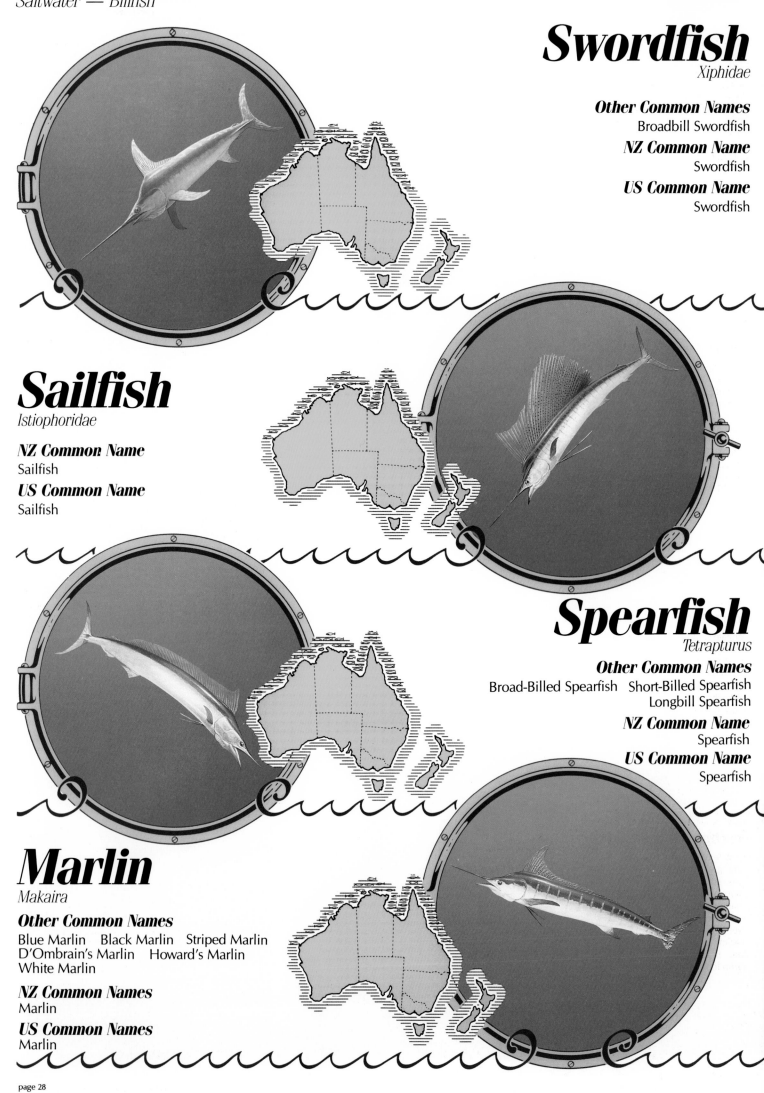

Swordfish
Xiphidae

Other Common Names
Broadbill Swordfish
NZ Common Name
Swordfish
US Common Name
Swordfish

Sailfish
Istiophoridae

NZ Common Name
Sailfish
US Common Name
Sailfish

Spearfish
Tetrapturus

Other Common Names
Broad-Billed Spearfish   Short-Billed Spearfish
Longbill Spearfish
NZ Common Name
Spearfish
US Common Name
Spearfish

Marlin
Makaira

Other Common Names
Blue Marlin   Black Marlin   Striped Marlin
D'Ombrain's Marlin   Howard's Marlin
White Marlin

NZ Common Names
Marlin

US Common Names
Marlin

Description

Long snout forming a flat sword. No teeth. No pelvic fin or scales in adults. Dark grey to black on top, lighter below. Up to 4.6m (15 feet).

Habitat

Both coastal waters and open seas to 60m (200 feet). Mainly tropical to temperate waters.

Underwater Behaviour

Fast swimmers with migratory habits. Feed on crustaceans and smaller fish, mainly Mackerel. Have been known to attack boats with sword, perhaps mistaking them for whales.

Table Qualities

Swordfish are highly sought-after commercially. Firm, white flesh with a distinct flavour. Usually sold in cutlets or steaks. Ideal for grilling or the barbecue, especially if prepared as kebabs. Can also be fried, baked or poached.

Recipes
Main: pages 212, 293

Description

Long snout forming a sword. Jaws with teeth. Scales present. Dorsal fins enlarged and retractable into grooves. Dark blue above, silver below. Up to 3.3m (11 feet).

Habitat

Surface to mid-depth in open seas. Tropical to temperate waters.

Underwater Behaviour

Fast swimmers. Feed on smaller fish, quite often forming groups to round up large schools.

Table Qualities

Sailfish are not fished commercially or particularly sought-after for the table.

Recipes
Main: page 293

Description

Elongate snout forming spear. Dense scales. Dark blue above, browny white on sides, silver below. Up to 1.8m (6 feet).

Habitat

Usually found near the surface in open seas. Tropical to temperate waters.

Underwater Behaviour

Fast swimmers. Feed on smaller fish.

Table Qualities

Spearfish, like Sailfish, are not particularly sought-after for the table.

Recipes
Main: page 293

Description

Elongate snout forming spear. Dense scales. Colouration usually blue or brown above, silver below. Up to 4.5m (15 feet). (Some Black Marlin longer.)

Habitat

Surface to mid-depth in open seas. Tropical to temperate waters.

Underwater Behaviour

Usually travel alone or in pairs — sometimes in small groups. Feed on small fish and larger crustaceans near the surface. Extremely fast swimmers with migratory habits.

Table Qualities

Marlin has high commercial value to Japan and Korea, where it is used fresh or processed. Some species are possibly endangered so not recommended for the table.

Recipes
Main: page 212

Comments

Marlin: Five species known in Australian and NZ waters: Blue Marlin, Black Marlin, Striped Marlin, Howard's Marlin and D'Ombrain's Marlin. Another species known in the US: White Marlin.

A spectacular view of Coromandel, New Zealand.

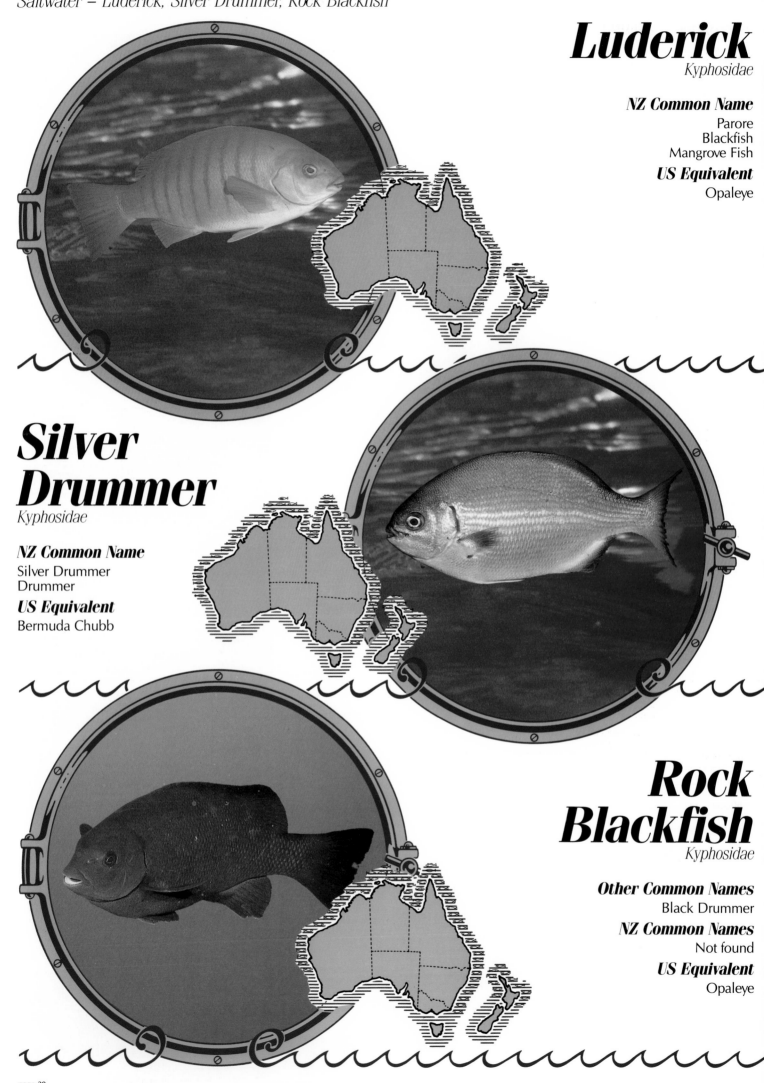

Luderick
Kyphosidae

NZ Common Name
Parore
Blackfish
Mangrove Fish

US Equivalent
Opaleye

Silver
Drummer
Kyphosidae

NZ Common Name
Silver Drummer
Drummer

US Equivalent
Bermuda Chubb

Rock
Blackfish
Kyphosidae

Other Common Names
Black Drummer

NZ Common Names
Not found

US Equivalent
Opaleye

Description

Small head, subterminal mouth. Deep, compressed body. Prominent scales. Dark olive green with vertical bars along body. Up to 51cm (1 foot 8 inches).

Habitat

Coastal reefs and estuaries to depths of 25m (83 feet).

Underwater Behaviour

Mainly herbivorous, feeding on various algae, occasionally feeding on Prawns and other crustaceans. A shy fish occurring in schools.

Table Qualities

The following fish, particularly the Silver Drummer, should be bled as soon as they are caught to decrease the weedy, earthy flavour. Flesh is soft, moist, oily and grey-pink in colour, changing to white when cooked. Flavour is distinct. Usually sold whole; best to fillet and remove skin as it is tough. The fat layer comes away with the skin. Fry in a small amount of oil or grill, barbecue or bake. Takes well to strong flavours.

Recipes
Main: pages 177, 229

Comments

Bermuda Chubb and Opaleye are slightly different to Australian species, but very similar in most respects and are of the same family.

Description

Small head and mouth. Deep, compressed body. Prominent scales. Dark silver to green/grey. Up to 75cm (2 feet 6 inches).

Habitat

Coastal reefs to depths of 35m (117 feet).

Underwater Behaviour

See above.

Table Qualities

See above

Recipes
Main: pages 177, 229

Comments

See above

Description

Small head and mouth. Deep, compressed body. Prominent scales. Black to dark brown. Up to 60cm (2 feet).

Habitat

Coastal reefs to depths of 25m (83 feet).

Underwater Behaviour

See above.

Table Qualities

See above.

Recipes
Main: pages 177, 229

Comments

See above.

'Peek a boo'.

Bream
Sparidae

Species
Black Bream   Pikey Bream   Southern Bream
Tarwhine   Yellowfin Bream

Other Common Names
Silver Bream

NZ Common Name
Not found

US Equivalent
Porgy

A serene morning spot near Port Douglas, Qld.

Description

Large head with steep profiled snout; single dorsal fin, long pectoral fins; silver to black; strong, fine teeth protruding from lips. Up to 60cm (2 feet) in length.

Habitat

Extremely varied; from offshore rocky reefs, to oceans and beaches, to high up in tidal estuaries. May enter and live in fresh water. Depth range to 25m (83 feet).

Underwater Behaviour

A very cunning and fast moving fish. Mostly bottom feeders. They will seek out shallow waters on moonless nights. Feed generally in small groups.

Table Qualities

Considered one of Australia's finest table fish. Flesh is white, with a fine texture and sweet flavour. Use whole or in fillets. Fry, grill, barbecue, bake or poach. Should be slightly undercooked to keep flesh moist.

Recipes
Entrée/Appetizer: page 204
Main: pages 157, 160, 228, 292

Comments

Porgies have a slightly different appearance to Australian Bream but are very similar and are members of the same family. "Bream" in NZ is used to describe the Snapper and the Luderick (Parore), while in Europe and the UK it describes a freshwater Carp.

A great place to relax in the waters of 'The Entrance', central coast, NSW.

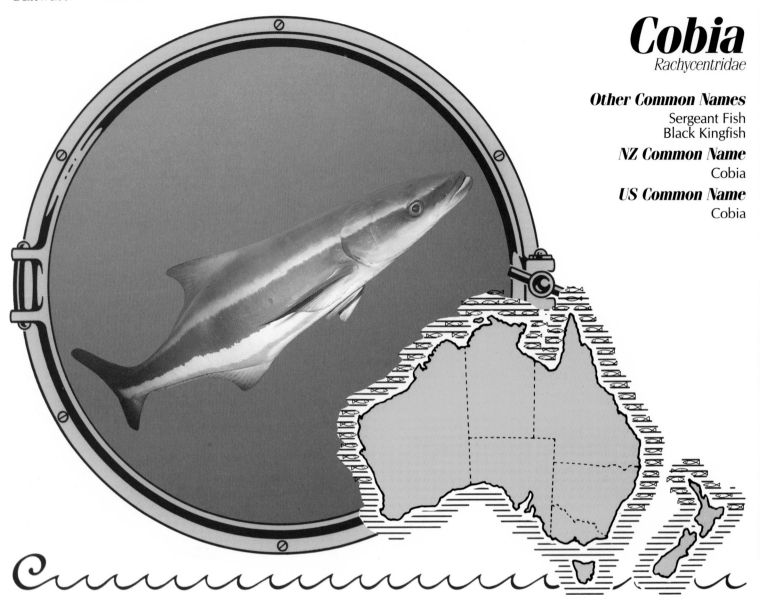

Cobia
Rachycentridae

Other Common Names
Sergeant Fish
Black Kingfish

NZ Common Name
Cobia

US Common Name
Cobia

Description
Elongate, almost cylindrical body. Large, broad, flattened head. Large mouth. First dorsal fin consists of 7-9 separate spines. Dark brown above, with 2 silvery lateral bands, yellowish/grey underside. Lunate caudal fin. Up to 2m (6 feet 7 inches).

Habitat
Open seas, island shores, reefs. Mainly tropical waters.

Underwater Behaviour
Usually feed by lingering around larger fish for food scraps. Often seen basking on the surface near boats or flotsam.

Recipes
Main: pages 129, 132

Table Qualities
Not a common table fish, but good to eat. Prepare in large, skinless fillets and slice these obliquely into steaks. Flesh is white and soft in texture, with a mild flavour. Fry, grill, barbecue or bake.

Comments
Represented by a single species worldwide — Rachycentron canadum.

Nudi Branch, Port Stephens, NSW.

A scenic outlook over the ocean surrounding North Stradbroke Island, Qld.

Coral Trout
Lutjanidae
Other Common Names
Leopard Cod
NZ Common Name
Not found
US Equivalent
Snapper

Description

Strong, sharp teeth. Large terminal mouth. Single, continuous dorsal fin. Small scales cover body except between mouth and eyes. Varying shades of red with blueish spots. Up to 90cm (3 feet).

Habitat

Found over coral and rocky reefs in tropical waters; sometimes off the continental shelf in open sea to depths of 180m (600 feet).

Underwater Behaviour

Feed in small schools on small fish.

Table Qualities

Sought-after table fish; white flesh is firm and moist, with a mild, slightly sweet flavour. Use whole or in fillets. Fry, grill, barbecue, bake, poach or steam. It is just as well to favour smaller Coral Trout for the table as large fish have occasionally been implicated in ciguatera poisoning — a result of eating smaller fish which have fed on organisms found on damaged coral, though this is highly unusual.

Recipes
Main: pages 128, 132

Comments

This particular species (Plectropoma maculatum) not found in the US. The US Snapper are all members of the same family and are very similar in all respects.

An underwater cave with beautiful blooming gorgonias.

Serene sunset over the waters of Lizard Island, Qld.

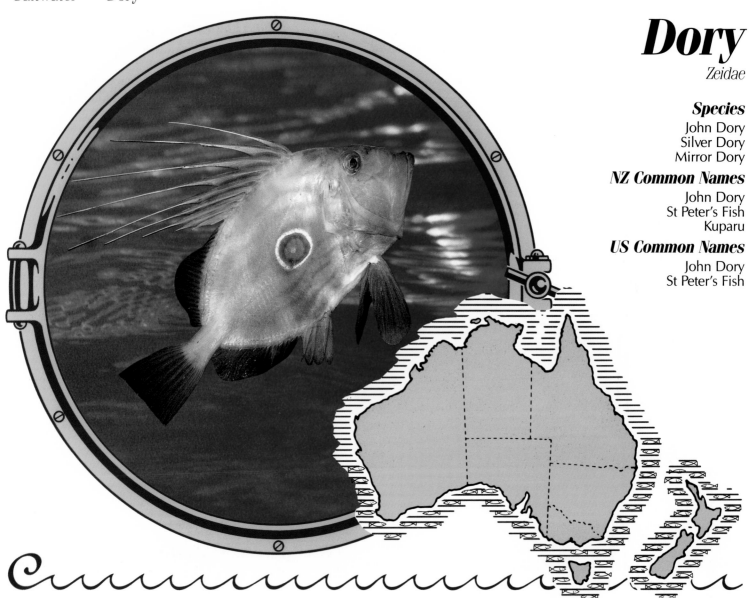

Dory
Zeidae

Species
John Dory
Silver Dory
Mirror Dory

NZ Common Names
John Dory
St Peter's Fish
Kuparu

US Common Names
John Dory
St Peter's Fish

Description
Pointed snout. Ovate, compressed body. Elongated spiny rays of dorsal fin. Mainly silvery species, (John Dory has a large yellow outlined black spot on either side of its body). Up to 60cm (2 feet) in length.

Habitat
Commonly found on offshore reefs; John Dory move into large estuaries and harbours around springtime.

Underwater Behaviour
Slow, sluggish swimmers; feed mainly on smaller fish by drifting close and snapping open extendible jaws to capture prey whole. Depth range to 100m (330 feet).

Table Qualities
One of the finest table fish; flesh is firm, white and finely textured, with a delicate, sweet flavour. Silver and Mirror Dory vary a little in texture and flavour. Use whole or in fillets. Fry, grill, barbecue, bake, poach or steam.

Recipes
Entrée/Appetizer: pages 204, 224
Main: pages 160, 210, 230

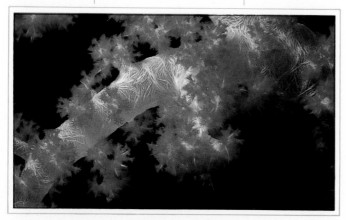

Spectacular Soft Coral on the Great Barrier Reef, Qld.

One of the many bushy Coral Atolls dotting the Queensland coast.

Emperor/Sea Perch
Lethrindae/Lutjanidae

Species
Red Emperor   Sweetlip Emperor
Spangled Emperor   Red-Finned Emperor
Scarlet Sea Perch   Mangrove Jack
Moses Perch   Striped Sea Perch

Other Common Names
See Comments

NZ Common Name
Not found

US Equivalent
Snapper
(See Comments)

'King of the Castle' in full splendour.

Description

Large mouth. Moderately compressed bodies. Brightly marked and coloured (from salmon pink in the case of the Red Emperor to olive green for the Sweetlip Emperor). Up to 1m (3 feet 3 inches).

Habitat

Coastal reefs to continental slope; tropical to temperate waters. Depth range to 180-200m (600-670 feet).

Underwater Behaviour

Feed in small schools on smaller fish and crustaceans.

Table Qualities

Excellent table fish with firm, white to pinkish flesh and a mild, sweet flavour. Use whole or in fillets. Fry, grill, barbecue, bake, poach or steam.

Recipes
Main: pages 129, 132, 195, 287, 291

Comments

This group of fish has suffered from a multitude of misnaming. Misleading names such as Red Bream, Red Snapper and Red Jew are used in some parts of Australia to describe some of these species. The US Snapper are members of the Lutjanidae family, as are the Australian Red Emperor, Scarlet Sea Perch, Striped Sea Perch and Moses Perch. The other Australian species are of the Lethrindae family and are very similar in all respects.

Sunset at Koolan Island, off the Kimberley coast, W.A.

Flathead
Platycephalus

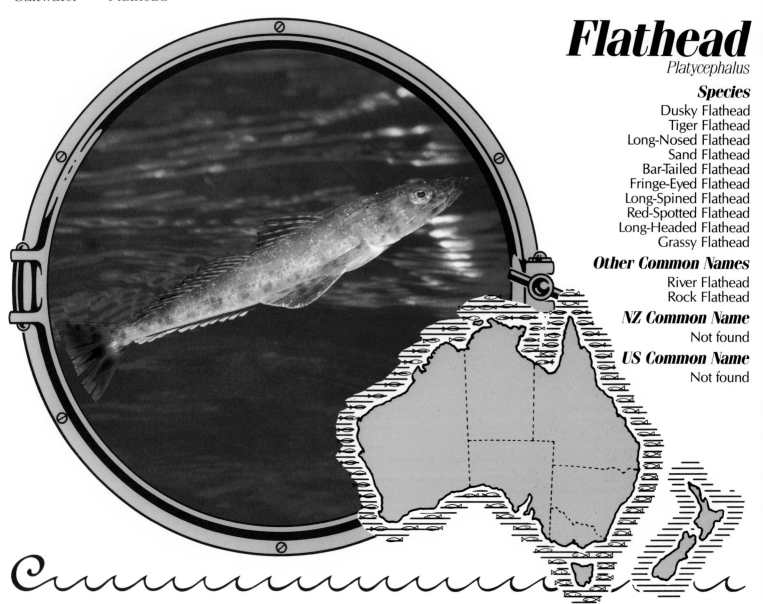

Species
Dusky Flathead
Tiger Flathead
Long-Nosed Flathead
Sand Flathead
Bar-Tailed Flathead
Fringe-Eyed Flathead
Long-Spined Flathead
Red-Spotted Flathead
Long-Headed Flathead
Grassy Flathead

Other Common Names
River Flathead
Rock Flathead

NZ Common Name
Not found

US Common Name
Not found

Description
Flattened, depressed head. Elongate, depressed body. Sharp spines at either side of head. Varying mottled markings. Up to 1.2m (4 feet), (Dusky Flathead).

Habitat
Bottom dwellers in estuaries and off-shore sand flats.

Underwater Behaviour
Feed by lying camouflaged on the bottom and ambushing their prey.

Table Qualities
An excellent table fish; has a mild flavour with firm, white flesh, fine in texture but can be dry. Use whole or in fillets. Fry, bake, poach or steam, taking care not to overcook. Can be barbecued if cooked on an oiled hotplate.

Recipes
Entrée/Appetizer: pages 189, 204
Main: pages 195, 230, 307

Comments
There is no near equivalent to these fish in the US or in New Zealand.

Fishing is a popular pastime around Sydney Harbour, NSW.

A 250 kilo spotted Cod makes a spectacular pet for a diver. Rowley Shoals, W.A.

Flounder
Bothidae/Pleuronectidae

Species
Large-Toothed Flounder   Greenback Flounder
Small-Toothed Flounder   Long-Snouted Flounder

NZ Equivalent
Black Flounder   Greenback Flounder
Sand Flounder   Yellowbelly Flounder
New Zealand Sole

US Equivalent
Three-Eye Flounder
Spotfin Flounder
Gulf Flounder
Diamond Turbot

Description

Small head, both eyes on one side. Deep, compressed body. Upper side of body usually brownish with markings; lower side white. Most species quite small, less than 30cm (1 foot); some larger, up to 60cm (2 feet). There are no very large species as found in Europe and US where they can reach lengths of up to 2.4m (8 feet).

Habitat

Bottom dwellers, usually on sand or mud flats to depths of 70m (233 feet).

Underwater Behaviour

Feed on worms, small crustaceans and molluscs. Effectively use camouflage, changing colour to match immediate environment.

Biscuit Sea Star (Vermillion Sea Star), Jarvis Bay, NSW.

Table Qualities

Excellent eating fish, with firm, white flesh and a delicate flavour. Use whole or in fillets, with or without skin. Grilled fish can be skinned on one side only, with this side presented on the plate. Fry, grill, barbecue, bake, poach or steam.

Recipes
Main: pages 213, 307

Comments

Numerous species of Flounder exist in Australian and NZ waters. More abundant in NZ where they are caught in commercial quantities. Members of Bothidae family are known as Lefteye Flounder and those of Pleuronectidae family as Righteye Flounder. In the US, the large California Halibut is a member of the former family, whilst the giant Pacific Halibut is a member of the latter. Sole are very similar to Flounder but are members of a different family — Soleidae. They are not commonly found in the markets.

An elevated view of the beautiful Auckland skyline, New Zealand.

Garfish
Exocoetidae

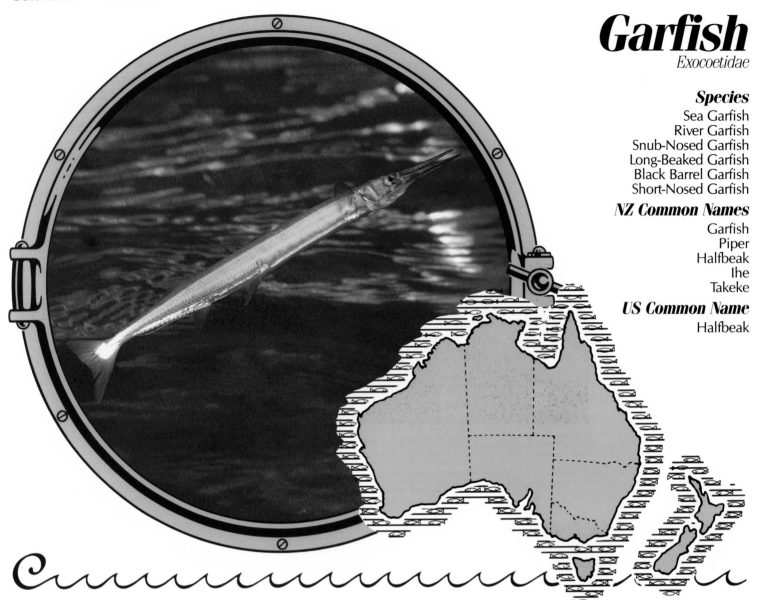

Species
Sea Garfish
River Garfish
Snub-Nosed Garfish
Long-Beaked Garfish
Black Barrel Garfish
Short-Nosed Garfish

NZ Common Names
Garfish
Piper
Halfbeak
Ihe
Takeke

US Common Name
Halfbeak

Description
Very elongate body. Lower jaw very long, extending into a needle point. Dorsal and anal fins opposite each other. Green/silver upper body; silvery below. Up to 45cm (1 foot 6 inches).

Habitat
Warmer seas. Usually on surface near shoreline, occasionally in estuaries. (River Garfish almost exclusively in estuaries.)

Underwater Behaviour
Herbivorous, feeding on microscopic vegetable matter near the surface. Large schools. Commonly eaten by large species such as Billfishes, Dolphins and Tuna.

Table Qualities
Very good eating, though the fine bones are considered a nuisance by many. White, fine textured, soft flesh with a sweet flavour. Use whole with backbone removed to stuff or butterfly. Fry, grill, barbecue or bake.

Recipes
Entrée/Appetizer:
page 273
Main: pages 277, 292

An elegant Flat Worm, Great Barrier Reef, Qld.

The famous Port Campbell cliffs, Vic.

Gemfish
Gempylidae

Other Common Names
King Barracouta
Hake   (See Comments)

NZ Common Names
Gemfish   Tikati
Silver Kingfish

US Common Name
Not found

Commercial Fishing fleet at sunny Cairns, Nth. Qld.

Description

Pointed snout; large eyes. Elongate body. Forked caudal fin. Silvery blue. Up to 1m (3 feet 4 inches).

Habitat

Deep sea fish to 600m (2000 feet).

Underwater Behaviour

Feed on smaller fish and crustaceans. Fast swimmers. Large schools.

Table Qualities

Very popular table fish. Flesh is creamy pink, moist and firm, with a mild flavour and large flake. It is a very important commercial catch in South-East Australia. Available in fillets or cutlets. Fillets can be skinned; thick fillets should be scored for even heat penetration. Also available smoked. Shallow fry, grill, barbecue, bake, poach or steam. Poach smoked Gemfish.

Recipes
Entrée/Appetizer: page 272
Main: page 277

Comments

This species (Rexea solandri) is no relation to the US Barracouta or Hake.

The cold eye and needle teeth of a Grey-nurse Shark belie its romantic nature, Moreton Bay, Qld.

Goatfish
Mullidae

Species
Blackspot Goatfish
Mottled Goatfish
Yellow Goatfish

Other Common Names
Red Mullet
Barbunya

NZ Common Names
Red Mullet
Goatfish
Ahuruhuru

US Common Name
Goatfish

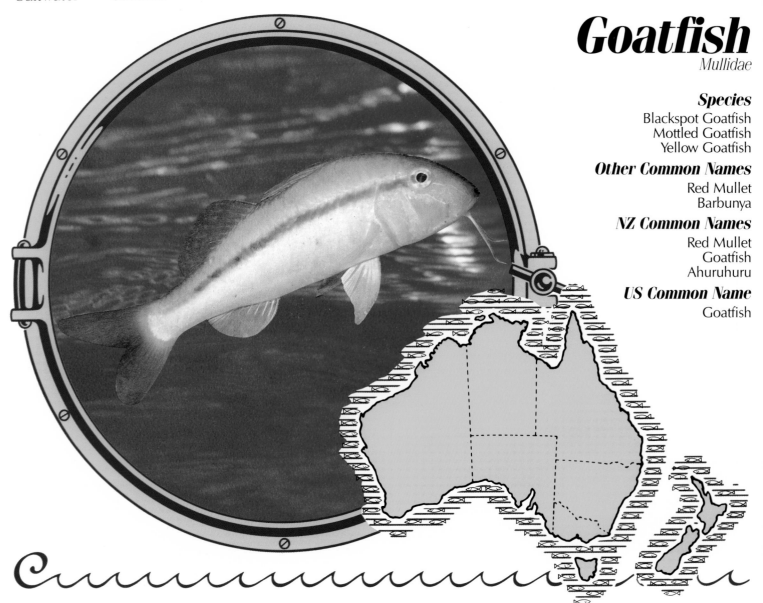

Description
Two long retractable barbels. Two distinct dorsal fins. Bright red colouring. Up to 38cm (1 foot 3 inches).

Habitat
Bottom dwellers in coastal waters to depths of 72m (240 feet). Most prevalent in tropical waters.

Underwater Behaviour
The long barbels are used to probe the bottom for food. Mainly invertebrates.

Table Qualities
Good eating fish, slightly fatty. Flesh is firm, white and soft with a mild flavour. Use whole; fillet large fish, leaving skin on. Shallow fry, grill, barbecue, bake, poach or steam.

Recipes
Main: pages 129, 132.

One of the splendid Nudi Branches, Great Barrier Reef, Qld.

Spectacular reflections on the Huon River, Castle Forbes Bay, Tas.

Groper
Various
(See Comments)

Species
Queensland Groper   Blue Groper

Other Common Names
Wrasse

NZ Equivalents
New Zealand Groper/Hapuku
Bass Groper

US Equivalents
Jewfish
Tautog
(See Comments)

Description

Large fish, up to 2.25m (7.5 feet) in the case of the Queensland Groper; up to 1m (3.3 feet) for the others. Generally have tough skin and scales and hemispherical body. Very large mouth with pointed snout.

Habitat

Quite often found in shallow waters of bays and estuaries, especially Queensland Groper. The New Zealand fish are found in deeper water to 240m (800 feet) and more. Blue Groper are rock dwellers.

Underwater Behaviour

Large variety in diet. Predatory feeders; quite often in shallow waters. Larger fish are solitary feeders while juveniles school.

Table Qualities

The larger fish are of no great table value. Blue Groper is endangered. Queensland Groper is good eating up to 20kg (40 pounds), although strong in flavour. Hapuku is fished commercially, average size around 8-10kg (16-20 pounds) and is excellent eating. Use in steak form with skin removed. The high fat content makes the fish ideal for the grill or barbecue; can also be baked or fried in a little oil.

Recipes
Entrée/Appetizer:
pages 124, 205
Main: page 213

Comments

NZ and Bass Gropers are related but are no relation to Queensland or Blue Gropers. The US "Groupers" are members of the Sea Bass Family — the US "Jewfish" is a member of this family, and though unrelated, is similar in many respects to the Queensland Groper. US "Tautog" is a member of the Wrasse Family and is similar to the Australian Blue Groper.

Coral Reef Clam, Great Barrier Reef, Qld.

Coastal Cliffs, W.A.

Hairtail
Trichiuridae

Species
Australian Hairtail
Northern Hairtail
Spiny Hairtail

NZ Common Name
Not commonly found

US Common Name
Cutlassfish

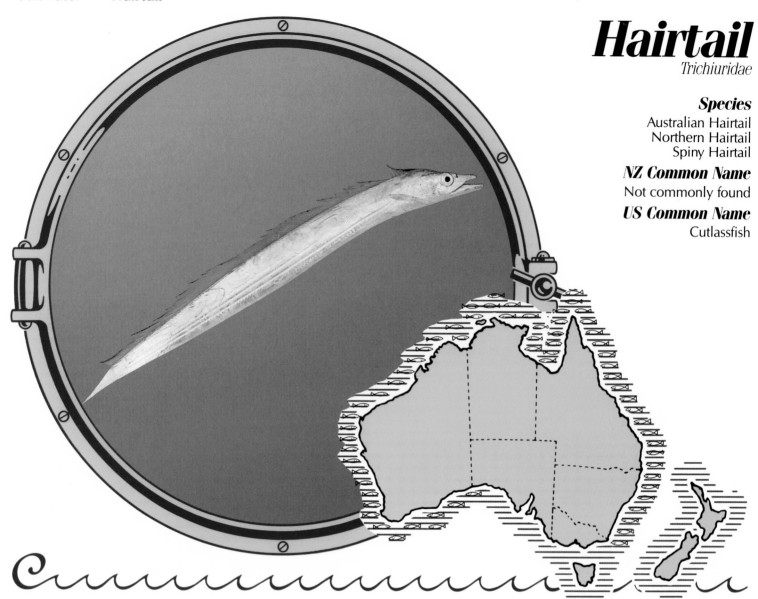

Description
Long jaws with large canine teeth in large mouth. Elongate bodies with continuous dorsal fin from back of head to tip of tail. Silvery blue in colour. Up to 2.25m (7.5 feet).

Habitat
Usually found in estuaries, sometimes in open sea — nearly always over a muddy bottom.

Underwater Behaviour
Feed in schools on small fish and crustaceans.

Table Qualities
An average table fish. White, soft flesh with a mild flavour, prepared in cutlets. Fry gently, grill, bake or poach; can be barbecued if cooked gently on a greased hotplate.

Recipes
Main: page 229

A diving adventure, Tryon Island, New Zealand.

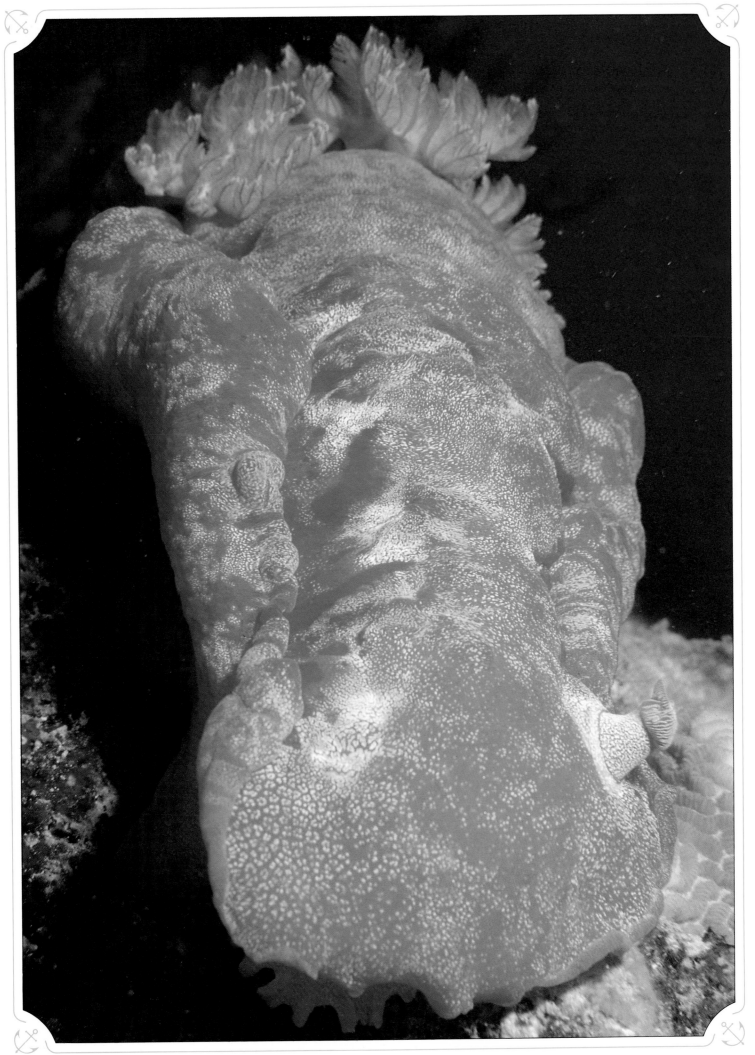

A graceful 'Spanish Dancer'. The Great Barrier Reef, Qld.

Jewfish
Sciaenidae

Species
Jewfish Teraglin

Other Common Names
Mulloway Trag

NZ Common Name
Not found

US Equivalent
Drums
Croakers
(White Seabass)
(See Comments)

Anemone fish make loving couples. When threatened they retreat into the anemones. Their obliging host is poisonous to other species.

Description

Elongate, moderately compressed body. Dorsal fins distinct and separate. Caudal fin convex on Jewfish, concave on Teraglin. Silvery grey. Jewfish up to 2m (6.6 feet); Teraglin up to 60cm (2 feet).

Habitat

Inshore waters and estuaries. Sometimes travel up rivers into freshwater and seek out deep holes.

Underwater Behaviour

Nocturnal feeders, resting during daylight in holes, caves or crevasses. Feed on smaller fish, Squid and Octopus.

Table Qualities

Good eating but large fish may lack flavour. Slightly dry with a large flake, pale pink in colour. Teraglin is considered the better of the two. Use whole, in fillets or cutlets. Shallow fry, bake, poach or steam. When grilling, baste with butter or oil to prevent flesh drying. Wrap in foil to barbecue.

Recipes
Main: pages 178, 228, 229

Comments

The US White Seabass is the member of the Sciaenidae family which is closest to the Australian Jewfish. Not to be confused with the US Jewfish which is a member of the Serranidae family (Sea Basses).

Cairns is a popular international tourist attraction, Qld.

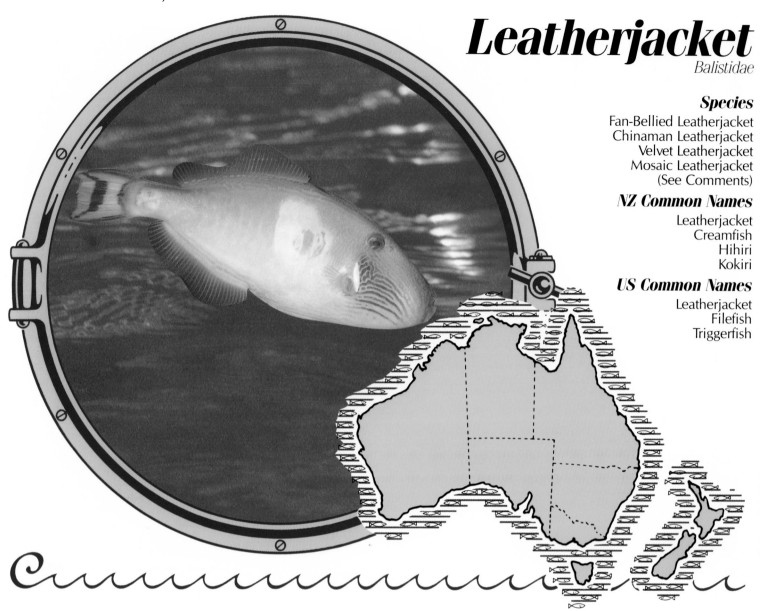

Leatherjacket
Balistidae

Species
Fan-Bellied Leatherjacket
Chinaman Leatherjacket
Velvet Leatherjacket
Mosaic Leatherjacket
(See Comments)

NZ Common Names
Leatherjacket
Creamfish
Hihiri
Kokiri

US Common Names
Leatherjacket
Filefish
Triggerfish

Description

Large incisor teeth. Prominent dorsal spine. Protruding pelvic spine, covered by skin flap. Colouring usually drab; some species brightly coloured. Velvet-like skin, comprising numerous, minute scales. Up to 90cm (3 feet).

Habitat

Inshore and estuaries; some species inhabit grass beds in open seas.

Underwater Behaviour

Voracious feeders on small crustaceans, algae and seagrasses. Small schools.

Table Qualities

Excellent eating, with white, soft flesh and a mild flavour. Use body whole, with head and tough skin removed. Cannot be filleted because of the large nodes on the skeleton. Flesh is easily separated from bones when cooked. Shallow fry, bake or poach. Baste well when grilling or barbecuing to keep flesh moist.

Recipes
Main: page 229

Comments

These are some of the more common Australian species. The different species are too numerous to list. Some species are inedible.

Hobart's busy harbour, Tasmania.

Sunset at Fog Dam, N.T.

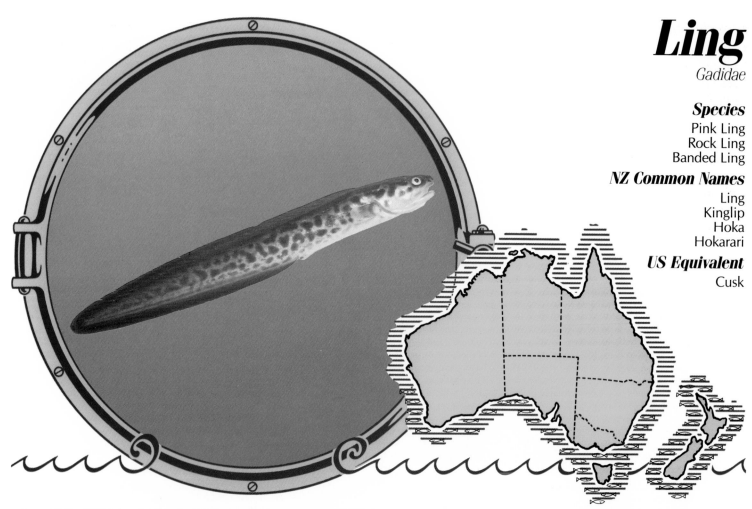

Ling
Gadidae

Species
Pink Ling
Rock Ling
Banded Ling

NZ Common Names
Ling
Kinglip
Hoka
Hokarari

US Equivalent
Cusk

Description

Single barb on chin. Long continuous dorsal fin. Body elongate and cylindrical, compressed towards tail. Rounded caudal fin. Mottled brown/yellow/orange/pink above; whitish below. Up to 1.5m (5 feet).

Habitat

Usually around hard rocky bottoms, often cave dwellers. To depths of 200m (670 feet).

Underwater Behaviour

Feed in small schools on small crustaceans and molluscs.

Table Qualities

Important fish commercially. Good eating with the advantage of large steak-like fillets with few bones. Flesh is white, firm and moist with a mild flavour. Remove any skin, score thick fillets to ensure even cooking. Fry, grill, barbecue, bake, poach or steam.

Recipes
Main: pages 178, 291

Comments

Ling are all members of the Cod family. The US Cusk (Brosme brosme) is the nearest equivalent in the Cod family to the Ling found in Australian waters.

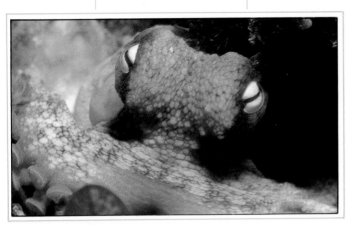

An observant Octopus off the coast, New Zealand.

An old grey jetty leans in tiredness at Abrolhos Islands off the W.A. coast.

Mackerel
Scombridae

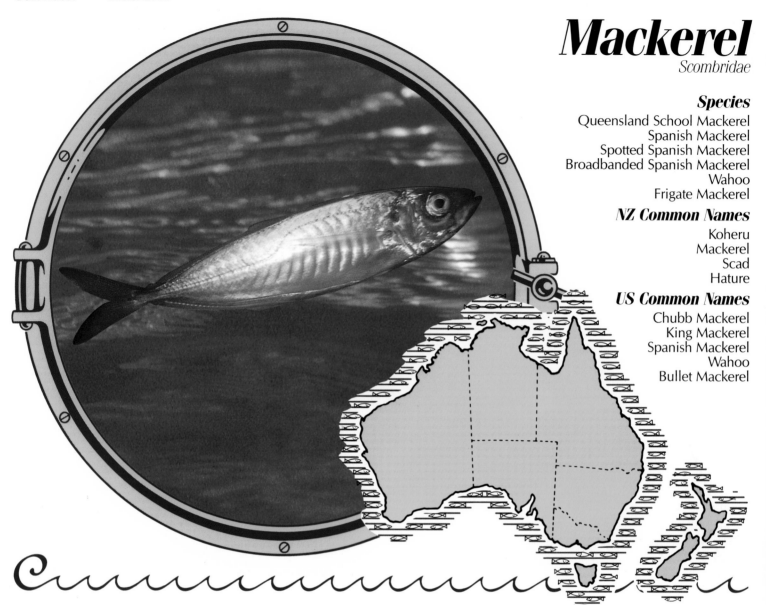

Species
Queensland School Mackerel
Spanish Mackerel
Spotted Spanish Mackerel
Broadbanded Spanish Mackerel
Wahoo
Frigate Mackerel

NZ Common Names
Koheru
Mackerel
Scad
Hature

US Common Names
Chubb Mackerel
King Mackerel
Spanish Mackerel
Wahoo
Bullet Mackerel

Description

Elongate, fusiform body. Two dorsal fins that depress into grooves. Series of finlets run from second dorsal and anal fins to caudal fin. Blueish green to black above, silver below. Up to 1.8m (6 feet), (Wahoo and Spanish Mackerel); Frigate and School Mackerel up to 50-60cm (1 foot 8 inches-2 feet).

Habitat

Mainly offshore fish, some smaller species inhabit coastal waters over continental shelf.

Underwater Behaviour

Fast swimmers. Larger species are migratory. Smaller species form large schools. Feed mainly on smaller schooling fish and sometimes on crustaceans.

Table Qualities

All fish are good eating. Flesh is soft but dry in texture, off-white with darker colouration with a distinct flavour. Larger species usually cut into cutlets. Even though fish is oily, it can be dry when cooked. Shallow fry with a protective coating of flour or crumbs, baste with butter or white wine when grilling, cover when baking. Also available smoked.

Recipes
Main: pages 178, 194

Comments

US species mentioned are closest equivalents of Scombridae family in US to Australian species. Wahoo is exactly the same.

A sunny island lying in a glassy ocean. Low Isles, Qld.

Morwong/ Sea Bream
Cheilodactylidae

Species
Jackass Morwong   Grey Morwong
Red Morwong   Banded Morwong

NZ Common Names
Tarakihi, Morwong
Porae
Red Moki, Nanua

US Common Name
Not found

Twilight Cove, North Esperance, W.A.

Description

Usually "rubbery" lips, Spiny rays along dorsal fin. Fifth ray from bottom of pectoral fins is elongated. Varying colours from green/grey to bright blue across top, silvery below. Up to 1m (3 feet 3 inches).

Habitat

Inshore and offshore reefs, quite often found in deep water. Temperate waters.

Underwater Behaviour

Feed mainly on molluscs and crustaceans, often using lips to suck molluscs off rocks. Grey Morwong takes in mouthfuls of sand, swallows organic matter and ejects residue through gills.

Table Qualities

Very good eating; an important commercial catch in South-East Australia. Pinkish flesh, moist and firm with a moderate fat content and a mild flavour. Use whole or in fillets. Fry, grill, barbecue, bake or poach.

Recipes
Entrée/Appetizer: page 170
Main: pages 176, 276, 307

Grey Nurse Shark.

Mullet
Mugilidae

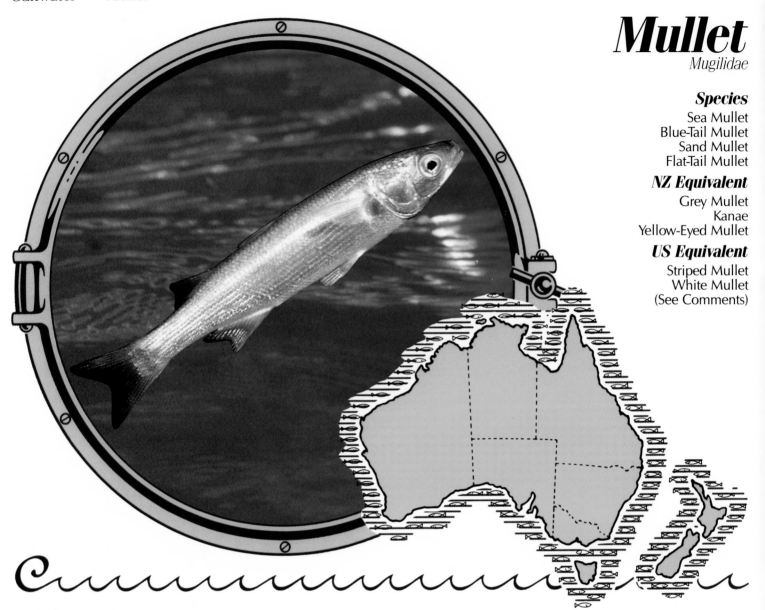

Species
Sea Mullet
Blue-Tail Mullet
Sand Mullet
Flat-Tail Mullet

NZ Equivalent
Grey Mullet
Kanae
Yellow-Eyed Mullet

US Equivalent
Striped Mullet
White Mullet
(See Comments)

Description
Small mouth and blunt snout. Elongate body, cylindrical near head, compressed towards tail. Pectoral fins placed high on body. Commonly blueish above, silvery below. Up to 80cm (2 feet 8 inches).

Habitat
Coastal waters and estuaries, often found in fresh water.

Underwater Behaviour
Schooling fish, often travelling long distances. Spawning in open sea. Feeds on algae, worms, small crustaceans.

Table Qualities
Flavour and oil content varies according to species and where caught. Generally has a distinct flavour and is oily. Flesh is pink, soft and moist. Use whole or in fillets. Fry, grill, barbecue or bake. Flavour much improved with the addition of a little brown sugar. A good fish for smoking.

Recipes
Main: pages 230, 291

Comments
There are six species of Mullet in the US; Striped Mullet is the most prevalent.

Sailing is a delight at Pindimar near Tea Gardens, N.S.W.

Parrot & Tusk Fish
Scaridae
Labridae

NZ Common Name
Not found
US Common Names
Parrot Fish
Tusk Fish
(See Comments)

Description

Large, strong teeth. Single, uninterrupted dorsal fin. Large scales. Brightly coloured. Up to 1.2m (4 feet).

Habitat

Shallow coastal waters and reefs.

Underwater Behaviour

Feeds on algae and small crustaceans in small groups.

Table Qualities

Good eating. White flesh is soft and moist with a delicate flavour. Presents attractively if cooked whole; can also be filleted as it is good shallow or deep fried with a batter or crumb coating. Can also be grilled, barbecued, baked or poached.

Recipes
Main: page 129

Comments

The Parrot and Tusk fishes are closely related. Tusk fish are members of the Labridae family (Wrasse). Both families are well represented in the US. There are many species of each of these fish in Australian waters.

Bubble Coral, Barrier Reef, Qld.

Tropical beach, water and trees at Cape Tribulation, Qld.

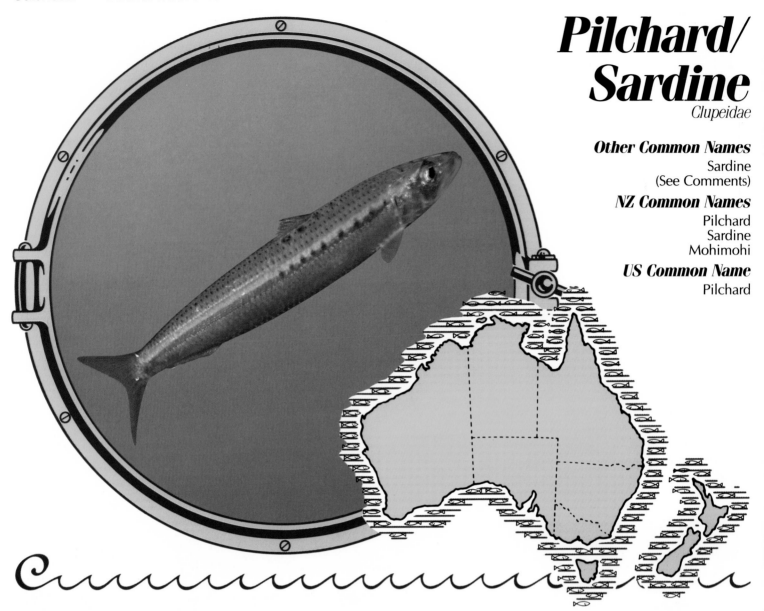

Pilchard/ Sardine
Clupeidae

Other Common Names
Sardine
(See Comments)

NZ Common Names
Pilchard
Sardine
Mohimohi

US Common Name
Pilchard

Description
Lower jaw not prominent. Elongate body. Forked caudal fin. Blue above, silver below. Up to 30cm (1 foot).

Habitat
Coastal waters, from cold to sub-tropical climates.

Underwater Behaviour
School in vast shoals, feeding on minute organisms. Spawn in open sea.

Table Qualities
Best known as processed fish, but a very interesting addition to the menu when fresh. Flesh is reddish, oily and soft with a strong flavour. Remove backbone and use whole or butterfly. Fry, grill, barbecue or bake.

Recipes
Entrée/Appetizer: page 188
Main: pages 194, 195

Comments
Generally the term "Sardine" is used for the young of any species in the Herring Family. There is only one species of Pilchard in Australian and NZ waters (Sardinops neopilchardus) and only one in US waters — the Pacific Sardine (Sardinops Sagax).

Soft Coral Pollyps, Port Stephens, NSW.

Commercial fishing fleet anchored at Bermagui Harbour, NSW.

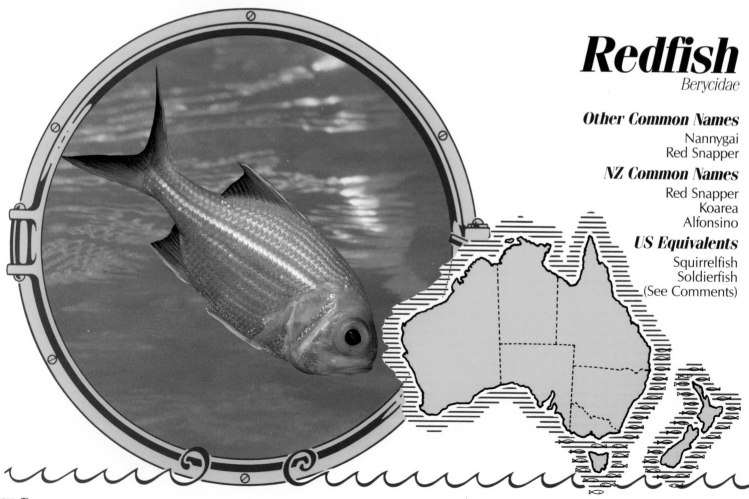

Redfish
Berycidae

Other Common Names
Nannygai
Red Snapper

NZ Common Names
Red Snapper
Koarea
Alfonsino

US Equivalents
Squirrelfish
Soldierfish
(See Comments)

Man working on model outriggers at Murray Island, Torres Strait, Qld.

Description

Very large eyes. Single dorsal fin. Head, back and fins red; other areas light red to silver. Up to 45cm (1 foot 6 inches)

Habitat

Coastal waters and reefs to depths of 400m (1320 feet).

Underwater Behaviour

Large schools feed on smaller fish and crustaceans. Daily migration of schools from sea bottom in early morning, dispersing throughout the day.

Table Qualities

A fine eating fish which is an important commercial catch. Delicate flesh, pale pink with a subtle flavour. A difficult fish to scale as scales are tightly knit, so cannot be used whole; sold filleted and skinned. Fry with a protective coating of flour, batter or crumbs, bake, or mince deboned fillets for fish loaves and patties.

Recipes
Entrée/Appetizer: pages 272, 273
Main: page 277

Comments

In the US, the closest species are within the Holocentridae Family, a member of the order Beryciformes. The Blackbar Soldierfish is very similar to Australia's most common variation (Centroberyx affinis).

Stinging Hydroid, Barrier Reef, Qld.

Shark, Skate & Ray

Subclass Elasmobranchii

Species
Gummy Shark
School Shark
Ray, Skate
(See Comments)

NZ Common Names
Rig
Shark
Ray
Skate

US Common Names
Shark
Ray
Skate

Description
Cartilaginous skeleton. Well developed jaws with numerous teeth in series. Placoid scales, toothlike in structure. Absence of an air or swim bladder. Five to seven pairs of separate, external gill openings.

Habitat
The majority of species live and breed in the relatively shallow waters on the continental shelf. Some species keep to open seas. More numerous in tropical areas.

Underwater Behaviour
All Sharks, with the exception of the Whale and Basking Sharks, are carnivorous. Most feed on fish, often attacking in schools. Rays and Skates are mostly bottom dwellers and are carnivorous.

Table Qualities
The flesh from these fish is generally very good. Flesh is white with pink tinges, moist and mild in flavour. The absence of bones is a very attractive feature. Shark and Ray sold as skinless fillets, which may have to be slit to make them thin enough for frying. However, Shark can have an ammonia taste; soak in water with lemon juice added to eliminate this. Deep-fry with a protective coating of batter or crumbs, grill, barbecue, bake, poach or steam.

Comments
There are many species of Shark, Ray and Skate which are marketed commercially. The two Shark species mentioned are the most prevalent at the markets. All are members of the subclass Elasmobranchii.

Recipes
Main: page 263

At 5 metres a Great White Shark is big enough to eat Lyn, and her famous diver husband Ben Croft, at a sitting. Albany Whaling Station, W.A.

A hot, hazy day emerging on Cambridge Gulf, Wyndham, W.A.

Snapper
Sparidae

Other Common Names
Schnapper

NZ Common Names
Snapper
Schnapper
Bream
Brim
Karati
Tamure

US Common Name
Porgy
(See Comments)

Description

Large head with steep profile and a distinctive hump on the forehead when fully grown. Well developed teeth. Single dorsal fin. Silvery with a pinkish tinge and blue markings. Up to 1.2m (4 feet).

Habitat

Younger fish inhabit estuaries, while the older fish are usually found on inshore reefs and in deep holes.

Underwater Behaviour

Younger fish are found in medium-sized schools feeding on very small crustaceans and plankton. Larger fish tend to feed on what is abundant in their locality, including small fish, and school in smaller groups.

Table Qualities

A very highly regarded table fish with firm, white flesh, mild but distinct flavour and a large flake. Use whole, in fillets or cutlets (large Snapper). Fry, grill, barbecue, bake, poach or steam. Fresh Snapper head and carcass make excellent fish stock.

Recipes
Entrée/Appetizer:
pages 204, 205
Main: pages 177, 211, 290, 292, 307

Comments

As with the Bream, also members of the Sparidae family, Porgies are the closest US equivalent. Also known in Australia as Cockney, Squire and Red Bream, according to maturity.

Marine Worm, Port Stephens, NSW.

Exotic Thursday Island, Qld.

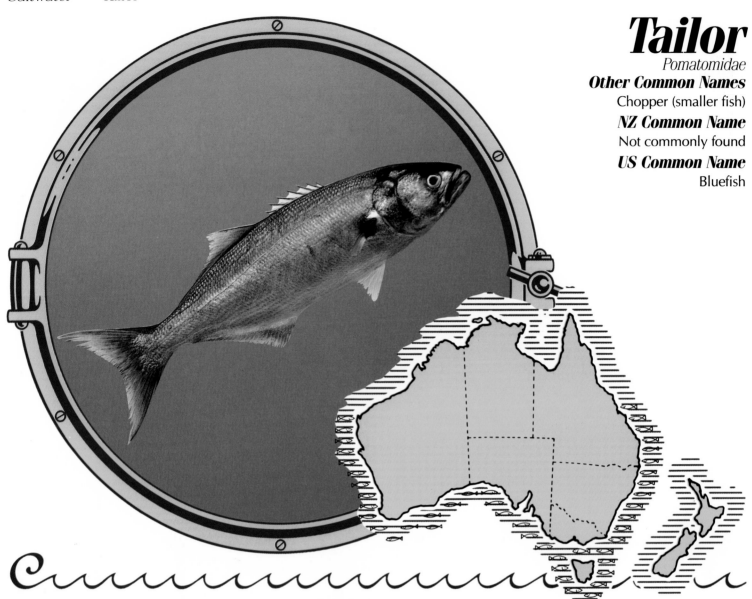

Tailor
Pomatomidae

Other Common Names
Chopper (smaller fish)

NZ Common Name
Not commonly found

US Common Name
Bluefish

Description
Large head and mouth. Sharp, well developed teeth. Elongate body. Forked caudal fin. Small scales. Blue/grey above, silvery below, yellow tinge to fins. Up to 1.2m (4 feet).

Habitat
Surface dwellers, mainly inshore waters.

Underwater Behaviour
Extremely voracious feeders, eating until gorged. In the US they have been known to attack people. Very fast swimmers. Migrate to open seas to spawn. Large schools common.

Table Qualities
A good eating fish if consumed very fresh. Must be bled immediately after it is caught. Slightly oily, pinkish, soft flesh with a distinct flavour. Use whole or filleted and skinned. Fry, grill, barbecue or bake. Also available smoked — poach.

Recipes
Entrée/Appetizer: page 257

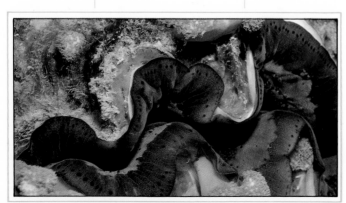
A beautiful Clam on the Great Barrier Reef, Qld.

Curious divers visit a wrecked crayfish boat, the 'Ross Serene'. Abrolhos Islands, W.A.

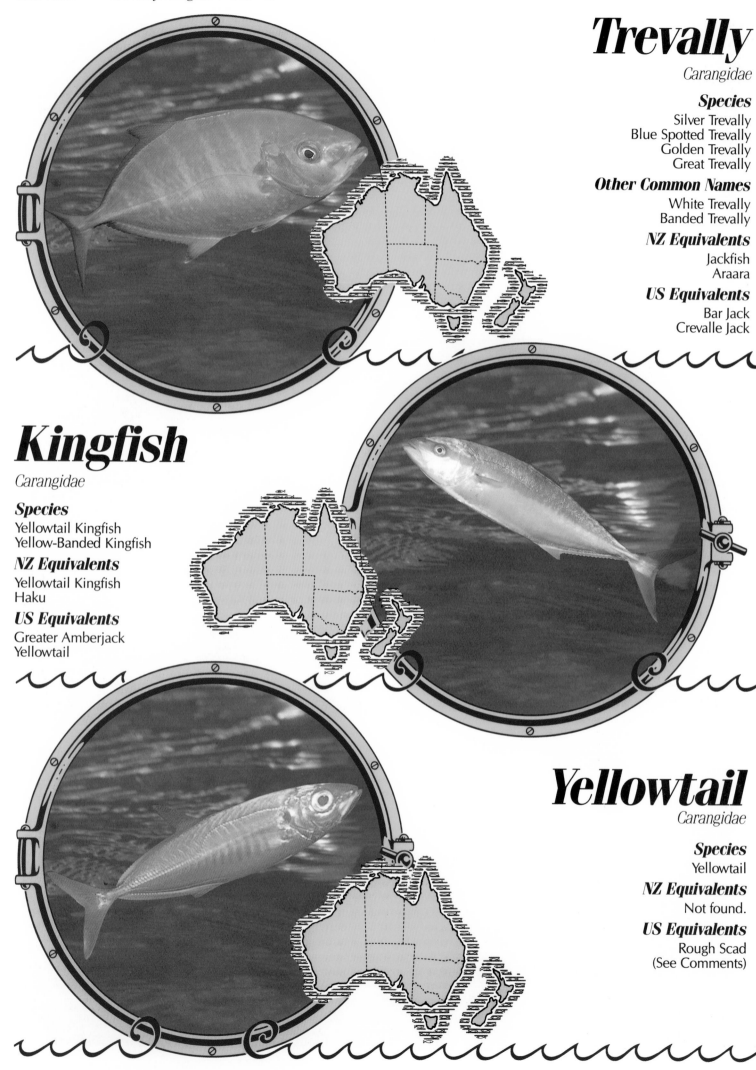

Trevally
Carangidae

Species
Silver Trevally
Blue Spotted Trevally
Golden Trevally
Great Trevally

Other Common Names
White Trevally
Banded Trevally

NZ Equivalents
Jackfish
Araara

US Equivalents
Bar Jack
Crevalle Jack

Kingfish

Carangidae

Species
Yellowtail Kingfish
Yellow-Banded Kingfish

NZ Equivalents
Yellowtail Kingfish
Haku

US Equivalents
Greater Amberjack
Yellowtail

Yellowtail
Carangidae

Species
Yellowtail

NZ Equivalents
Not found.

US Equivalents
Rough Scad
(See Comments)

Description

Elongate, moderately compressed body. Separate dorsal fins. Forked caudal fin. Yellow/green/silver colouring. Up to 1.2m (4 feet).

Habitat

From deep water of continental shelf to shallow bays and estuaries.

Underwater Behaviour

Found in largish, fast swimming schools; older fish more solitary. Voracious feeders — small fish and crustaceans. A powerful, fighting fish.

Table Qualities

Generally very good eating; larger fish are not as flavoursome and tend to be dry. Very firm, slightly pink flesh, delicate, sweet flavour. Use whole or filleted and skinned.

Recipes
Entrée/Appetizer: page 171
Main: pages 178, 195

Comments

"Jack" is the common name for the Carangidae Family in the US. The Bar Jack (Caranx ruber) and the Crevalle Jack (Caranx hippos) are very similar to the Australian Trevallies while the Greater Amberjack (Seriola dumerili) is similar to both Kingfish.

Description

Elongate, moderately compressed body. Large head. Forked caudal fin. Blueish above, silver underside with a yellow/green band laterally. Up to 1.5m (5 feet).

Habitat

Reefs, rocky shores. Surface dwellers.

Underwater Behaviour

Often in very large schools. Feed on small fish, Squid and Crabs. Fast swimmers.

Table Qualities

Very good eating, with soft, dry, pink flesh, flavoursome and slightly sweet. Use whole, in cutlets or fillets. Very good served raw for sashimi.

Recipes
Entrée/Appetizer: page 256
Main: pages 178, 194, 263

Comments

See above.

Description

Large eyes. Lateral lines made prominent by the hard plates or scutes attached. Forked caudal fin. Greenish, yellow. Up to 30cm (12 inches).

Habitat

Shallow waters of bays, harbours and estuaries.

Underwater Behaviour

Large fast-moving schools. Feed on juvenile fish and small crustaceans.

Table Qualities

Tasty, but generally not worth the effort due to small size and bones. Excellent bait.

Comments

See above.

A picturesque scene on the waters of Milford Sound, New Zealand.

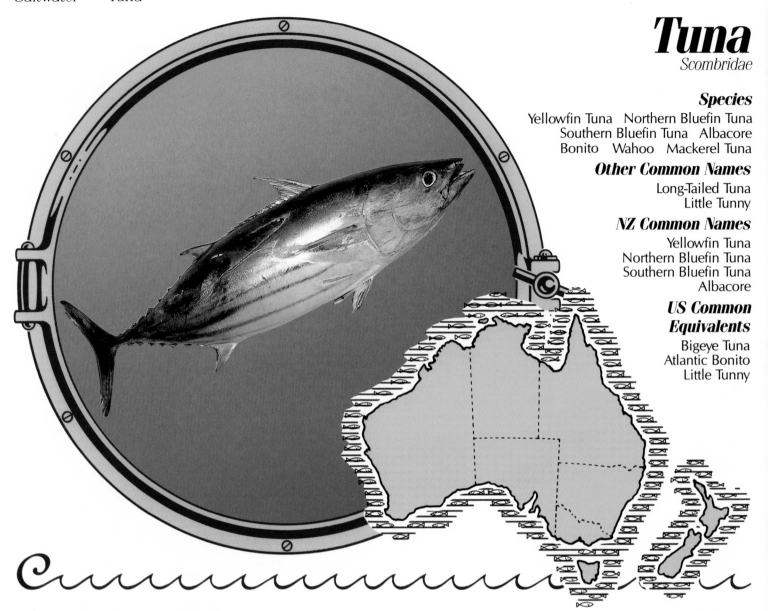

Tuna
Scombridae

Species
Yellowfin Tuna   Northern Bluefin Tuna
Southern Bluefin Tuna   Albacore
Bonito   Wahoo   Mackerel Tuna

Other Common Names
Long-Tailed Tuna
Little Tunny

NZ Common Names
Yellowfin Tuna
Northern Bluefin Tuna
Southern Bluefin Tuna
Albacore

US Common Equivalents
Bigeye Tuna
Atlantic Bonito
Little Tunny

Description

Large head, eyes and mouth. Compressed, fusiform body. Two dorsal fins which depress into grooves for streamlining. High pectoral fins — forked caudal fin. Numerous small scales which give the impression of plating. Blue-green above, silvery below; quite often with stripes or other markings. Wahoo, Southern Bluefin and Yellowfin up to 1.8m (6 feet); Albacore up to 1.5m (5 feet); Bonito up to 90cm (3 feet); Mackerel and Tuna up to 1.2m (4 feet).

Habitat

Surface dwellers; open seas to inshore reefs and islands.

Underwater Behaviour

Very fast swimmers. Larger species migratory. Voracious feeders with fast metabolism hence frequent feeders. Schooling fish. Diet includes fish, Squid, crustaceans.

Table Qualities

Tuna is a highly prized commercial catch. Albacore is very important to the canning industry, while Yellowfin is the most valuable species, being highly prized for the Japanese sashimi market. Flesh is oily and richly flavoured; red in colour turning white when cooked. There is a dark strip of musculature which is more strongly flavoured. Sold whole, in cutlets or steaks. Grill, barbecue, pan fry or bake. May be poached to use in place of canned Tuna.

Recipes
Entrée/Appetizer: pages 124, 170, 240, 256
Main: pages 157, 160, 211

Comments

US: The Atlantic Bonito is a slightly different species to the Australian Bonito. The Bluefin Tuna is a much larger fish than the Australian species of the same name. The Yellowfin Tuna (Thunnus albacares), Albacore (Thunnus alaluuga) and Wahoo (Acanthocybium solanderi) are identical to the Australian species, while the Southern Bluefin Tuna (Thunnus maccoyi) is very similar to the Bigeye Tuna and the Mackerel Tuna (Euthynnus aletteratus) is called Little Tunny.

NZ: The species mentioned are identical to the Australian species of the same names.

This Beaver floatplane explores the Drysdale River for monster Barramundi in an exotic, untouched fishing spot, W.A.

Westralian Jewfish/
(Dhu-Fish)
Pearl Perch
Glaucosomidae

Species
Westralian Jewfish   Pearl Perch

Other Common Names
Westralian Pearl Perch
Westralian Dhu-Fish
(See Comments)

NZ Common Name
Not found

US Common Name
Not found

Long gone are days at sea for this old vessel in a mangrove creek on the Pearling Coast. Broome, W.A.

Description

Large head, mouth and eyes. Single dorsal fin, increasing in size towards tail. Concave caudal fin. Pearlish green/grey colouring. Westralian fish larger, up to 1.2m (4 feet); Pearl Perch up to 60cm (2 feet).

Habitat

Coastal waters; Pearl Perch only along eastern coast down to mid-northern NSW; Westralian Jewfish west coast only — north up to Shark Bay.

Underwater Behaviour

Enter shallow waters to spawn where they may form large schools. Neither fish found in very large numbers. Feed on smaller fish and crustaceans.

Table Qualities

Considered by anglers to be one of the finest eating fish in the country, especially the Westralian Jewfish. Flesh is white, moist and tender with a sweet, delicate flavour. Use whole or filleted. Panfry, grill, bake, poach or steam. Slightly undercook to retain moistness.

Recipes
Main: page 195

Comments

There appears to be some controversy over the spelling of the WA species — "Dhu-Fish" is commonly used, but the WA Department of Fisheries lists "Jewfish" as the correct name. More importantly, we should remember, "What is in a name? That which we call a rose by any other name would smell as sweet"!

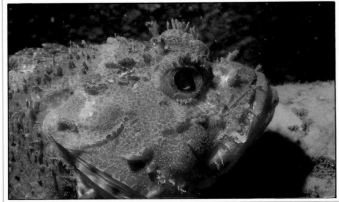

The grim face of a Scorpion Fish.

Whitebait
Various
(See Comments)

NZ Common Name
Whitebait
Inanga

US Common Name
Whitebait

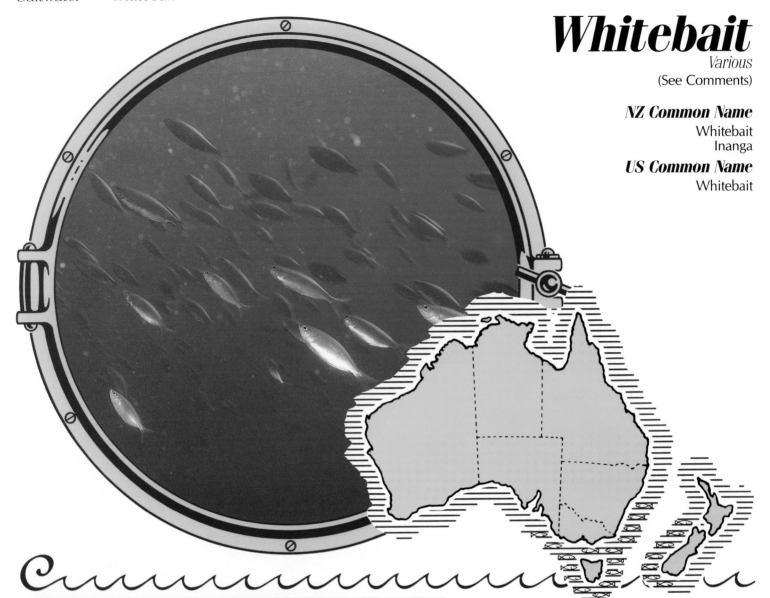

Table Qualities

Traditionally a gourmet dish; a great delicacy of long-standing in Britain, the Mediterranean, and more recently New Zealand and Australia.

As the tiny fish are eaten whole, it is not a dish that appeals to everyone. Best if prepared very fresh. May be stored for 2 days in the refrigerator, providing the fish are rinsed, drained well and placed in a colander which is in turn placed in a larger bowl. This will keep the fish dry. Cover with a plate (plastic film causes sweating). Prepare as fritters, or coat with flour and deep-fry until crisp. Outstanding in flavour and texture.

Comments

Whitebait is a dish rather than a type of fish. Originating from 18th Century England, a mixture of several species of immature fish, rolled in flour and deep-fried golden brown. In New Zealand, Whitebait comprises one Family — Galaxias. This is often exported for sale in Australian markets.

Recipes
Entrée/Appetizer: page 205
Main: pages 210, 211, 212

The umbrella Tube Worm at the Great Barrier Reef, Qld.

In the gloom of 60 metres depth, a Sea Fan spreads itself on the current of the Great Barrier Reef, Qld.

Whiting
Sillaginidae

Species
Sand Whiting   King George Whiting
School Whiting   Trumpeter Whiting
Yellow-finned Whiting   Stout Whiting

Other Common Names
Silver Whiting
Spotted Whiting
Bass Strait Whiting

NZ Common Name
Not found

US Common Name
Not found

Description

Long snout, small teeth, elongate, hemispherical body and concave caudal fin. Colouring brown/yellow/green above; silvery below and on fins; quite often mottled. Up to 50cm (1 foot 8 inches).

Habitat

Shallow waters of beaches, bays, estuaries. Sand or mud bottom dwellers.

Underwater Behaviour

Schooling fish, feeding on worms, crustaceans and molluscs. Highly active.

Table Qualities

Very highly regarded for its tasty flesh. Slightly sweet, with finely textured, delicate white flesh. Use whole or in fillets. Leave skin on when cooking whole to retain moisture. Pan fry with a protective coating of flour or crumbs, grill, barbecue, bake or poach.

Recipes
Entrée/Appetizer: pages 171, 204
Main: pages 176, 178

Comments

Not to be confused with the unrelated English Whiting.

A Sea Star reminiscent of Smarties, Jarvis Bay, NSW.

The foreground of abundant tropical plants masking the beauty of Murray Island, Torres Strait, Qld.

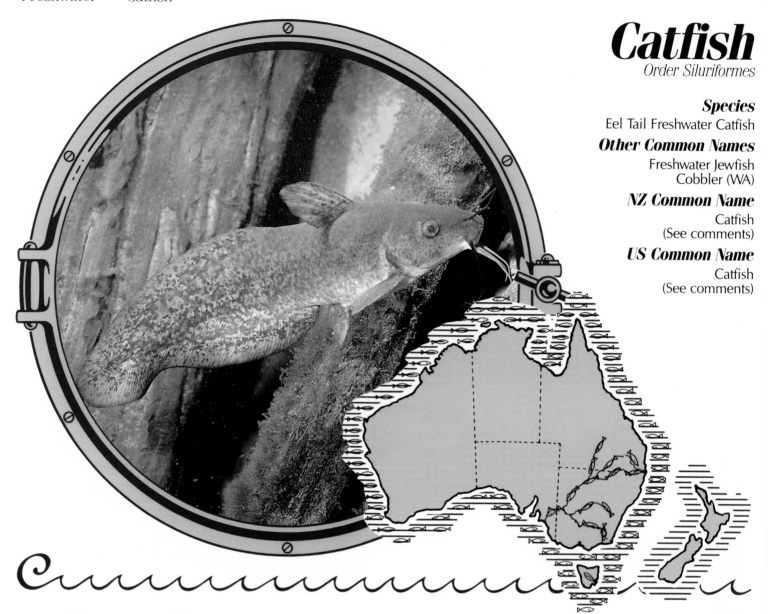

Catfish
Order Siluriformes

Species
Eel Tail Freshwater Catfish

Other Common Names
Freshwater Jewfish
Cobbler (WA)

NZ Common Name
Catfish
(See comments)

US Common Name
Catfish
(See comments)

Description

Mouth encircled by 8 long feelers (hence name). No scales present. Concealed spines in dorsal and pectoral fins. Caudal fin continuous with dorsal and anal fins and truncate. Brown/olive with mottling; white below. Up to 60cm (2 feet).

Habitat

Sandy and muddy bottoms of tidal estuaries and far reaches of rivers; often found around roots of willow trees.

Underwater Behaviour

Bottom dwellers, feeding on Shrimps, Yabbies, Mussels, worms, or whatever food is found locally.

Table Qualities

Excellent eating; best to buy fillets with spine and tough skin removed. Moist, white, firm flesh with a "clean" flavour. Combines well with sauces.

Recipes
Main: page 240

Comments

Catfish are an extremely extensive group of fish in both marine and freshwater environments. The most common freshwater Catfish in Australian waters is the Eel Tail (Tandanus tandanus) which is not found in US or NZ.

Surfers Paradise, playground of the well-known Goldcoast, Qld.

A reflective scene of Australia's great Murray River, Vic.

Eel
Anguillidae

Species
Long-Finned Eel
Short-Finned Eel

NZ Common Name
Freshwater Eel

US Common Name
Freshwater Eel

Description

Large head. Long, snake-like body, compressed towards tail. Small scales and pectoral fins present. Caudal fin continuous with dorsal and anal fins. Painted tail. Colour varies with sexual maturity — green/brown/yellow/silver. Up to 1.5m (5 feet).

Habitat

Found far up river, often in land-locked ponds, down to river mouth. Found in open seas when spawning.

Underwater Behaviour

Inhabits river systems feeding on small invertebrates. In order to spawn, they make their way slowly downriver and out to sea — always to the same breeding ground. The young hatch, drift for a while in the larval stage, then make their way to the nearest freshwater system, where they move upriver seeking out the source, often crossing wet land to reach land-locked lakes and ponds.

Table Qualities

Considered a true delicacy. Soft white flesh, slightly oily. Fresh Eel sold whole or in cutlets; remove skin before cooking. Eel can be marinated before cooking; pan fry, grill, bake or braise. Smoked Eel is readily available and very popular for appetizers and snacks.

Recipes
Entrée/Appetizer: page 240
Main: pages 246

An old building resting on the banks of a river near Yass, NSW.

Golden Perch
Serranidae

Other Common Names
Callop
Freshwater Bream
Yellowbelly
Murray Perch

NZ Common Name
Not found

US Equivalent
White Perch
(See Comments)

Description
Deep, compressed body. Superior mouth. First dorsal fin has prominent spines and is connected to second dorsal fin. Convex caudal fin. Olive green to black on top; gold to white underneath. Up to 60cm (2 feet) but occasionally reported much bigger, up to 1.2m (4 feet).

Habitat
Turbid, slow moving waters of inland rivers. In lagoons and dams, they tend to seek out weed beds and tree roots.

Underwater Behaviour
Solitary fish, feed on worms, grubs, frogs, Yabbies etc.

Table Qualities
Very good table fish. Flesh is firm, white and slightly oily, with a delicate flavour. Use whole or as skinless fillets. Shallow fry, grill, barbecue, bake, poach or steam.

Recipes
Entrée/Appetizer: page 241

Comments
The US White Perch (Marone americana) is closest equivalent to the Australian Golden Perch (Plectroplites ambigius).

Cattle crossing the Tweed River, NSW.

Big Nellie, a spectacular area near Taree, NSW.

Murray Cod

Serranidae

Species
Murray Cod
Trout Cod

NZ Common Name
Not found

US Common Name
No equivalent

A Heron watches its own reflection in Kakadu National Park.

Description

Very large mouth, large head. Spiny first dorsal fin, connected to second dorsal. Convex caudal fin. Green with a mottled pattern; Trout Cod blue or white and spotted. Up to 2m (6 feet 8 inches).

Habitat

Mainly inhabits Australia's largest inland waterway — The Murray-Darling system; also found in east coast rivers.

Underwater Behaviour

Voracious feeder on practically anything edible, commonly seeking out rotting carcasses. Heavy fish, they are slow movers. Mainly nocturnal, seeking out holes, crevasses, logs etc. during daylight hours.

Table Qualities

Considered a gourmet fish. Flesh is white, moist and firm and is mild in flavour. Use whole or filleted. From very large fish, cut fillets obliquely into steaks. Shallow fry, grill, barbecue, bake or poach.

Recipes
Entrée/Appetizer:
page 302
Main: page 246

Comments

These two members of the Bass family are unique to Australia's south east. The Murray Cod (Maccullochella macquariensis) is justifiably famous in its country of origin, the Trout Cod (Maccullochella mitchellii) being slightly less well known.

A mystic scene of the Murray River, NSW.

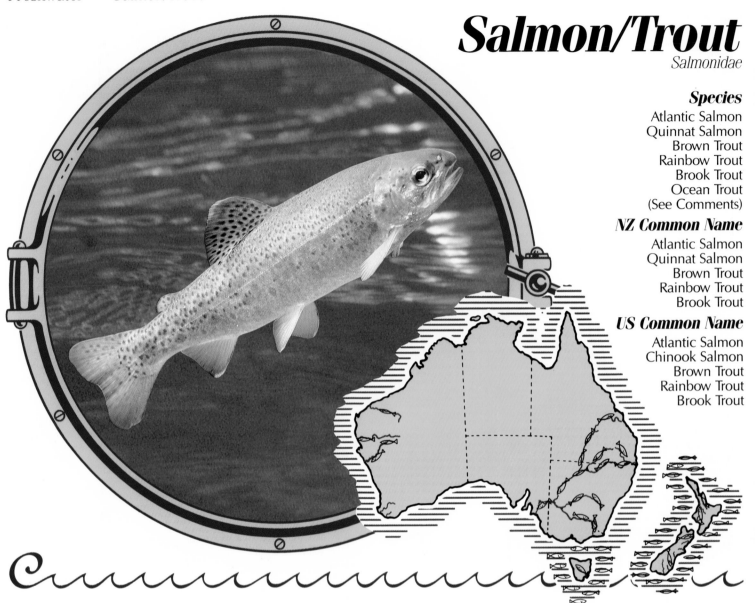

Salmon/Trout
Salmonidae

Species
Atlantic Salmon
Quinnat Salmon
Brown Trout
Rainbow Trout
Brook Trout
Ocean Trout
(See Comments)

NZ Common Name
Atlantic Salmon
Quinnat Salmon
Brown Trout
Rainbow Trout
Brook Trout

US Common Name
Atlantic Salmon
Chinook Salmon
Brown Trout
Rainbow Trout
Brook Trout

Description
Elongate, fusiform body. Large head. Low pectoral fins. Spotted, colouration varies from freshwater to marine and from species to species. Atlantic Salmon up to 1.3m (4 feet 4 inches); Quinnat up to 1.6m (5 feet 4 inches); Rainbow Trout and Brown Trout up to 1m (3 feet 4 inches); Brook Trout up to 53cm (21 inches).

Habitat
Trout: Cool, clear, fast moving freshwater streams; sometimes saltwater (not in Australia or New Zealand).

Atlantic Salmon: Coastal waters to freshwater streams and lakes.

Quinnat Salmon: Ocean, from surface to mid-depth; spawning in large rivers. Often found in "landlocked" lakes.

Underwater Behaviour
Atlantic Salmon and Trout: Solitary feeders on small organisms, insects, worms, grubs and small fish. May live in salt or fresh water.

Quinnat Salmon: Feed on small crustaceans and fish. May enter fresh water at any time, but most noticeably during the main spawning seasons (Spring and Autumn). Attempts at breeding "landlocked" fish in Australia have been unsuccessful, but similar attempts in NZ have succeeded.

Table Qualities
All are excellent table fish and can be used whole, filleted or in cutlets. Pan-fry, grill, barbecue, bake, poach or steam. Also available smoked. Flesh is fine, moist, salmon-pink to white in colour, and a little oily. Exquisite flavour. Quinnat Salmon is a little more oily and slightly richer in flavour.

Recipes
Entrée/Appetizer: pages 152, 302
Main: pages 157, 247, 292, 306

Comments
None of these fish are native to Australia or NZ, all having been introduced from the northern hemisphere. Atlantic Salmon and Rainbow Trout are both now farmed commercially in Tasmania — the Rainbows being marketed as "Ocean Trout", as the farms are in salt water.

Reeling in a catch of Trout.

Abalone
Genus Haliotis

Species
Blacklip Abalone
Greenlip Abalone

NZ Common Name
Paua
Abalone

US Common Name
Abalone
(See Comments)

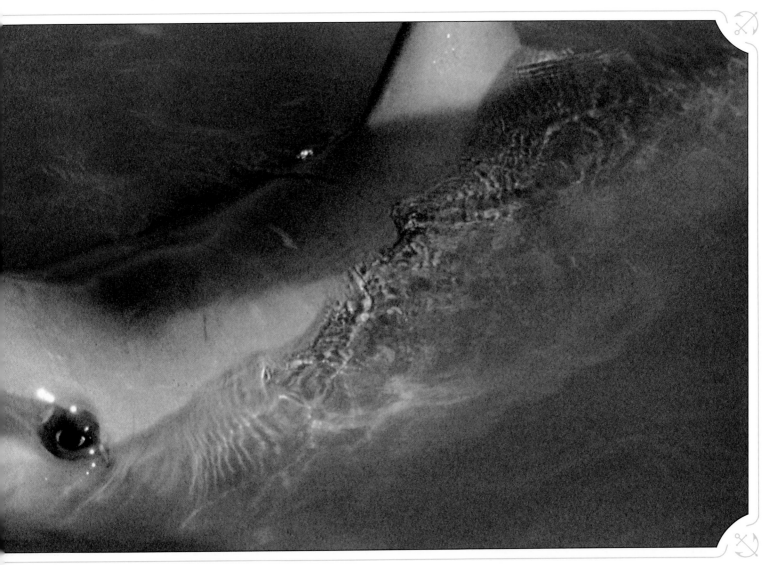

Dolphins delight in communicating with people in the unique situation of Shark Bay, W.A.

Description

Single, ear-shaped shell, lined with Mother-of-Pearl. Actual animal is a type of snail, from 6cm (2 inches) to 25cm (10 inches) across, and up to 8cm (3 inches) thick. A large "sucker" foot is featured. Blacklip has a red shell with a black frill across the bottom of the snail's foot; Greenlip has a red shell, streaked with green; green frill across foot.

Habitat

Found clinging to rocks or seaweed in shallow to deep inland waters. Those in deeper water are usually much larger.

Underwater Behaviour

Virtually sedentary. Maximum recorded movement is 200m (660 feet).

Table Qualities

High market prices and modern day scarcity testify to Abalone's popularity for the table. Delicious, rich flavour. May be steamed for several hours; overcooking by any other method will toughen the meat. Usually bought live; check by touching flesh — it should move. The fresh meat is also sold, as is canned Abalone. For storage details, see page 316, for preparation, see page 314.

Recipes
Main: page 262

Comments

In the US the common Abalone are the Red Abalone, Pink Abalone, Green Abalone and Black Abalone.

Balmain Bug & Moreton Bay Bug
Scyllaridae

Species
Balmain Bug   Moreton Bay Bug

Other Common Names
Shovel-Nosed Lobster
Bay Lobster

NZ Common Name
Not found

US Common Name
Not found
(See Comments)

Description

Two plate-like structures in front of head. Distinctive, almost triangular-shaped body. Wide, fan-like tail. Eyes in centre of head for Balmain Bug; on outer edges of head for Moreton Bay Bug. Balmain Bug green; Moreton Bay Bug browny with spots.

Habitat

Coastal waters and bays.

Underwater Behaviour

Soft bottom dwellers; scavengers. Plates used to burrow into sea floor.

Table Qualities

Very similar to the Rock Lobster.

Recipes
Entrée/Appetizer:
page 224
Main: pages 178, 277

Comments

These animals are closely related to the Rock Lobsters. Similar species exist in US waters, but are not commonly eaten.

A spotted Nudibranch, Port Stephens, NSW.

Crested terns in council on the Ningaloo Reef, W.A.

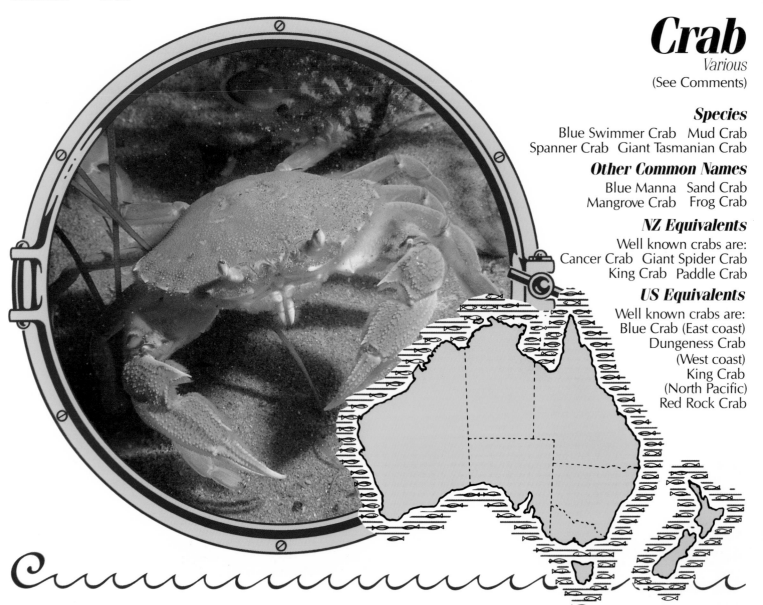

Crab
Various
(See Comments)

Species
Blue Swimmer Crab   Mud Crab
Spanner Crab   Giant Tasmanian Crab

Other Common Names
Blue Manna   Sand Crab
Mangrove Crab   Frog Crab

NZ Equivalents
Well known crabs are:
Cancer Crab   Giant Spider Crab
King Crab   Paddle Crab

US Equivalents
Well known crabs are:
Blue Crab (East coast)
Dungeness Crab
(West coast)
King Crab
(North Pacific)
Red Rock Crab

Description

Body triangular or oval in outline. Five pairs of legs; first pair usually more massive and ending in pincers. Eyes on moveable stalks which can retract into sockets. Abdomen narrow and triangular in males; broad and rounded in females.

Habitat

Spanner and Blue Swimmer found in bays, estuaries and open seas. Tasmanian Crab found generally in Bass Strait at moderate depths. Mud Crabs found in mud flats of estuaries and bays.

Underwater Behaviour

Usually omnivorous scavengers; some predatory. Locomotion by means of walking with a sidelong gait; open sea species able to swim surprisingly rapidly.

Table Qualities

Absolute delicacy; best bought live to retain freshness, especially Mud Crab. The flesh goes off rapidly after dying. See page 316 for storage, page 313 for preparation and page 315 for cooking.

Recipes
Entrée/Appetizer:
pages 124, 125, 152, 306
Main: pages 128, 144, 161, 291

Comments

There are numerous species of Crab found around the world. All are members of the Order Decapoda.

A tropical sunset. Darwin Harbour.

An aerial view of Sydney's beautiful harbour.

Crayfish-Freshwater
Parastacidae

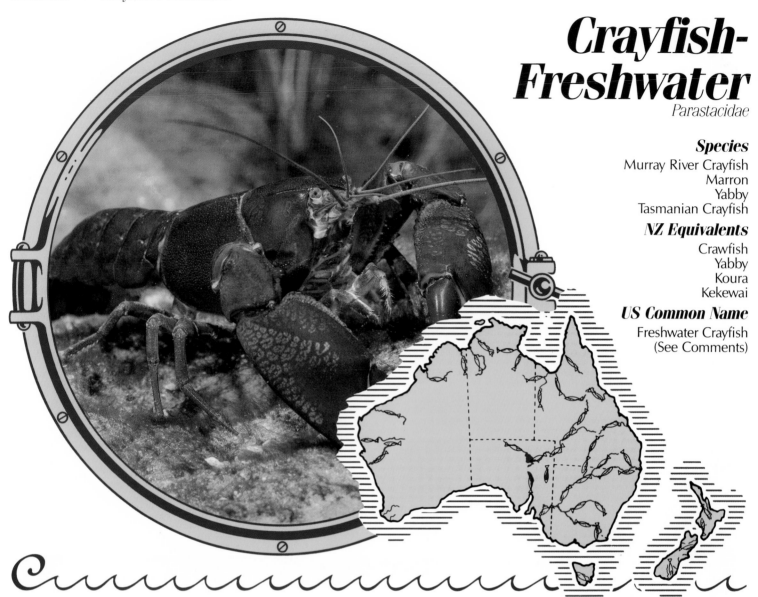

Species
Murray River Crayfish
Marron
Yabby
Tasmanian Crayfish

NZ Equivalents
Crawfish
Yabby
Koura
Kekewai

US Common Name
Freshwater Crayfish
(See Comments)

Description

Five pairs of legs, the foremost are much more developed and have large pincers at the ends. The foremost of the remaining four pairs of legs also have pincers, but less developed. From blue to green to brown above; white below. The Tasmanian Crayfish is the world's largest, growing up to 40cm (16 inches) long; other species up to 30cm (1 foot).

Habitat

Rivers, streams and waterholes; commonly on farm dams.

Underwater Behaviour

Bottom scavengers, feeding on whatever small animals or scraps are around.

The serene beauty of a water lily on a billabong in the Northern Territory.

Table Qualities

Flesh is fine, moist and beautifully flavoured. The meat is in the tail and the claws. Usually sold live; for storage, see page 316, for preparation, page 313. Grill, barbecue or boil (page 315).

Recipes
Entrée/Appetizer:
pages 153, 240
Main: page 247

Comments

There are many species of freshwater Crayfish in the US — all are similar to the Australian varieties, though generally smaller.

The Ashburton River in the rugged outback of Nanntarra, Pilbara, W.A.

Cuttlefish
Class Cephalapoda

NZ Common Name
Cuttlefish

US Common Name
Cuttlefish

Octopus

Class Cephalapoda

NZ Common Name
Octopus

US Common Name
Octopus

Squid/ Calamari
Class Cephalapoda

NZ Common Name
Squid

US Common Name
Squid

Description

Flattened body. Fin down each side, from head to tail. Eight arms and two tentacles, tentacles encircle mouth and may be retracted into pouches. Thick, internal calcified shell (cuttlebone).

Habitat

Shallow, coastal water, often migrate to deeper waters in winter.

Underwater Behaviour

Active animals, swim by moving fins, aided by a central water jet — jet enables rapid backward movement when in danger. Able to secrete an ink cloud for protection. Feed on small crustaceans, small fish and are known to be cannibalistic. Tentacles used to catch prey.

Table Qualities

White, firm flesh with a subtle flavour. Sold whole — see page 314 for preparation. Pan fry or barbecue quickly, otherwise stew slowly for an hour or so. Often cooked in their own ink.

Recipes
Entrée/Appetizer:
page 170

Comments

Cuttlefish, Squid and Octopus are all members of the Phylum Mollusca and so come under the broad classification of Molluscs. More specifically, they are all members of the Class Cephalaphoda, more commonly known as Cephalapods.

Description

No apparent body, eight arms or tentacles hang from a skirt around the bottom of the rounded head. Two rows of suckers on each arm. Generally grey/brown.

Habitat

Varies from shallow waters of bays and estuaries to the extremely deep water of the oceans for some of the large species.

Underwater Behaviour

Generally move about on the bottom by means of their arms; may move through the water by using its central funnel as a water jet. Favourite food is Crab, though will feed opportunistically; commonly eat their own arms. Paralyses victims then engulfs them.

Table Qualities

Needs to be tenderised by beating on rocks. Commercially octopuses are tenderised by tumbling in a washing machine or cement mixer. Flesh is firm and white with a distinct flavour. Sold whole — see page 314 for preparation. Grill, barbecue or fry quickly, or simmer slowly for 1-1½ hours in its own juice

adding wine etc. if desired.

Recipes
Entrée/Appetizer:
pages 152, 286
Main: page 263

Comments

See above.

Description

Elongate, slender body, edged by triangular fins. A short head with well developed eyes. Eight arms and two tentacles. A long horn-like structure sits inside the mantle: the rudiment of a shell.

Habitat

Shallow coastal water to open seas. Some large species are found in very deep water.

Underwater Behaviour

Same as for Cuttlefish; see above.

Table Qualities

White, firm flesh, mild flavour. May be bought whole, in tubes (hoods) or rings; for preparation see page 314. Delicious and tender if not overcooked. Pan fry quickly, deep-fry with batter coating quickly, bake or stew slowly.

Recipes
Entrée/Appetizer:
page 170
Main: pages 160, 263

Comments

See above.

The violent ocean battering the shores of Western Australia.

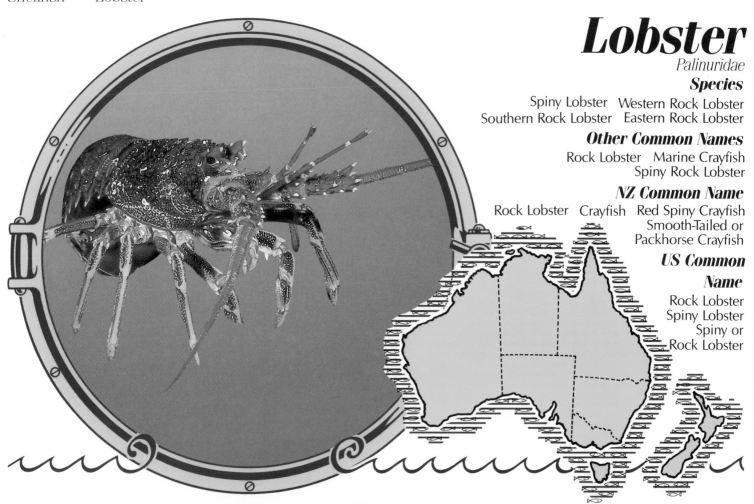

Lobster
Palinuridae
Species
Spiny Lobster   Western Rock Lobster
Southern Rock Lobster   Eastern Rock Lobster
Other Common Names
Rock Lobster   Marine Crayfish
Spiny Rock Lobster
NZ Common Name
Rock Lobster   Crayfish   Red Spiny Crayfish
Smooth-Tailed or
Packhorse Crayfish
US Common Name
Rock Lobster
Spiny Lobster
Spiny or
Rock Lobster

Description

Five pairs of legs, foremost of which are elongated into spines. Spiny body, with typical plate-like fantail shape.

Habitat

Close to shore at depths of up to 160m (530 feet). Prefer rock or reef habitats.

Underwater Behaviour

Bottom dwelling scavengers, generally feeding on small crustaceans, molluscs, scraps and dead animals. Breeding occurs in deep water during winter. The female can carry up to two million eggs under her abdomen.

Table Qualities

Extremely popular table fare; most of the meat is in the tail, consequently they are often marketed as frozen tails. White, moist meat with a rich, sweet flavour. Whole Lobster sold live or cooked. See page 316 for storage, page 313 for preparation for the table. Grill, barbecue or boil (page 315).

Recipes
Entrée/Appetizer: page 256
Main: pages 132, 157, 262, 291

Comments

Much confusion exists as to the naming of these crustaceans. True Lobsters are members of the family Homaridae — Australia and New Zealand have none of these. The species of the family Palinuridae are variously described as Rock Lobsters, Spiny Lobsters or marine Crayfish. They are easily distinguished from Lobsters and freshwater Crayfish by the absence of pincers on the first pair of legs. Panulirus argus and Panulirus interruptus are the most common species in the US.

Murray Islanders enjoy sailing their model outriggers. Torres Strait, Qld.

Everyone has seen the Triton shell, but not many people have been lucky enough to meet its inhabitant. The owner of the shell is shy, retiring and nocturnal by habit.

Molluscs (Bi-Valve)
COCKLE-CLAM-MUSSEL-OYSTER-PIPI-SCALLOP
Class Lamellibranchia

Species
Cockle   Clam
Mussel   Oyster
Pipi   Scallop

NZ Common Name
As Australia

US Common Name
As Australia

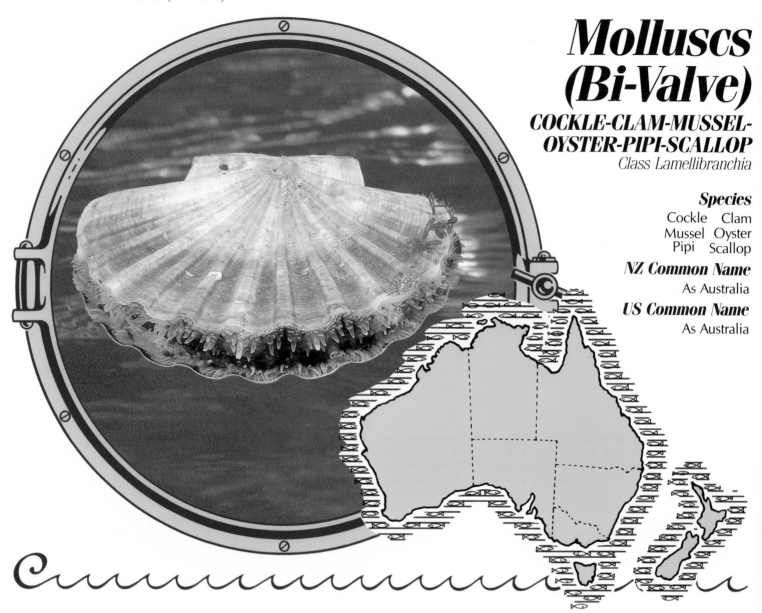

Description

Calcareous shell, which consists of two hinged pieces (valves). Internally and externally symmetrical. Valves joined by a tough ligament and a set of interlocking teeth. Two gills and a rudimentary head. Well developed foot (not present in Oyster).

Habitat

Sandy or muddy bottoms from shallow inland waters to the deeper waters of the continental shelf. Some species prefer very deep water.

Underwater Behaviour

Mainly sedentary and lives buried in sand or mud, or clinging to rocks; feeds on minute plankton and organic debris. Scallops are unusual in being highly active — and able to swim away when in danger.

Table Qualities

The meat of all these Molluscs can toughen easily when cooking. Oysters are delicious eaten raw with a little lemon juice. All Bi-valves bought live should have tightly closed shells, although Pipis may be slightly open. For storage of live Molluscs, see page 317, for preparation, page 314. Pan fry, steam, barbecue or poach, cooking for 2-3 minutes only, otherwise meat will toughen.

Recipes
Entrée/Appetizer:
pages 170, 189, 205, 224, 225, 272, 286, 302, 303
Main: pages 157, 161, 177, 211, 263, 276, 277, 290

The sun goes down in crimson glory at the coral atolls of the Rowley Shoals, west of Broome, W.A.

Great Oyster Bay, Tas.

Prawn
Penaeidae

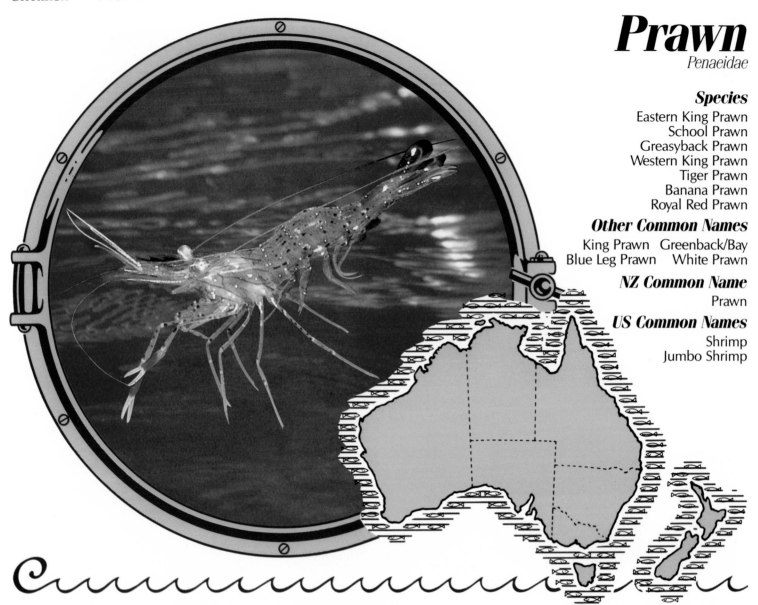

Species
Eastern King Prawn
School Prawn
Greasyback Prawn
Western King Prawn
Tiger Prawn
Banana Prawn
Royal Red Prawn

Other Common Names
King Prawn   Greenback/Bay
Blue Leg Prawn   White Prawn

NZ Common Name
Prawn

US Common Names
Shrimp
Jumbo Shrimp

Description
Five pairs of legs. Thin and fragile shell. Dark, prominent eyes. Long, fine feelers at front of head. Up to 30cm (1 foot) for the King Prawn; 12-25cm (5-10 inches) for the other species.

Habitat
Muddy bottoms of inshore and offshore waters.

Underwater Behaviour
Agile swimmers, propelling themselves by means of the paddle-like limbs of the abdomen — can leap from the water when in danger. Bottom feeding scavengers.

Table Qualities
Extremely popular the world over; flesh is white, finely textured and extremely tasty. Sold whole, cooked or uncooked (green), or shelled as Prawn meat. Uncooked Prawns can be fried, grilled, barbecued, baked or poached; cooked Prawns can be served cold or heated gently for a variety of dishes. For boiling uncooked Prawns, see page 315.

Recipes
Entrée/Appetizer:
pages 140, 141, 170, 225, 256, 286, 302
Main: pages 132, 229, 230, 263, 276, 292

Comments
''Prawns'' in the US refer to the freshwater species. There are many varieties of this marine species in the US.

Male sea lions in territorial display, dispute a sun-baking spot at Carnac Island, W.A.

A Prawn trawler in action off the Gulf of Carpentaria, Qld.

Sea Urchin
Class Echinoidea

NZ Common Name
Sea Urchin
US Common Name
Sea Urchin

Description

Spherical shell of calcareous plates. Numerous sharp spines protrude from perforations in shell. Underside of shell has a large hole covered with skin where mouth is situated. The top surface has a smaller opening for the waste vent.

Habitat

Mainly shallow coastal waters. Some species found in deep water.

Underwater Behaviour

Creep on sea bottom feeding mainly on vegetable matter. Some species feed on small animals.

Table Qualities

The edible parts are actually the roes or gonads. Mustard in colour, with a fluid texture and a subtle nut-like flavour. Sea Urchin roes are available ready prepared for the table; if you have obtained whole Sea Urchins, great care must be taken in removing the gonads from the spiny shell. For preparation, storage and serving, see page 314.

Rock art at Nambucca Heads, NSW.

Tropical mangroves and water at Tunning Fork Bay, Cape York, Qld.

Smoked Fish

Fish Roes

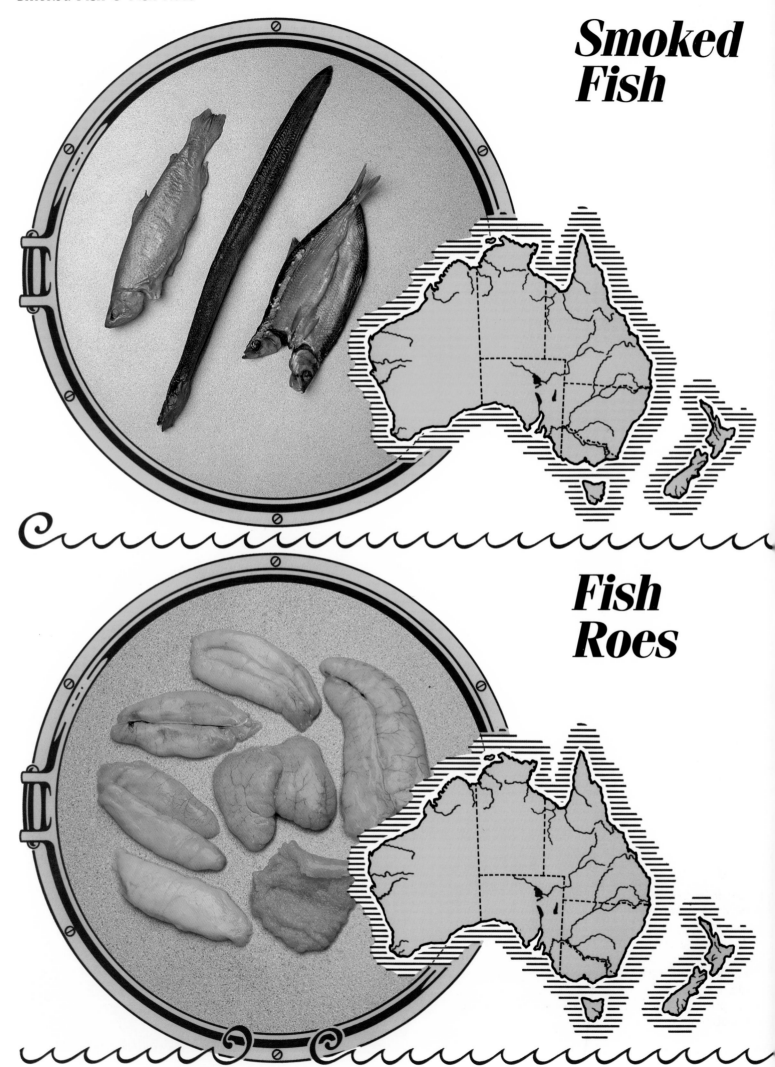

Cold-Smoked Fish

In Australia, Gemfish, Tailor, Salmon and Sea Trout are cold-smoked. Other cold-smoked fish are imported — Cod, Herring (Kippers) and Haddock (Finnan Haddie).

Table Qualities

The outside of the fish is orange in colour, with resilient flesh, almost dry to the touch. Smoked Salmon and Sea Trout flesh is a uniform orange-pink in colour. Reject any fish with a sticky feel and rancid smell.

Hot-Smoked Fish

Eel, Gemfish, Mackerel, Tailor and Freshwater Trout are prepared in Australia.

Table Qualities

Hot-smoked fish is usually dark bronze in colour and firm when pressed as the flesh is cooked.
For storage, preparation and serving see page 315.

Fish Roes

Soft roes (milt) are obtained from male fish, hard roes (fish eggs) from female fish. Both types of roe are considered delicacies, and are very high in nutrients. The better-known roes are all imported — Salmon Roe (orange-red globules, salted and packed in jars), Caviar (small grey globules, salted, from the Sturgeon) and Lumpfish Caviar (tiny orange or black globules, salted and dyed, from the Lumpfish).

Soft Roes

Creamy white in colour with a soft, creamy texture. Care should be taken not to puncture the fine membrane. Shape varies according to the fish from which they are removed. Usually obtained from Flathead, Gemfish, Mullet and Snapper.

Hard Roes

Roes from the grey Mullet are the only ones of culinary merit and commercial value in Australia. When removed from the fish, the actual eggs are contained in two elongated, oval sacs, joined at the top, and care must be taken that the membrane is not punctured. They are orange-yellow in colour, with a grainy texture. These are salted, pressed, dried and sometimes cold-smoked, to make a popular Mediterranean snack food called Botargo, available in Australia as Smoked Fish Roe.

A scuba diver flanked by a school of fish, at Heron Island, Australia.

A romantic end to a hard day of fishing.

Shady beach, Great Barrier Reef, Qld.

The Great Barrier Reef

*I*f there's only one place you visit in your lifetime, make it The Great Barrier Reef. More than the coral kaleidoscope, more than the countless perfect palm fringed beaches, more than the clear blue waters and skies; more than all this, is the direct link with nature's ancient and enduring strength. The past lives of infinite organisms running back through the ages greet you at every turn illustrating countless years passed and the hopes for the years to come.

"Davey Jones Locker", where the dead ships lie.
Abrolhos Islands, W.A.

Australia's greatest national treasure is probably the world's most important "living museum". The Great Barrier Reef is like an immense storehouse of knowledge with information on the countless species of flora and fauna and precious insight into the intricate and vital relationships between these multivarious life forms.

In a sense, the Reef itself is one great organism. A massive, living, breathing creature, always parts growing, always parts dying. A fantastic symbiotic whole which has shaped the environment to its needs and has learned, over its ancient life, how to weather the most torrid of nature's tempests.

The awesome power of its lifeforce is reflected in its awesome and timeless beauty. Through the crystalline splendour of the transparent waters beat the ever deepening hues of blues and greens. Colours vivid from some wild dreamland, creatures with unfathomable purpose, geometric fish with designer patterns, curious squid and aggressive plants. A world removed from our reality, but perhaps a world closer to the realities of life.

The importance of the Reef cannot be over emphasised. It is a great relief to know that this importance has been recognised by its inclusion on the World Heritage List — a move which has ensured the continued preservation of this unique area for posterity.

The recipes in this chapter relate to species that are plentiful on the Reef and that are in no way endangered. Many of these species are also found in waters outside the Reef and you will find that a great number are readily available in fish markets around the country.

The meal that is shown in the photograph opposite is truly a tropical treat! The Groper and Tomato combine superbly to make for an extremely tasty soup, while the Red Emperor and Prawns in a Pastry Roll will delight your senses with its complementary blend of subtle flavours. The Avocado Lime Cream is a most refreshing way to complete a well-rounded meal.

Surely, if nothing else, the food from this chapter will inflame your desires for a little travel north. Make that visit soon!

Top: AVOCADO LIME CREAM, Recipe page 135. *Middle*: GROPER TOMATO SOUP, Recipe page 124.
Below: RED EMPEROR & PRAWNS IN A PASTRY ROLL, Recipe page 129.

Groper Tomato Soup

(Photograph page 123)

INGREDIENTS

500g (1lb) Groper or Hapuku fillets
1 tablespoon oil
2 medium onions, finely sliced
2 large potatoes, peeled and diced
3 x 425g (15oz) cans tomatoes
½ teaspoon sugar
salt and pepper to taste
2 tablespoons finely chopped fresh basil or 1 teaspoon dried
2 cups fish stock or water (page 315)
finely chopped parsley to garnish

METHOD

Skin the fillets. Cut into small pieces, removing any bones. Heat oil in a large saucepan and gently cook onions. Add potatoes, tomatoes, sugar, salt, pepper, basil and stock. Bring to the boil then simmer for 20 minutes, crushing the tomatoes to break them up. Add fish pieces and simmer gently until flesh flakes. Serve soup sprinkled with parsley. Note: Groper is only available commercially in North Queensland; use Hapuku elsewhere.

Serves 6

Crunchy Vegetable Salad

INGREDIENTS

1 cup chick peas
1 capsicum, diced
1 cup finely sliced celery
1 tablespoon finely chopped capers
½ cup finely sliced pickled onions
¼ cup finely sliced olives
2 tablespoons oil
1½ tablespoons lime or lemon juice
2 tablespoons finely chopped fresh basil
salt and pepper to taste
assorted salad greens

METHOD

Wash chick peas and place in a saucepan. Cover with water and soak overnight. Drain. Cook in boiling water for 45-60 minutes until tender, adding salt towards end of cooking; drain and chill well.
In a bowl combine chick peas, capsicum, celery, capers, onions and olives. Mix well. Combine oil, lime juice, basil and seasonings, pour over salad. Arrange over salad greens and serve.

Serves 6

Cheese Puffs

INGREDIENTS

1 cup self-raising flour
pinch salt
pinch cayenne pepper
1 tablespoon butter
1 cup grated cheddar cheese
3 tablespoons milk
1 egg, beaten
½ cup ghee

METHOD

In a bowl, sift self-raising flour, salt and cayenne pepper. Rub in butter, add cheese, reserving 2 tablespoons. Add combined milk and egg to form a soft dough. Knead lightly. Roll into a long roll about 2.5cm (1 inch) in diameter. Cut evenly into 12 portions. Heat ghee in a pan and fry portions until golden, around 3-4 minutes, turning halfway through cooking time. Drain and sprinkle with reserved cheese. Serve hot with salad garnish.

Serves 6

Avocado and Pawpaw Salad

INGREDIENTS

1 large pawpaw, firm but ripe
2 avocados
3 tomatoes
⅓ cup lime or lemon juice
¼ teaspoon salt
¼ teaspoon ground coriander
white pepper to taste
watercress, well washed
endive, well washed
pine nuts, toasted

METHOD

Cut pawpaw in half, remove seeds and skin. Cut into bite-size pieces. Cut avocados in half, remove stone. Ball with a melon baller.
Peel and seed tomatoes and cut into quarters.
In a bowl mix lime juice, salt, coriander and pepper. Place pawpaw, avocado and tomatoes in this dressing and toss gently.
Place watercress and endive sprigs onto appetizer plates and spoon fruits and dressing on top. Garnish with toasted pine nuts.

Serves 6

Tuna Rice Salad

INGREDIENTS

1 x 500g (16oz) can Tuna, or 500g (1lb) poached fresh Tuna
3 cups cooked rice
¾ cup finely sliced celery
2 tablespoons finely chopped pickled onions
¼ cup diced capsicum
2 tablespoons finely chopped parsley
½ cup mayonnaise
2 tablespoons lime or lemon juice
salt and pepper to taste
lettuce leaves
lemon wedges

METHOD

Drain and flake Tuna. In a bowl combine Tuna, rice, celery, onions, capsicum, parsley, mayonnaise and lime juice. Season with salt and pepper. Mix well and chill. Place lettuce leaves on a platter, pile on salad, garnish with lemon wedges and serve.

Serves 6

Crab and Mushroom Salad

INGREDIENTS

500g (1lb) cooked Crab meat
250g (8oz) mushrooms, finely sliced
2 tablespoons finely chopped parsley
2 teaspoons finely chopped fresh tarragon
3 tablespoons lime or lemon juice
1 ½ tablespoons hazelnut oil
salt and pepper to taste

METHOD

Flake Crab meat. In a bowl combine Crab meat, mushrooms, parsley and tarragon. Mix well. Combine lime juice and hazelnut oil and pour over the Crab salad. Season with salt and pepper. Serve on a bed of lettuce or in individual lettuce cups.

Serves 6

CRAB QUICHE, Recipe page 125.

Crab Quiche

(Photograph page 125)

INGREDIENTS

Pastry
250g (8oz) flour
125g (4oz) butter or margarine, cubed
1 egg, beaten
water

METHOD

Sift flour and salt into a bowl. Rub in butter until mixture resembles breadcrumbs. Add beaten egg and enough water to combine mixture to a firm dough. Knead lightly, cover and rest in a cool place for 30 minutes. Roll out pastry and line a quiche pan. Prick pastry and blind bake for 10 minutes in oven preheated at 200ºC (400ºF). Allow to cool slightly. Flake Crab meat. In a

Filling
2 cups cooked Crab meat
2 tablespoons finely chopped parsley
2 tablespoons dry sherry
salt and pepper to taste
5 eggs
1 ½ cups milk
pinch cayenne pepper
paprika

bowl combine Crab meat, parsley, sherry, salt and pepper. Mix well. In another bowl lightly beat eggs, milk and cayenne pepper.
Place Crab meat mixture into the pastry shell and pour over custard mixture. Sprinkle with paprika and return to oven, reduce to 180ºC (350ºF), and cook for 30-35 minutes or until custard sets. Custard is set when a knife, inserted in the centre, comes out clean. Serve hot.

Serves 4 to 6

Giant trees at Cape Tribulation, Qld.

CORAL TROUT WITH MACADAMIAS AND BANANAS, Recipe page 128.

Coral Trout with Macadamias and Bananas

(Photograph page 128)

INGREDIENTS

2 x 750g (1½lb) Coral Trout
3 tablespoons butter
2 tablespoons lime or lemon juice
2 large bananas, sliced diagonally
½ cup macadamia nuts
1 tablespoon dark rum
1 tablespoon brown sugar
½ cup cream

METHOD

Scale and clean fish, rinse and pat dry. In a large frying pan melt half the butter, add half the lime juice and add Trout. Cover and simmer gently for 15 minutes or until flesh flakes. Lift out fish and keep warm. Add remaining butter and lime juice to pan juices, and heat until reduced a little. Add banana slices and macadamia nuts, toss over medium heat for 1 minute. Stir in rum, brown sugar and cream and simmer for 2-3 minutes. Serve alongside the fish.

Serves 6

Crab with Water Chestnuts

INGREDIENTS

3 medium size cooked Mud Crabs
2-3 tablespoons oil
2 garlic cloves, crushed
1 medium onion, finely sliced
24 water chestnuts, thinly sliced
1 cup fish or chicken stock
1 tablespoon soy sauce
pepper to taste
2 teaspoons cornflour
2 tablespoons sherry

METHOD

Remove meat from Crabs, incluaing the claws and cut into bite-size pieces.
Heat oil in a pan and stir-fry garlic and onion. Add water chestnuts, stock and Crab meat. Season with soy sauce and pepper. Mix cornflour with sherry, add to Crab mixture, stirring until thickened and bubbling. Serve with noodles or rice.

Serves 6

Red Emperor and Prawns in a Pastry Roll

(Photograph page 123)

INGREDIENTS

500g (1lb) Red Emperor or
Cobia fillets
water
250g (8oz) shelled cooked
Prawns
2 tablespoons butter or
margarine
1 medium onion, finely
chopped
60g (2oz) mushrooms, finely
chopped
3 tablespoons flour
1¼ cups milk
½ cup grated cheddar cheese
2 tablespoons lemon juice
1 teaspoon finely grated
lemon rind
salt and pepper to taste
10 sheets filo pastry
melted butter
sesame seeds

METHOD

Skin the fillets. Place fillets in pan and just cover with water. Poach gently until flesh flakes, about 3-4 minutes. Remove and flake fish. Wash and devein Prawns, chop roughly. In a saucepan melt butter and gently cook onion, add mushrooms and cook for 2-3 minutes. Stir in flour, cook for 2 minutes. Gradually pour in milk and stir over heat until sauce boils and thickens. Remove from heat, add cheese, lemon juice, rind, salt and pepper, mix well. Fold in flaked fish and Prawns.
To assemble: Brush and stack filou sheets with melted butter, brush top sheet with butter. Place filling toward bottom longer edge, keeping 4cm (1 ½ inch) of sides clear of filling. Fold base and sides over filling and roll up. Place seam side down onto greased baking sheet, brush top with butter and sprinkle with sesame seeds. Bake in a preheated 180ºC (350ºF) oven for 20 minutes until golden. Serve hot cut in thick slices.

Serves 6

Parrot Fish in Apricot Rum Nectar

INGREDIENTS

2 x 1kg (2lb) whole Parrot Fish
or Goatfish
1 cup apricot nectar
¼ cup rum
½ teaspoon cinnamon
8cm (3 inch) piece green
ginger, finely grated
2 tablespoons honey

METHOD

Scale and clean fish. Trim fins. With a sharp knife score the fish by cutting twice diagonally on each side. Place fish in a greased ovenproof dish. Meanwhile, in a bowl combine apricot nectar, rum, cinnamon, ginger and honey. Mix well. Pour marinade over fish and rest in refrigerator for 1 hour. Place fish with marinade in oven and bake at 180ºC (350ºF) for 25-30 minutes or until flesh flakes.

Serves 6

When you catch a Crayfish like this it's worth holding it up for the camera.

Left: FISHERMAN'S BASKET WITH MANGO SAUCE, Recipe page 132. *Right:* GARLIC PRAWNS, Recipe page 132.

Fisherman's Basket with Mango Sauce

(Photograph pages 130 & 131)

INGREDIENTS

3 green Lobster tails
500g (1lb) Coral Trout fillets
500g (1lb) green King Prawns
500g (1lb) Scallops
1 cup seasoned cornflour
3 eggs, beaten
2 cups fine dry breadcrumbs
1 cup desiccated coconut
oil for deep frying

Sauce

⅔ cup fresh mango pulp purée
⅓ cup coconut milk
2 tablespoons fresh lime or lemon juice
1 tablespoon chopped fresh coriander

METHOD

Halve Lobster tails, lift out flesh and remove intestinal tract. Cut fish in 2cm (3/4 inch) strips. Shell and devein Prawns, leaving tails on. Toss each piece of prepared seafood in seasoned cornflour, dip in egg and coat with combined breadcrumbs and coconut. Place on a tray, cover loosely and refrigerate for 1 hour. Combine sauce ingredients and set aside.
Heat oil to 180ºC (350ºF) and fry Lobster tails for 2-3 minutes, until golden, drain on kitchen paper and keep warm. Fry Trout fillets and Prawns for approximately 2 minutes and Scallops for 1 minute.
Serve immediately in a basket with Mango Sauce served separately.

Serves 6

Garlic Prawns

(Photograph pages 130 & 131)

INGREDIENTS

1kg (2lb) green Prawns
8 large garlic cloves
125g (4oz) butter, melted
1 cup light olive oil
1 cup dry white wine
2 tablespoons lemon juice
2 tablespoons finely chopped parsley
1 teaspoon salt

METHOD

Shell Prawns, leaving tails on, devein. Chop garlic finely and combine with remaining ingredients, being sure to coat Prawns well.
Pile mixture evenly into heavy cast-iron pots or individual casserole dishes, cover and bake at 220ºC (425ºF) for 15 minutes. Serve with crusty bread to mop up the juices.

Serves 2 to 3

Coral Trout with Julienne of Orange

INGREDIENTS

750g (1½lb) Coral Trout fillets
2 medium size oranges
1 tablespoon butter or margarine
3 shallots, finely chopped
¼ cup lemon juice
2 tablespoons sherry
¾ cup fish or chicken stock
salt and pepper to taste

METHOD

Skin the fillets and place in a greased ovenproof dish. Wash oranges, peel thinly removing any pith from the peel. Cut peel into fine julienne strips. Melt butter in a pan and sauté orange strips and shallots. Add lemon juice, sherry and stock. Season with salt and pepper, cool. Pour over fillets and bake at 180ºC (350ºF) for 20-25 minutes or until flesh flakes.

Serves 6

Coral Trout with Fresh Crab Topping

INGREDIENTS

750g (1½lb) Coral Trout or Goatfish fillets
1 cup cooked Crab meat
¾ cup fresh breadcrumbs
4 shallots, finely sliced
1 egg, beaten
1½ tablespoons sherry
salt and pepper to taste
1 tablespoon lemon juice

METHOD

Skin the fillets and lay in a greased ovenproof dish. Flake Crab meat removing any small pieces of shell. In a bowl combine Crab meat, breadcrumbs, shallots, egg, sherry and salt and pepper. Mix well. Mixture should be well moistened and come together easily. Spoon mixture evenly over fillets and sprinkle lemon juice. Bake at 180ºC (350ºF) for 20-25 minutes or until flesh flakes and top is golden.

Serves 6

Coral Trout Rolled with Prawns

INGREDIENTS

750g (1½lb) Coral Trout fillets
4 shallots, finely chopped
2 tablespoons finely chopped parsley,
125g (4oz) mushrooms, finely chopped
250g (8oz) cooked Prawns, cut into very small pieces
salt and pepper to taste
½ cup white wine

METHOD

Skin the fillets. In a bowl combine shallots, parsley, mushrooms and Prawns. Mix well. Place spoonfuls of mixture onto each fillet and roll up. Secure with toothpicks. Lay rolled fillets in a greased baking dish and pour over wine. Cover and bake at 180ºC (350ºF) for 20-25 minutes until flesh flakes. These rolled fillets can be masked with any delicately flavoured sauce.

Serves 6

Red Emperor Fillets with Capers and Lemon

INGREDIENTS

750g (1½lb) Red Emperor or Cobia fillets
¼ cup capers, drained well
3 tablespoons lemon juice
salt and pepper to taste
parsley, finely chopped

METHOD

Skin the fillets. Place fillets in a greased ovenproof dish. Sprinkle capers over fish and pour over lemon juice. Season with salt and pepper. Cover and bake at 180ºC (350ºF) for 10-15 minutes or until flesh flakes. Sprinkle with parsley before serving. This is a good recipe for a low-fat meal; if more flavour is desired, dot top with small pieces of butter or margarine before cooking.

Serves 6

The Great Barrier Reef, protected by the World Heritage, Port Douglas, Nth Qld.

Pineapple Tropicale

(Photograph pages 134 & 135)

INGREDIENTS

3 small pineapples
2 mangoes, peeled and flesh cubed
2 bananas, peeled and sliced thinly
2 tablespoons lime juice
2 tablespoons finely chopped crystallized ginger
6 egg whites
¼ cup castor sugar
3 tablespoons slivered almonds
icecream for serving

METHOD

Leave top on pineapple. Halve lengthways, cutting through the leaves. Cut flesh from shell and dice. In a bowl combine pineapple, mango, banana, lime juice and ginger. Mix well. Place mixture back into the pineapple shells. Beat egg whites until stiff, gradually beat in sugar to form a meringue. Pile meringue over top of fruit, sprinkle with almonds and bake at 180ºC (350ºF) till golden. Serve warm with ice cream.

Serves 6

Baked Pawpaw

(Photograph pages 134 & 135)

INGREDIENTS

2 medium size ripe pawpaws
1 cup coconut milk
3 tablespoons sugar
2 tablespoons rum
shredded coconut

METHOD

Peel and cut pawpaw into cubes, discarding seeds. Place pawpaw into a greased ovenproof dish and pour over combined coconut milk and sugar. Bake at 180ºC (350ºF) for 20 minutes or until heated through and slightly golden. Remove and add rum.
Serve warm or chilled, garnished with shredded coconut.

Serves 6

Left: BAKED PAWPAW, Recipe page 134. *Right*: PINEAPPLE TROPICAL, Recipe page 134.

Avocado Lime Cream

(Photograph page 123)

INGREDIENTS

3 large avocados
¼ cup castor sugar
¾ cup cream, lightly whipped
¾ cup natural yoghurt
extra whipped cream and
grated lime rind to decorate

METHOD

Cut avocados in half, remove stone and scoop out flesh. Finely grate limes and juice the fruit. In a food processor or blender purée avocado flesh, add sugar, lime rind and juice. Fold in the cream and yoghurt. Spoon into dessert bowls. Chill well before serving. Decorate with whipped cream and lime rind.

Serves 6

Golden Bananas

INGREDIENTS

6 firm medium size bananas
2 tablespoons butter
2 tablespoons sugar
½ cup apricot jam, sieved
2 tablespoons brandy or rum
cream for serving

METHOD

Peel bananas and slice in half lengthways. Melt butter in frying pan, sprinkle on the sugar and cook over a medium heat for 1-2 minutes shaking the pan constantly until the mixture has lightly caramelized. Stir in the apricot jam and brandy. Keep stirring until the mixture is smooth. Add bananas, cook gently to heat them through, spooning the sauce on top. Do not let bananas become too soft. Place two halves and sauce in each dessert dish and serve with pouring cream.

Serves 6

Competitors gathering for a sailing race at sunny Green Island, Qld.

The splendor of the Manderin fish.

Top End Treats

The "top end" is without doubt Australia's most exotic destination. This is the land of the monsoon, fearsome cyclone, thick and oppressive, hot moist air, palm-fringed blinding white sand, impenetrable jungle and steamy mangrove.

With such extraordinary surroundings, it comes as no surprise that the cuisine can also be quite remarkable — ask for a steak and it may just be water buffalo that arrives at your table! Or a succulent portion of crocodile! Or even a thick, juicy slice from that most exotic of Australian fish — the Barramundi.

By far the most renowned fish from Australia's far north, Barramundi is one of those highly adaptable species that can be found in both salt and freshwater. It is certainly the delight of the true angling enthusiast, who appreciates the thrill of fighting with a powerful fish that often leaps out of the water when hooked.

This magnificent fish is also the delight of the true lover of fine food. Its firm, white flesh is tender and has a subtle but distinctive flavour. In this chapter you will find a multitude of interesting recipes for this delicious catch. From the stunning Barramundi and Prawn Chowder, to the tangy Chambord, there are recipes to delight the most discerning diner. Perhaps individual Barramundi Ramekins appeal, or the Poached Fillets with oysters?

For those who like the Amber Brew, try the Barramundi in Beer. However the Baked Barramundi, with its delicious stuffing of prawns, sherry, mushrooms and cream, is every bit as tantalising as the photograph on page 144 suggests.

Naturally Barramundi is not the only delectable seafood found in the far north. You would be hard-pressed to find Prawns anywhere else in the world that are quite as spectacular, both in the net and on the plate, as those that are taken from the Gulf of Carpentaria. The giant Tiger and Banana Prawns of this region are commonly 25 cm (10 ins) in length.

Other common catches in our northern waters are Sharks, Crabs, Mullet, and Anchovies, which school in immense numbers off the shores of our tropical coast and are of growing commercial interest.

For a true taste of our exotic northern reaches, close your eyes and relax. Think of balmy moonlit nights and let the thick, salty air fill your lungs. A glass of your favourite wine or beer, and sit down to a meal chosen from this chapter. Perhaps you've been tempted by the mouth-watering photograph opposite — a definitely "moreish" entrée of Prawn Tempura (page 140) with the superb Crab in Blackbean Sauce recipe (page 144) for mains, followed by the absolutely scrumptious Pistachio Nut Cream. What could possibly beat it? Don't delay! Take yourself to the top end — NOW!

The gathering storm. Thunder clouds promise a squally night at an anchorage in the outer Abrolhos.

Top right: PISTACHIO NUT CREAM, Recipe page 146. *Left*: CRAB IN BLACK BEAN SAUCE, Recipe page 144.
Below right: PRAWN TEMPURA, Recipe Page 140.

Prawn Tempura

(Photograph page 139)

INGREDIENTS

1kg (2lb) medium King Prawns
oil for deep frying
Batter
1 cup flour
pinch salt
1 egg, lightly beaten
1 cup mineral water or soda water

METHOD

Peel and devein Prawns, leaving tails on. Slit down the back, clean and flatten out like a butterfly. Set aside in refrigerator until required.
To make batter, sift flour and salt together in a bowl; add beaten egg. Gradually pour in mineral water, stirring to make a smooth batter. Stand batter for at least 30 minutes. Just before using, check consistency, add a little more mineral water if necessary to make a thin batter. Heat oil in a deep frying pan. Dip Prawns into batter, drop into oil and fry until golden brown. Drain on kitchen paper and serve hot with a dipping sauce such as Teriyaki mixed with chopped chili.

Serves 6

Shirred Anchovies

INGREDIENTS

500g (1lb) fresh Anchovies
2 cups fish stock (page 315)
1½ tablespoons lemon juice
6 eggs
3 tablespoons milk
salt and pepper to taste

METHOD

Preheat oven to 150°C (300°F). Wash and clean Anchovies well, small heads can be removed if desired. Divide Anchovies between 6 greased, ovenproof ramekin dishes. Add to each dish a third of a cup of fish stock and a little lemon juice. Beat eggs with milk, season with salt and pepper and pour evenly into each dish. Bake for 20-25 minutes or until golden and set. Unmould and serve hot with toast triangles.

Serves 6

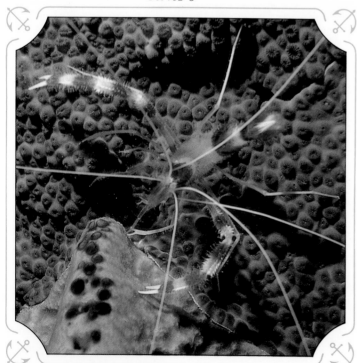

Banded Coral Shrimp, Lady Musgrave Islands.

Pasta with Walnut Sauce

INGREDIENTS

500g (1lb) pasta (tagliatelle, spiral etc)
2 garlic cloves, crushed
125g (4oz) ground walnuts
500g (1lb) ricotta cheese, crumbled
125g (4oz) Parmesan cheese, grated
salt and pepper to taste

METHOD

Cook pasta in boiling water until tender. Drain, keeping a little of the pasta water, and return pasta to pan. In a bowl combine garlic and walnuts and mix in ricotta cheese, Parmesan cheese, salt and pepper. Pour two-thirds of the sauce over the hot, drained pasta, toss well to coat, adding a little pasta water if too dry. Turn into a large serving bowl or serve on individual plates, spooning remaining sauce on top. Serve immediately with extra grated Parmesan cheese served separately.

Serves 6

Barramundi and Prawn Chowder

INGREDIENTS

500g (1lb) Barramundi fillets
250g (8oz) cooked Prawn meat
2 tablespoons butter or margarine
2 bacon slices, chopped
1 medium onion, finely chopped
2 medium potatoes, cubed and parboiled
pepper to taste
1L (4 cups) milk
3 tablespoons flour, blended with water
2 tablespoons chopped parsley

METHOD

Cut fillets into 2cm (¾ inch) cubes. Devein Prawns. Melt butter in a saucepan and gently cook the bacon and onion until onion is soft. Add parboiled potatoes, pepper, fish and milk. Simmer over a low heat for 10 minutes until fish is nearly cooked. Stir in blended flour and parsley, stirring constantly until thickened and bubbling gently. Fish is cooked when flesh flakes. Add Prawns and heat through without boiling. Serve garnished with chopped parsley.

Serves 6

Barramundi Chambord

INGREDIENTS

750g (1½lb) Barramundi cutlets
½ cup tarragon wine vinegar
½ cup white wine
½ teaspoon Worcestershire sauce
salt and pepper to taste
¾ cup tomato puree
grated Parmesan cheese

METHOD

Wipe over Barramundi cutlets with damp kitchen paper. Combine vinegar, wine, Worcestershire sauce, salt and pepper. Marinate the fish in this mixture for 1 hour, turning occasionally. Drain fish and place on greased grill tray. Spread with half the tomato purée and sprinkle with Parmesan cheese. Grill lightly for 2-3 minutes then turn. Spread the other side with remaining tomato purée and cheese and continue to grill for 2-3 minutes. Serve immediately.

Serves 6

GRILLED SKEWERED PRAWNS, Recipe page 141.

Grilled Skewered Prawns

(Photograph page 141)

INGREDIENTS

*1kg (2lb) medium, green King Prawns
24 button-size mushrooms
6 bacon slices, cut into small pieces
12 skewers
2 tablespoons Worcestershire sauce*

METHOD

Peel and devein Prawns, leaving tails on. Wipe mushrooms with kitchen paper. Thread Prawns, mushrooms and bacon slices alternately onto skewers, allowing two skewers per person.

Place skewered Prawns onto a grill plate and cook for 2-3 minutes on each side, basting with Worcestershire sauce. Serve on a bed of fluffy rice.

Serves 6

Avocado and Apple Dip

INGREDIENTS

*500g (1lb) green cooking apples
2 limes, juiced and rind finely grated
3 ripe avocados
2-3 drops Tabasco sauce
250g (8oz) cream cheese, softened
salt and pepper to taste*

METHOD

Peel, core and slice apples. Place in a pan, add lime rind and juice. Cook until soft; cool and purée. Cut avocados in half and remove stone. Remove flesh and mash well. Add to the apple purée with the Tabasco sauce. Beat the cream cheese until smooth and fold through purée mixture. Season with salt and pepper. Serve with cracker biscuits or fresh vegetable sticks.

Serves 6

The beauty of nature is reflected in the waters of Ormiston Gorge, N.T.

BAKED BARRAMUNDI, Recipe page 144.

Crab in Black Bean Sauce

(Photograph page 139)

INGREDIENTS

1kg (2lb) cooked Crab meat
2 tablespoons oil
2 garlic cloves, crushed
2 tablespoons salted black beans, mashed well
2 teaspoons grated fresh ginger
4 shallots, finely sliced
1 capsicum, finely sliced
1 Chinese cabbage, washed and shredded
1 tablespoon soy sauce
2 tablespoons sherry
¾ cup fish or chicken stock
salt and pepper to taste
2 teaspoons cornflour
2 tablespoons water

METHOD

Flake Crab meat. Heat oil in a wok or large frying pan and stir-fry garlic, beans, ginger and shallots. Add capsicum, cabbage, soy sauce, sherry and fish stock. Simmer for 5 minutes. Add Crab meat, salt and pepper. Mix cornflour and water, add to Crab mixture and stir until thickened and bubbling. Serve immediately with rice.

Serves 6

Baked Barramundi

(Photograph page 144)

INGREDIENTS

1 x 2kg (4lb) whole Barramundi
2 cups finely ground cooked Prawn meat
1 egg, beaten
½ cup cream
2 tablespoons sherry
2 tablespoons finely chopped mushrooms
salt and pepper
extra ½ cup cream

METHOD

Preheat oven to 180ºC (350ºF). Scale, clean and rinse Barramundi. Wipe dry with paper towels. In a bowl, mix together Prawn meat, egg, cream, sherry, mushrooms, salt and pepper. Stuff the cavity of the fish with this mixture and secure with skewers. Place fish in a greased baking dish. Pour over the extra cream and bake for 45-60 minutes or until flesh flakes. Carefully lift fish onto serving platter, remove skewers. Strain pan juices over fish and serve immediately.

Serves 6

Grilled Anchovies

INGREDIENTS

1kg (2lb) fresh Anchovies
2 eggs, lightly beaten
2 tablespoons milk
3 cups fine, soft breadcrumbs
lemon wedges
fried parsley (page 315)

METHOD

Wash and clean Anchovies well, small heads can be removed if desired. Pat dry with paper towels. Stir Anchovies into egg mixture, lift out individually and coat with breadcrumbs. Rest in refrigerater for 30 minutes.
Arrange Anchovies on an oiled foil tray under preheated griller and grill for 1-2 minutes on each side.
Do not have Anchovies too close to heat source.
Arrange on a platter with lemon wedges and fried parsley. Serve with a dipping sauce of soy and fresh tomato purée seasoned with basil or a curry sauce.

Serves 6

Baked Anchovies with Herbs and Red Wine

INGREDIENTS

1kg (2lb) fresh Anchovies
2 tablespoons finely chopped parsley
2 tablespoons finely chopped chives
1 tablespoon finely chopped fresh tarragon
125g (4oz) mushrooms, finely sliced
salt and pepper to taste
½ cup red wine
1 cup fresh breadcrumbs
2 tablespoons finely grated Parmesan cheese

METHOD

Preheat oven to 180ºC (350ºF). Wash and clean Anchovies well, small heads can be removed if desired. In a greased ovenproof dish place parsley, chives, tarragon, mushrooms, salt and pepper. Lay the fish on the herbs and mushrooms, pour over red wine and bake uncovered for 10-15 minutes or until liquid is slightly reduced. Top fish with breadcrumbs and cheese. Return to oven to lightly brown. Serve hot.

Serves 6

Individual Barramundi Ramekins

INGREDIENTS

500g (1lb) Barramundi fillets
2 cups court bouillon (page 315)
2 medium potatoes, peeled and cubed
good pinch nutmeg
salt and pepper to taste
1½ tablespoons finely chopped parsley
½ cup sour cream
buttered fine breadcrumbs

METHOD

Poach Barramundi fillets in court bouillon for 10 minutes. Remove fillets, flake and keep aside. Place potatoes in a pan of boiling water and cook until tender. Drain water from potatoes and add nutmeg, salt, pepper, parsley and cream. Stir in flaked fish and heat pan contents thoroughly until piping hot. Adjust seasoning and spoon mixture into individual, greased ramekin dishes or scallop shells. Sprinkle with breadcrumbs. Mixture should be hot to serve. Grill until crumbs become golden brown. Serve immediately.

Serves 6

Poached Fillets of Barramundi with Oysters

INGREDIENTS

750g (1½lb) Barramundi fillets
12 bottled Oysters
2 tablespoons butter or margarine
3 shallots, finely chopped
2 tablespoons finely chopped parsley
pepper to taste
⅓ cup white wine
1 cup fish stock (page 315)
3 tablespoons cream

METHOD

Wipe fillets with damp paper towels. Remove any grit from drained Oysters. Melt butter in a large shallow pan, add shallots, parsley and a little pepper. Cook gently for 1-2 minutes. Arrange fillets in pan, add wine and stock. Cover and simmer until flesh flakes easily with a fork. Remove fish from pan and keep warm. Reduce the liquid by half over a high heat. Reduce heat and add cream and Oysters to heat through. Do not boil. Pour sauce and Oysters over the fish. Serve immediately.

Serves 6

Barramundi in Beer

INGREDIENTS

1 x 2kg (4lb) whole Barramundi
4 tablespoons butter or margarine
4 tablespoons flour
3 cups beer
2 tablespoons brown sugar
4 whole peppercorns
2 whole cloves
2 tablespoons lemon juice

METHOD

Preheat oven to 180ºC (350ºF). Scale, clean and rinse Barramundi. Wipe dry with paper towels. In a large baking dish melt butter, stir in flour and cook for 3 minutes. Gradually pour in beer, stirring constantly until smooth and thickened. Add brown sugar, peppercorns and cloves. Add Barramundi and cover with foil, tucking edges under rim of dish. Bake for 45-60 minutes or until flesh flakes. Place fish on a warm serving platter. Stir lemon juice into pan juices and strain over the fish.

Serves 6

Butterfly Cod, Great Barrier Reef, Qld.

Pistachio Nut Cream

(Photograph page 139)

INGREDIENTS

125g (4oz) unsalted, shelled pistachio nuts
1 tablespoon gelatine
4 tablespoons water
2½ cups cream
½ cup castor sugar
1 teaspoon vanilla essence

METHOD

Blanch shelled pistachio nuts and remove skins, if desired. Reserve a few for garnish, grind remainder to a coarse meal in blender or food processor. Soften gelatine in water and dissolve over hot water; cool. Whip cream, fold in sugar, vanilla, cooled gelatine and pistachio meal. Pour into 6 individual dessert glasses and chill until set. Coarsely chop reserved pistachio nuts. Serve with chopped pistachios sprinkled on top of the dessert.

Serves 6

Date and Ginger Cake

INGREDIENTS

1 cup chopped dates
1 cup boiling water
1 teaspoon bicarbonate of soda
125g (4oz) butter
1 cup castor sugar
1 egg
1 cup plain flour
1 teaspoon vanilla essence
½ cup chopped walnuts
250g (8oz) preserved ginger, chopped

METHOD

Mix dates with boiling water and soda. Let stand 10 minutes. Cream butter, sugar and egg until light and fluffy. Fold in flour, add vanilla and mix in dates, nuts and ginger. Pour into a greased and floured 20cm (8 inch) fluted ring tin. Bake in a preheated 190°C (375°F) oven for 35-40 minutes or until cooked when tested. Turn out and cool a little. Dust with sifted icing sugar and serve warm, cut in slices, with whipped cream.

Persimmon and Pineapple Salad with Coconut

(Photograph page 147)

INGREDIENTS

3 ripe persimmons
1 pineapple
1 cup pineapple juice
2 tablespoons finely chopped mint
½ cup shredded coconut

METHOD

Cut persimmons in half and scoop out flesh into a bowl. Slice pineapple in half lengthways, cutting through leaves and down to the stalk end. Cut out pineapple flesh, chop into bite-size pieces and add to persimmon flesh, reserving pineapple skins for serving. Mix juice and mint together and pour over fruit. Chill. To serve, spoon salad into pineapple skins and sprinkle with coconut. Serve with cream or ice cream.

Serves 6

Macadamia Nut Ice Cream

INGREDIENTS

3 large whole eggs
3 egg yolks
1 cup castor sugar
250g (8oz) macadamia nuts, finely chopped
600ml (1 pint) cream, lightly whipped

METHOD

Using a rotary beater or hand-held electric mixer, beat eggs and egg yolks in a heat-proof bowl. Gradually beat in sugar, then place bowl over simmering water and beat until thick and creamy. Cool completely, then fold in macadamia nuts and cream. Pour into freezer trays and freeze partially. Turn into a chilled bowl and beat with electric mixer until smooth and light. Turn into a freezer container, cover and freeze until firm.

Serves 6

Tropic greenery surrounds the Katherine River, Low level reserve, near Katherine, N.T.

PERSIMMON & PINEAPPLE SALAD WITH COCONUT, Recipe page 146.

Like members of a football team ready for the game, these striped Sweetlips display their colourful patterns on a Coral Sea Reef.

Sea Lions raise their heads in curiosity.

The Taste of Tasmania

Australia's Island State is, in many ways, its forgotten jewel. Tasmanians are often justifiably resentful of the mainland's seeming neglect. But no doubt there are many Tasmanians who secretly rejoice at this lack of attention, for the smallest Australian State is a place of a great and serene beauty.

The mystique of Tasmania lies in many areas; its isolation, its proximity to the Antarctic, its political history, possibly the most remarkable and spectacular wilderness regions left on this earth, its resemblance, in parts, to "Mother England" and not least of all, its unique wildlife, both past and present.

No doubt most people have heard of the Tasmanian Devil and of course the Tasmanian Tiger, which is now thought to be extinct. Yet few are aware of some equally fascinating wildlife which is from "Tassie's" waters. For example, the Giant Tasmanian Crab which grows up to 15 kg (33lbs), with pincers up to 45 cm (18 ins) long! Another giant is the Tasmanian Freshwater Crayfish, which can grow up to 40 cm (16 ins) in length, weighing as much as 6 kgs (14 lbs).

Of the introduced wildlife, the Trout has to be the most renowned. It was in Tasmania that the first Brown Trout to be spawned in the Southern Hemisphere was hatched — in 1864, at a place called Plenty, not far from Hobart. From this stock originated all the Brown Trout which have since been established in Australia and New Zealand.

Rainbow Trout were also established early, having been introduced from California in 1896. Interestingly, it has not been possible to establish self-sustaining colonies of Rainbows in any rivers, only in lakes and reservoirs. Whenever they are released in rivers they always make their way out to sea. Consequently, river stock are regularly replenished by the Tasmanian Inland Fisheries Commission.

Rainbow Trout are also farmed commercially in saltwater and marketed as Ocean Trout. Another successfully farmed species is the Atlantic Salmon.

The fishing in this State extends beyond its many beautiful freshwater streams and lakes. Tasmanian Scallops, for example, have long been sought after as a true delicacy of the sea, and a major industry has evolved around this tasty little mollusc.

The beach fishing on the east coast is as good as anywhere in the country. If the wild and rugged west coast was more easily accessible, the results would no doubt see many a tall fishing tale beaten "hands down"! Game fishing is also very popular, Tuna being highly sought after by many enthusiasts.

As an introduction to the wonderful world of Tasmanian seafood, you could not do better than try the Poached Atlantic Salmon (shown opposite). With Spinach Soup for starters and the Poached Pears to follow, you have a very healthy meal with a fantastic combination of flavours.

Australia's "Apple Isle" certainly has a lot to offer, so why not let your palate travel south and savour the taste of Tasmania?!

Top: SPINACH SOUP, Recipe page 152. *Middle:* POACHED ATLANTIC SALMON, Recipe page 157.
Below: POACHED PEARS WITH CITRUS JUICES, Recipe page 162.

Spinach Soup

(Photograph page 151)

INGREDIENTS

6 cups chicken stock
60g (2oz) pasta shells
250g (8oz) cooked, chopped spinach
salt and pepper to taste
¼ teaspoon nutmeg
2 egg yolks
⅔ cup grated Parmesan cheese
6 cheese toasts (see end of Method)

METHOD

Put stock into a large saucepan and bring to the boil. Add pasta and simmer for 5 minutes. Add spinach, salt, pepper and nutmeg. Simmer for a further 5 minutes or until pasta is tender. Remove from heat. Add a little of the boiling broth to the egg yolks, mix well. Add this to the simmering soup, stirring over gentle heat for a minute or so. Stir in Parmesan cheese, remove immediately from heat and serve in bowls, each with a cheese toast floated on top.
Cheese Toasts:
Cut 6 small rounds from a French bread stick. Toast under grill, spread with butter and sprinkle thickly with shredded tasty cheese. Return to grill until cheese is melted and bubbly.

Serves 6

Cheese Filled Apricots

INGREDIENTS

24 fresh apricots
125g (4oz) cream cheese, softened
4 tablespoons sour cream
60g (2oz) smoked almonds, finely chopped
2 teaspoons finely chopped chives
black pepper to taste
extra smoked almonds to garnish

METHOD

Wash and halve apricots, removing stones. In a bowl combine cream cheese, sour cream, almonds, chives and pepper. Mix well. Fill each apricot half, garnish with a piece of almond. Chill well before serving.

Serves 6

Fresh Salmon and Dill Tart

INGREDIENTS

Pastry

175g (6oz) flour
pinch salt
125g (4oz) butter or margarine, cut into cubes
water to bind

Filling

500g (1lb) fresh Atlantic Salmon cutlets or fillets
2 whole eggs
2 egg yolks
600ml (1 pint) cream
2 tablespoons sour cream
salt and pepper to taste
½ cup roughly chopped fresh dill

METHOD

Pastry:
In a bowl, sift flour and salt. Rub in butter until mixture resembles fine breadcrumbs. Add enough water to bind. Mix to a dough. Wrap in plastic film and rest in refrigerator for 30 minutes. Roll out to fit a 20cm (8 inch) flan dish. Blind bake at 200ºC (400ºF) for 15 minutes.
Filling:
Remove skin from fish and remove all bones. Cut fish into bite-size pieces and arrange evenly over the cooked pastry. In a bowl, beat together whole eggs, yolks, cream, sour cream, salt and pepper. Pour over fish. Scatter dill over the surface and bake at 180ºC (350ºF) until the filling is just firm, about 30 minutes. Serve immediately.

Serves 6

Octopus and Rice Salad

INGREDIENTS

1kg (2lb) small Octopus (see page 314)
½ cup red wine
4 cups cooked rice
1 capsicum, finely diced
½ cup chopped black olives
⅓ cup corn kernels
1 tablespoon finely chopped pimiento
pepper to taste
6 lettuce cups
½ cup chopped walnuts

Mustard Vinaigrette

1 tablespoon Dijon mustard
¼ cup white wine vinegar
½ cup olive oil
1 tablespoon lemon juice
salt and pepper

METHOD

Prepare Octopus as directed, leaving body and tentacles uncut. Wash and place in saucepan. Add wine, cover tightly and simmer gently for 45-60 minutes or until tender. (Octopus is tender when cut easily with a knife.) Remove from heat and cool. Cut Octopus into small pieces.
In a bowl combine rice, capsicum, olives, corn, pimiento and pepper to taste. Add Octopus pieces. Mix vinaigrette ingredients, pour over salad and toss lightly. Chill well. Serve in lettuce cups, sprinkled with walnuts.

Serves 6

Potted Crab

INGREDIENTS

500g (1lb) cooked Crab meat
125g (4oz) unsalted butter
1 tablespoon lemon juice
2-3 drops Tabasco sauce
pinch paprika
salt and pepper to taste

METHOD

Flake Crab meat and remove any small bones. Melt butter in a saucepan, add Crab meat, lemon juice, Tabasco sauce, paprika, salt and pepper. Mix well. Remove from heat, place mixture in a food processor and purée. Spoon mixture into individual pots and chill well. Serve with crisp bread or water crackers.

Serves 6 to 8

A diver adds a Rock Lobster to the menu tonight.

CRAYFISH SOUP, Recipe page 153.

Crayfish Soup

(Photograph page 153)

INGREDIENTS

18 cooked Yabbies or 1
medium-size cooked Crayfish
500g (1lb) cooked Prawns
3 cups fish stock (page 315)
2½ cups milk
½ cup cream
salt and pepper to taste
¼ teaspoon dry mustard
2 tablespoons sherry
½ cup sour cream
chopped chives

METHOD

Wash Yabbies well and remove meat.
Shell and devein Prawns. In a
saucepan place fish stock, milk,
cream, salt, pepper and mustard.
Bring slowly to a simmer, do not boil.
Cut Yabby flesh into bite-size pieces
and cut Prawns in half. Add the
seafood to the soup and simmer to
heat through. Add sherry just before
serving.
Garnish each bowl with a dollop of
sour cream and sprinkle with chives.

Serves 6

Iced Fruit Soup

INGREDIENTS

250g (8oz) dried apricots
4 medium green apples
2½ cups of water
1 punnet strawberries, hulled
and puréed
2 cups fresh orange juice
⅓ cup lemon juice
½ cup sugar
¼ teaspoon cinnamon
2 cups apple cider
1 cup sweet white wine
mint leaves to garnish

METHOD

Rinse apricots. Peel, core and slice
apples. In a saucepan, bring apricots,
apples and water to the boil, reduce
heat and simmer for 15 minutes or
until fruit is soft.
Purée apricot and apple mixture.
Combine with remaining ingredients
except mint. Chill well. Serve in soup
bowls, garnish with mint leaves. Ice
cubes may be floated in soup if
desired.

Serves 6 to 8

Reflected skies in the water aglow with the sunset at Mt. Wellington, Derwent River, Tas.

LOBSTER CANTONESE, Recipe page 157.

Poached Atlantic Salmon

(Photograph page 151)

INGREDIENTS

1 x 2kg (4lb) whole Atlantic Salmon
6 tablespoons butter or margarine
1 medium lemon, sliced thinly
¾ cup parsley sprigs
6 whole peppercorns
water

METHOD

Scale and clean fish. Trim fins. Smear butter over fish. Place a few lemon slices in cavity of fish and sprinkle over parsley. Place fish in a fish kettle and just cover with water. Place remaining lemon slices and peppercorns in kettle and poach for 40-45 minutes. Fish is cooked if skin can be gently lifted and flesh flakes. This can be served hot or cold, but if serving cold allow to cool in poaching liquid. Carefully lift fish onto a baking tray and gently remove skin from body section on both sides. Lift onto serving platter with the aid of 2 egg lifters.
Serve simply with a mild flavoured sauce such as Hollandaise.

Serves 6

Lobster Cantonese

(Photograph page 156)

INGREDIENTS

2 medium Lobsters, cooked
2 tablespoons vegetable oil
2 teaspoons sesame oil
500g (1lb) minced pork
2 tablespoons finely chopped water chestnuts
2 tablespoons chopped bamboo shoots
1 cup Chinese dried mushrooms, soaked
1½ cups fish or chicken stock
2 eggs, beaten
1 tablespoon cornflour
2 teaspoons soy sauce
⅓ cup water

METHOD

Split Lobsters, clean and remove flesh and claws. Slice the flesh. In a frying pan, heat the oils. Add pork mince and cook, stirring often until broken up and browned. Add water chestnuts, bamboo shoots and mushrooms. Cook for 12-15 minutes, stirring frequently. Reduce heat and add fish stock. Gradually stir in beaten eggs. Add Lobster flesh and claws. Heat through. Blend cornflour with soy sauce and water and slowly add to Lobster mixture. Cook over low heat until sauce thickens. Serve with rice.

Serves 4 to 6

Pan-fried Tuna with Bacon

INGREDIENTS

6 medium size Tuna slices each about 125g (4oz)
seasoned flour
oil for shallow frying
3 garlic cloves, crushed
1 medium onion, finely sliced
3 bacon slices, chopped coarsely

METHOD

Remove any skin from Tuna. Coat Tuna with flour. Heat oil in a frying pan and gently cook garlic, onion and bacon. Add Tuna and cook for 2-3 minutes each side or until flesh flakes. Serve with rice and salad.

Serves 6

Poached Ocean Trout with Lemon and Chive Sauce

INGREDIENTS

750g (1½lb) Ocean Trout fillet
⅓ cup water
3 tablespoons lemon juice
salt to taste
1 cup cream
2 tablespoons finely chopped chives

METHOD

Skin the fillets. Place fillets in a pan and pour over combined water and 2 tablespoons of the lemon juice, adding salt to taste. Cover and cook gently for 5-6 minutes or until flesh flakes.
Remove fish from pan and keep warm. Add cream to pan juices, heat gently without boiling, stir in remaining lemon juice and chives. Simmer gently for 2-3 minutes without boiling. Arrange fillets on a serving platter and pour over sauce. Serve garnished with additional chives tops.

Serves 6

Chilled Bream with Crab Mayonnaise

INGREDIENTS

750g (1½lb) Bream fillets
1 cup fish or chicken stock
250g (8oz) cooked Crab meat, flaked
1½ tablespoons tomato paste
1 cup mayonnaise
2 teaspoons chopped chives
3 canned Anchovy fillets, drained and mashed
pepper to taste

METHOD

Remove skin and bones from fillets. Place in a pan, pour over stock and simmer gently until flesh flakes, 5-6 minutes. Drain and flake flesh. In a bowl combine fish, Crab meat, tomato paste, mayonnaise, chives, Anchovies and pepper. Mix well. Chill well and serve with salad.

Serves 6

Scallops with Avocado

INGREDIENTS

1kg (2lb) Scallops
seasoned flour
2 tablespoons butter or margarine
1 medium onion, finely sliced
2 tablespoons lime juice
2 tomatoes, skinned and chopped
2 tablespoons sherry
3 large avocados, peeled and quartered
300ml (½ pint) cream
salt and pepper to taste
lime wedges for garnish

METHOD

Remove any dark membrane from scallops, rinse lightly and drain well. Coat in seasoned flour. Melt butter in pan, add onion and cook 2-3 minutes. Add lime juice, tomatoes, sherry and Scallops. Cook gently for 2 minutes then add avocado, cream, salt and pepper. Heat through, do not boil. Serve immediately and garnish with lime wedges.

Serves 6

A dove's view of Dove Lake, Tas.

Whole Dory Stuffed with Cucumber and Capers

INGREDIENTS

6 small, whole Dory
1 medium onion, finely diced
2 cups small bread cubes, without crusts
1 cup shredded cucumber
2 teaspoons finely chopped capers
2 bacon slices, finely chopped
pinch cinnamon
pinch ground cloves
salt and pepper to taste
½ cup white wine

METHOD

Clean and wash Dory, trim fins. In a bowl combine onion, bread, cucumber, capers, bacon, cinnamon, cloves, salt and pepper. Mix well. Fill the cavity of each fish evenly with mixture, secure opening with toothpicks. Place fish in a greased baking dish and pour over wine. Bake at 180ºC (350ºF) for 20-25 minutes or until flesh flakes.

Serves 6

Stuffed Squid Hoods

INGREDIENTS

6 medium size Squid (see page 314)
4 shallots, finely chopped
125g (4oz) mushrooms, finely chopped
4 slices bread, crumbed
2 teaspoons finely chopped fresh basil or ½ teaspoon dried
1 teaspoon finely chopped fresh oregano or ½ teaspoon dried
3 tablespoons tomato paste
salt and pepper to taste
½ cup red wine

METHOD

Preheat oven to 180ºC (350ºF). Prepare Squid as directed, leave hoods intact. Mince the tentacles. In a bowl combine shallots, mushrooms, breadcrumbs, basil, oregano, tomato paste, salt, pepper and tentacles. Mix well. Fill each Squid hood with mixture and secure openings with toothpicks or skewers. Place filled Squid hoods in a greased baking dish, pour over wine and cover. Bake for 40-45 minutes or until Squid is just tender. Serve immediately.

Serves 6

Fresh Tuna Kedgeree

INGREDIENTS

750g (1½lb) fresh Tuna slices
½ cup white wine
¼ cup water
1 bay leaf
3 cups cooked rice
2 tablespoons butter or margarine
2 tablespoons flour
1 cup fish or chicken stock
1 cup milk
1 teaspoon mild curry powder
2 teaspoons lemon juice
salt and pepper to taste
buttered breadcrumbs

METHOD

Preheat oven to 180ºC (350ºF). Remove any skin from Tuna. In a pan, combine wine, water and bay leaf. Add Tuna slices and poach until flesh flakes. Remove and flake Tuna. In a bowl combine Tuna with cooked rice, lightly fork through. In a saucepan melt butter and stir in flour, cooking for 1-2 minutes Gradually add stock and milk, stirring until thick and smooth. Add curry powder, lemon juice, salt and pepper. Mix sauce into Tuna and rice mixture and place into a greased ovenproof dish. Sprinkle with buttered breadcrumbs and bake until heated through and golden.

Serves 6

Bream with Ginger and Coconut Milk

INGREDIENTS

6 plate-size Bream
seasoned flour
oil for shallow frying
3 tablespoons finely grated fresh ginger
2½ cups coconut milk
salt and pepper to taste
½ teaspoon ground coriander

METHOD

Scale and clean fish, trim fins. Coat fish in seasoned flour. Heat oil in a large frying pan and gently cook half of the ginger, add fish (you may have to fry 2-3 fish at a time) and cook for 3-4 minutes each side or until flesh flakes. Turn fish once only. When all the fish are cooked place on a platter and keep warm. Meanwhile drain off excess oil, add remaining ginger to pan and gently cook for 1 minute. Add the coconut milk to the pan juices and heat through. Add coriander and season to taste. Pour over fish when serving.

Serves 6

Sunset at Magician Bay, Bicheno, Tas.

SCALLOPS IN WALNUT SAUCE, Recipe page 161.

Scallops with Walnut Sauce

(Photograph page 161)

INGREDIENTS

1kg (2lb) Scallops
2 tablespoons butter or margarine
2 tablespoons flour
1½ cups fish or chicken stock
½ cup finely ground walnuts
2 garlic cloves, crushed
¼ cup finely chopped parsley
2 tablespoons lemon juice
salt and pepper to taste
walnut halves to garnish

METHOD

Remove any dark membrane from Scallops, rinse lightly and drain. Melt butter in a pan, stir in flour and cook gently for 2-3 minutes. Gradually pour in stock, stirring constantly until thick and smooth. Add Scallops, walnuts, garlic, parsley, lemon juice, salt and pepper. Cook gently for 3-4 minutes; do not boil as Scallops will toughen. Serve immediately garnished with walnut halves.

Serves 6

Crab with Sour Cream

INGREDIENTS

1kg (2lb) cooked Crab meat
2 cups sour cream
3 cups fresh breadcrumbs
1 cup grated cheddar cheese
½ teaspoon curry powder
salt and pepper to taste
1 tablespoon lemon juice
Parmesan cheese, grated

METHOD

Preheat oven to 180ºC (350ºF). Flake Crab meat. In a large bowl combine Crab meat, sour cream, breadcrumbs, cheese, curry powder, salt, pepper and lemon juice. Mix well. Place mixture in a greased, ovenproof dish and sprinkle with Parmesan cheese. Bake for 15-20 minutes or until heated through. Serve with fresh green salad.

Serves 6

Poached Pears with Citrus Juices

(Photograph page 151)

INGREDIENTS

6 pears
4 medium oranges
1 large lemon
5 tablespoons brown sugar
1 tablespoon honey
6 whole cloves

METHOD

Preheat oven to 180ºC (350ºF). Choose pears of uniform size that are ripe, but firm. Grate the rind from all the oranges over a bowl. Squeeze the juice from 2 of the oranges and the lemon and add to the orange rind, stir in 1 tablespoon of the brown sugar. Set aside. With a sharp knife peel the remaining oranges, removing all the pith. Segment the oranges by cutting between each membrane line. Cut each segment into 3 and place into a bowl, add 1 tablespoon of brown sugar and honey. Core and peel the pears and set them upright in a greased ovenproof dish. Fill the pear cavities with the chopped orange, pour over the sugared juices and rind. Top each pear with a clove. Cover and bake for 35-40 minutes or until pears are tender. Baste the pears with the juice during cooking. Serve chilled with cream.

Serves 6

SPICY APPLE DESSERT CAKE, Recipe page 163.

Spicy Apple Dessert Cake

(Photograph pages 162 & 163)

INGREDIENTS

125g (4oz) unsalted butter
125g (4oz) brown sugar
1 egg, lightly beaten
2 cups self-raising flour
500g (1lb) green apples, peeled and cored
½ cup sultanas
1 teaspoon ground ginger
1 teaspoon cinnamon
2 tablespoons brown sugar, extra
custard or whipped cream

METHOD

Preheat oven to 180ºC (350ºF). Melt butter in a saucepan. Cool. Add sugar and egg and beat well. Stir in flour and mix to a soft dough. Press half of the dough into the base of a 20cm (8 inch) spring form tin. Thinly slice the apples and arrange slices on top, scatter sultanas over and sprinkle with combined ginger, cinnamon and brown sugar. Cover with remaining dough and bake for 35-40 minutes or until golden. Serve with pouring custard or whipped cream.

Serves 6

Brandied Peaches

INGREDIENTS

6 large fresh peaches (canned may be used)
3 tablespoons brown sugar
300ml (½ pint) cream, lightly whipped
3 tablespoons brandy

METHOD

Peel peaches and remove stones; if using canned peaches, drain them. Slice peaches thinly, reserving a few slices for garnish. Place a layer of peaches into 6 individual glass dessert dishes, sprinkle with brown sugar, add a layer of whipped cream and a few drops of brandy. Repeat layers, finishing with a layer of cream. Chill for at least 2 hours to allow flavours to blend. Garnish with reserved peach slices before serving.

Serves 6

Tourists visiting the 'Powder Magazine' in Launceston, Tas.

Boiling waves crashing onto the rocks
of the Southern Australian Coastline.

Down by
the Seaside

Australia and New Zealand have, together, over 25,000 kilometres of tremendously variable coastline. Towering rocky headlands, large rolling sand dunes, jutting rock platforms, blow holes, and, of course, an endless procession of enormous, golden sanded beaches.

Much of this coastline is largely untouched and so provides an ideal opportunity to observe the many ecosystems that exist in these environments. And, of course, a large part of these ecosystems is in the sea life.

To the untrained eye, coastal environments can appear to be largely devoid of life. Nothing could be further from the truth! A closer look can reveal an enormous variety of life in a very small area. From the minute and colourful algae of the rock pools, the myriad of tenacious shellfish, the wily octopus, the scuttling crab, the swaying weeds, to the cleverly hidden Pipis and worms. Further out into the surf zone, the life forms get larger; Bream, Whiting, Flathead, Tailor, Jewfish . . . right up to the more serious-sized Rays and, of course, the well-loved Sharks!

Amongst this abundant life, there is, of course, an abundance of food. Many a keen beach and rock fishermen will testify to that! Seafood, it goes without saying, is very popular along this busy coastal stretch. Fortunately, for those of us

without the necessary fishing skills, the cities and many of the larger towns have thriving fish markets which provide an enormous range of fresh produce.

All of the fish and shellfish in this chapter are readily available. Here you will discover some delicious ways to prepare and cook this fresh coastal food. The Crispy Fried Trevally in Beer Batter (page 171) is a quick and easy way to whip up a delicious fish meal. And don't miss the Rolled Fillets of Whiting with Oysters (page 176) for an exciting combination of textures with an extremely flavoursome result.

You shouldn't go past the suggested meal shown in the photograph opposite. Skewered Shellfish is an extremely easy and rewarding entree, while the Sea Bream and Mushroom Pie provides a spectacular presentation with a glorious taste. The Chilled Strawberry Cream provides a nice light finish to a perfect summer meal.

Next time you're down by the seaside, spare some thought for the sealife around you. And let's hope that this delicious source of nutrition endures for many years to come.

A magnificent aerial view of Sydney's metropolitan and harbour area, NSW.

Top: CHILLED STRAWBERRY CREAM, Recipe page 180. *Middle*: SEA BREAM & MUSHROOM PIE, Recipe page 176. *Below*: SKEWERED SHELLFISH, Recipe page 170.

The headlands, beach and water of popular Lord Howe Island, NSW.

Skewered Shellfish

(Photograph page 167)

INGREDIENTS

500g (1½lb) medium green King Prawns
3 prepared Squid hoods (see page 314)
500g (1½lb) Scallops
250g (8oz) button mushrooms
1 large capsicum cut into 3cm (1¼ inch) pieces
12 small, whole spring onions, cut in 2
6 slices pineapple, cut into bite-size pieces
bamboo or metal skewers
¼ cup soy sauce
2 tablespoons lime juice

METHOD

Peel and devein Prawns, removing heads and leaving tails on. Cut cleaned Squid hoods into rectangles; wash and devein Scallops. Arrange Prawns, Squid and Scallops alternately with mushrooms, capsicum, onion and pineapple onto skewers. Place skewers under grill and cook for 2-3 minutes on each side, basting with a mixture of soy sauce and lime juice. Serve.

Serves 6

Tuna with Tomatoes and Pasta

INGREDIENTS

500g (1lb) fresh Tuna slices
1 teaspoon oil
1 large onion, finely sliced
2 garlic cloves, crushed
2 x 425g (15oz) cans tomatoes
1 capsicum, finely diced
2 tablespoons finely chopped fresh basil
125g (4oz) shelled green peas
salt and pepper to taste
500g (1lb) spaghetti or other pasta

METHOD

Remove skin from Tuna and cut into bite-size pieces.
Heat oil in a pan and gently cook onion and garlic. Add tomatoes, capsicum, basil and peas. Cook for 3-4 minutes. Add Tuna pieces, cover and simmer gently until flesh flakes. Meanwhile cook pasta in boiling water until tender. Drain pasta and place onto a serving platter. Pour over Tuna and tomato sauce, toss and serve.

Serves 6

A close relationship between a Clown Fish and nature.

Sea Bream Soufflé

INGREDIENTS

500g (1lb) Sea Bream fillets
½ cup water
1½ tablespoons butter
2½ tablespoons flour
½ cup milk
4 eggs, separated
2 tablespoons finely chopped parsley
1 tablespoon lemon juice
¼ teaspoon Tabasco sauce
salt and pepper to taste
Parmesan cheese, grated

METHOD

Preheat oven to 180°C (350°F). Wash and skin fillets. Place fillets in a pan with water, cover and simmer gently until flesh flakes. Remove fish and reserve stock. Flake flesh, removing any bones. Melt butter in a saucepan, stir in flour and cook 2 minutes over gentle heat. Remove from heat and gradually stir in reserved fish stock and milk. Return to heat and stir until thick and smooth. Pour into a bowl and add flaked fish with beaten egg yolks, parsley, lemon juice, Tabasco, salt and pepper. Mix well.
Beat egg whites until stiff and gently fold through fish mixture.
Spoon into individual greased soufflé dishes, sprinkle with Parmesan cheese. Stand in a baking dish, add hot water to the dish to come half way up sides of soufflé dishes. Bake for 20-25 minutes, until risen and golden. Serve immediately.

Serves 6

Cuttlefish and Squid in Garlic Sauté

INGREDIENTS

500g (1lb) Cuttlefish (see page 314)
500g (1lb) Squid (see page 314)
3 tablespoons olive oil
6 garlic cloves, crushed
½ cup finely chopped parsley

METHOD

Prepare Cuttlefish and Squid as directed. Cut Cuttlefish flaps and Squid hoods into strips and thin rings. In a pan heat olive oil, add garlic and sauté for 2-3 minutes. Add parsley and prepared seafood. Stir-fry for 3-5 minutes until tender, taking care not to overcook as the seafood will toughen. Serve immediately.

Serves 6

Guacamole

INGREDIENTS

3 large ripe avocados
2 medium tomatoes, skinned and finely chopped
1 small onion, finely chopped
2 garlic cloves, crushed
½ capsicum, diced
½ teaspoon chili powder
2 tablespoons lemon juice
salt and pepper to taste

METHOD

Peel avocados, remove stones and mash flesh. In a bowl combine avocado flesh, tomatoes, onion, garlic, capsicum, chili, lemon juice, salt and pepper. Mix well. Serve with crusty bread.

Serves 6

CRISPY FRIED TREVALLY IN BEER BATTER, Recipe page 171.

Crispy Fried Trevally in Beer Batter

(Photograph page 171)

INGREDIENTS

500g (1lb) Trevally fillets
oil for deep-frying
lemon wedges
fried parsley (page 315)

Beer Batter

1½ cups flour
pinch salt
1 tablespoon butter or margarine, melted
2 eggs, separated
1¼ cups flat beer

METHOD

Skin the fillets. Cut into bite-size pieces or strips and refrigerate until required. In a bowl sift flour and salt, stir in melted butter and egg yolks. Add beer, mixing well to form a smooth batter. Cover and stand for at least 30 minutes. Just before using, beat egg whites until stiff and fold into batter. Coat fish pieces in batter and deep-fry in heated oil until golden. Drain on kitchen paper. Serve immediately on individual plates, garnished with lemon wedges and fried parsley.

Serves 6

Mousseline of Fish in Mushroom Caps

INGREDIENTS

500g (1lb) Whiting fillets
¼ teaspoon salt
pepper to taste
pinch nutmeg
2 egg whites, lightly beaten
2 cups heavy cream
12 medium size mushroom caps
½ cup white wine

METHOD

Skin Whiting fillets and remove bones. Place in a food processor and blend until fish flesh is very fine. Add salt, pepper and nutmeg. Gradually add egg whites. Push mixture through a sieve and place in a bowl over ice. With a wooden spoon gradually work in about 2 cups of heavy cream. Place spoonfuls of mixture into each mushroom cap. Place mushrooms in an ovenproof dish, pour in wine. Bake in preheated oven, 150ºC (300ºF), for 15-20 minutes. Serve hot or cold.

Serves 6

Left : WHOLE SNAPPER ON A BED OF VEGETABLES, Recipe page 177.
Right: SCALLOPS IN MORNAY SAUCE, Recipe page 177.

Seven Mile Beach, near Cape Byron (the extreme eastern point of Australia), NSW.

ROLLED FILLETS OF WHITING WITH OYSTERS, Recipe page 176.

Rolled Fillets of Whiting with Oysters

(Photograph page 176)

INGREDIENTS

1kg (2lb) Whiting fillets
2 cups fish stock (page 315)
¼ cup white wine
2 dozen Oysters, coated with seasoned flour
oil for frying
2 tablespoons butter
2 tablespoons flour
½ cup cream
salt and pepper to taste

METHOD

Skin the Whiting fillets. Roll fillets and secure with toothpicks. Place the rolled Whiting in a greased ovenproof dish. Pour over combined fish stock and wine, cover and bake for 15-20 minutes or until flesh flakes. Meanwhile lightly fry the Oysters in oil, remove and keep warm. Remove fish from oven dish and arrange on a serving platter. Keep warm.
Knead the butter and flour together. Pour liquid from oven dish into a saucepan and place over heat. Gradually stir the kneaded flour mixture into the liquid until all is incorporated, then let sauce boil gently for 1 minute. Stir in cream, season to taste with salt and pepper and mask the fillets of Whiting with the sauce. Pile Oysters in the centre of the platter and garnish with lemon slices.

Serves 6

Sea Bream and Mushroom Pie

(Photograph page 167)

INGREDIENTS

1kg (2lb) Sea Bream fillets
2 cups thick white sauce (page 315)
1 cup finely sliced mushrooms
1 tablespoon chopped chives
2 teaspoons chopped capers
2 tablespoons lemon juice
½ teaspoon Anchovy essence or
2 teaspoons Anchovy paste
1-2 sheets frozen puff pastry, thawed
milk

METHOD

Preheat oven at 230ºC (450ºF).
Skin fillets, removing any bones. Cut into small pieces. In a bowl combine fish pieces, white sauce, mushrooms, chives, capers, lemon juice and Anchovy essence. Mix well. Transfer to a 23cm (9 inch) pie plate or deep pie dish. If necessary join 2 pastry sheets together—overlap and press lightly with rolling pin. Cut out a piece slightly larger than top of dish and cut narrow strips from trimmings. Moisten edge of dish and place strips around rim. Lift top in position, press lightly and trim off excess with a sharp knife. Decorate with leaves from trimmings and knock up edge with the back of a knife. Glaze with milk and cut a vent in the centre. Bake for 10 minutes in preheated oven, then reduce temperature to 180ºC (350ºF) and continue to bake for 20 minutes or until golden. Serve hot.

Serves 6

Whole Snapper on a Bed of Vegetables

(Photograph pages 172 & 173)

INGREDIENTS

1 x 2kg (4lb) whole Snapper, cleaned and scaled
60g (2oz) butter
2 large potatoes, peeled and thinly sliced
1 large onion, peeled and thinly sliced
salt and pepper
¼ cup olive oil
¼ cup finely chopped parsley
¼ cup lemon juice

METHOD

Grease a large shallow ovenproof dish liberally with butter and cover with layers of potatoes and onions. Dust with salt and pepper and toss through oil and parsley.
Place Snapper on top, cut 3 diagonal slits across the top and pour over lemon juice.
Cover with foil and bake at 180ºC (350ºF) for 45 minutes, until flesh flakes and potatoes are tender when tested.

Serves 4 to 6

Blackfish with Bacon and Mustard Sauté

INGREDIENTS

750g (1½lb) Blackfish or Drummer fillets
seasoned flour
2 teaspoons oil
6 shallots, finely chopped
6 bacon slices, chopped
2 teaspoons prepared mustard

METHOD

Skin the fish fillets and wipe over with damp paper towels. Coat with flour. Heat oil in a frying pan, add shallots and bacon. Cook for 2 minutes. Stir in mustard and add fish fillets. Gently fry for 3 minutes on each side or until flesh flakes, enabling the fish to cook and absorb the bacon and mustard flavours. Serve immediately with bacon mixture spooned onto fillets.
Note: Blackfish and Drummer are oily fish; only a little oil is required for cooking.

Serves 6

Drummer Loaf

INGREDIENTS

1kg (2lb) Drummer or Blackfish fillets
4 bacon slices, chopped
¾ cup fresh breadcrumbs
2 eggs, lightly beaten
2 tablespoons finely chopped parsley
2 teaspoons finely chopped mint
salt and pepper to taste

METHOD

Preheat oven to 180ºC (350ºF). Skin fish fillets. Place in a pan, just cover with water and poach for 5 minutes or until flesh flakes. Remove and flake the flesh. In a bowl combine fish, bacon, breadcrumbs, eggs, parsley, mint, salt and pepper. Mix well. Place mixture into a greased loaf tin and bake for 30-35 minutes. Serve hot or cold.

Serves 6

Scallops in Mornay Sauce

(Photograph pages 172 & 173)

INGREDIENTS

500g (1lb) Scallops
60g (2oz) butter
1 small leek, finely sliced
2 tablespoons dry white wine
2 tablespoons plain flour
1 cup milk
salt and pepper
⅓ cup cream
½ cup grated cheddar cheese
⅓ cup soft breadcrumbs
1 tablespoon melted butter

METHOD

Melt butter in a shallow pan, add leeks and cook gently for 1 minute. Add Scallops and cook lightly for a further 2 minutes. Remove leeks and Scallops with a slotted spoon, place in a bowl and cover with wine. Stir flour into butter mixture and cook over a gentle heat for 2 minutes. Stir in milk, salt and pepper and stir constantly over heat until mixture boils and thickens. Stir in cream, fold through Scallop mixture, spoon into medium sized Scallop shells or individual ovenproof dishes, top with combined cheese, breadcrumbs and melted butter and place under griller to brown. Serve with a crisp green salad.

Serves 2 to 3

Wreck of the Ethel at Innes National Park, S.A.

Balmain Bugs In Green Mayonnaise

INGREDIENTS

24 medium-large Balmain or Moreton Bay Bugs, cooked
½ cup roughly chopped fresh spinach leaves
1 cup watercress sprigs
2 teaspoons Pernod
2 teaspoons fresh tarragon leaves
1 teaspoon French mustard
1 garlic clove, crushed
4 egg yolks
½ cup oil
2 tablespoons tarragon vinegar
salt and pepper to taste
1 teaspoon sugar
extra watercress to garnish

METHOD

Split underneath tail section of bugs and remove meat. Wash spinach and watercress and place in pan with 2 tablespoons water. Cook briefly until wilted. Drain and squeeze out any remaining moisture. Purée in food processor or blender, add Pernod, tarragon, mustard and garlic and process briefly.

To prepare mayonnaise, beat egg yolks in a bowl with a little of the vinegar, then beat in oil drop by drop until thick. Beat in remaining vinegar and puréed greens. Season to taste with salt, pepper and sugar. Slice prepared Bug meat into medallions and arrange on watercress sprigs. Lightly coat with green mayonnaise.

Note: Mayonnaise is easily prepared in a food processor, providing the oil is added slowly.

Serves 6

Whole Whiting Sauté Meunière

INGREDIENTS

6 small whole Whiting
seasoned flour
¾ cup milk
1 cup dry breadcrumbs
3 tablespoons oil
2 tablespoons butter or margarine
½ cup finely chopped parsley
½ cup lemon juice

METHOD

Scale and clean fish, leaving the heads and tails on. Dip fish into seasoned flour, milk then breadcrumbs. Place in refrigerator for 30 minutes to allow breadcrumbs to firm.

Heat oil in a frying pan and fry fish for 3 minutes on each side, or until flesh flakes. Remove and set aside. Drain oil from pan and add butter. Heat until slightly brown, add parsley and lemon juice. Pour over fish and serve immediately.

Serves 6

Oven-Baked Kingfish with Anchovy and Cucumber

INGREDIENTS

6 Kingfish cutlets or Mackerel
125g (4oz) butter or margarine
1 tablespoon Anchovy paste or essence
2 cups skinned and finely diced cucumber
black pepper

METHOD

Preheat oven to 180ºC (350ºF). Wipe over cutlets with damp kitchen paper. Beat butter till soft and add Anchovy paste or essence. Mix well. Coat each cutlet with Anchovy mixture and place in a greased ovenproof dish. Top with cucumber and sprinkle with black pepper. Bake for 30-35 minutes or until flesh flakes. Serve hot.

Serves 6

Trevally Croquettes

INGREDIENTS

750g (1½lb) Trevally fillets
2 tablespoons butter or margarine
3 tablespoons flour
1 cup fish or chicken stock
½ cup milk
1 tablespoon finely chopped parsley
1 tablespoon finely chopped onion
⅔ cup grated carrot
salt to taste
pinch cayenne pepper
flour
1 egg, beaten
dry breadcrumbs
oil for shallow frying

METHOD

Skin the fillets and remove bones. Mince finely using a food processor, set aside. In a saucepan melt butter, stir in flour and cook gently for 2 minutes. Gradually add stock and milk, stirring constantly until sauce boils and thickens. Remove from the heat and add parsley, onion, carrot, salt, cayenne pepper and minced fish. Mix well. Chill mixture well then mould into croquette shapes. Coat with flour, beaten egg and breadcrumbs. Rest in refrigerator for 30 minutes. Heat oil in pan and gently fry croquettes for 2-3 minutes on each side or until golden brown.

Serves 6

Jewfish Casserole

INGREDIENTS

750g (1½lb) Jewfish or Teraglin cutlets
2 tablespoons finely grated fresh ginger
4 whole peppercorns
2 cups water
1 tablespoon oil
1 medium onion, finely chopped
1 garlic clove, crushed
3 large tomatoes, skinned and roughly chopped
salt and pepper to taste

METHOD

Place cutlets in a large pan with ginger, peppercorns and water. Cover and simmer for 5-6 minutes or until flesh flakes. Remove pan from heat, leaving fish in the liquid. Meanwhile, heat oil in a frying pan and gently cook onion and garlic until onion is soft. Add tomatoes, cover and simmer for 10 minutes. Add salt and pepper to fish and poaching liquid. Cover and simmer for 5 minutes. Lift fish carefully onto serving platter, pour sauce over and garnish with rosemary sprigs.

Serves 6

Flaming Kingfish Cutlets

INGREDIENTS

750g (1½lb) Kingfish cutlets or Ling fillets
4 oranges
¼ cup brandy
1 tablespoon brandy, extra, for flaming

METHOD

Wipe over cutlets. Juice 2 oranges and combine juice with brandy. Marinate cutlets in this mixture for 1 hour. Place cutlets under griller and cook 2-3 minutes each side, basting frequently with marinade. Peel and slice remaining 2 oranges. Towards the end of cooking time place orange slices under griller and heat through. Arrange cutlets on platter, place orange slices on top. Warm remaining brandy, flame, pour over cutlets. Serve immediately.

Serves 6

A ferry returning from the Hawkesbury River to Sydney Harbour, passing North Head, NSW.

Passionfruit Torte

(Photograph page 181)

INGREDIENTS

Crumb Crust

2 cups sweet biscuit crumbs
125g (4oz) butter or margarine
½ teaspoon cinnamon

Filling

1⅓ cups castor sugar
3 tablespoons cornflour
1 cup water
1 tablespoon butter or margarine
¼ cup lemon juice
½ cup passionfruit pulp
2 eggs, separated
1 tablespoon gelatine
¼ cup water
1 cup cream, lightly whipped

METHOD

Crumb crust:
Preheat oven to 200ºC (400ºF).
Combine biscuit crumbs, butter and cinnamon in a bowl and mix well. Press over the base and sides of a greased 20cm (8 inch) spring form tin. Bake for 5-8 minutes. Cool.
Filling:
Put sugar and cornflour into a saucepan, blend with water. Stir constantly over a medium heat until mixture thickens and begins to bubble. Stir in butter, lemon juice and passionfruit pulp. Add the beaten egg yolks, stir well, remove from heat and cool, stirring occasionally. Mix gelatine with water and dissolve over hot water. Stir gelatine into cooled sauce. Fold stiffly beaten egg whites and cream into the sauce. Pour sauce into cooled crumb crust and refrigerate to set. Serve well chilled with extra whipped cream.

Serves 6 to 8

An ornate Surgeon-Fish. The Great Barrier Reef.

Chilled Strawberry Cream

(Photograph page 167)

INGREDIENTS

2 punnets strawberries
¾ cup sugar
2 tablespoons lemon juice
1 tablespoon gelatine
2 tablespoons water
2 egg whites, stiffly beaten
1 cup thin cream, lightly whipped
extra whipped cream for serving

METHOD

Wash and hull strawberries. Reserve 6 for garnish. Put strawberries and the sugar in a saucepan and bring slowly to the boil. Add lemon juice and stir over a low heat until sugar dissolves. Remove from heat and cool. Purée berry mixture in a blender or food processor.
Soften the gelatine in water, dissolve over hot water and stir into purée. Fold stiffly beaten egg whites, and whipped cream through the purée and pour into 6 champagne glasses. Chill until set. Garnish with extra whipped cream and reserved strawberries.

Serves 6

Ricotta Coffee Cream

INGREDIENTS

500g (1lb) ricotta cheese
¼ cup icing sugar, sifted
1½ teaspoons instant coffee powder
4 tablespoons rum
⅔ cup cream
chocolate shavings

METHOD

In a bowl or food processor beat or process the ricotta cheese until smooth. Blend in icing sugar, coffee and rum.
In a separate bowl beat the cream until just thick, then fold in the ricotta mixture. Cover and chill for at least 1 hour.
When ready to serve, divide the mixture evenly between 6 glass dishes. Top with chocolate shavings and serve with brandy snap biscuits.

Serves 6

Chocolate Ice Cream Bars

INGREDIENTS

125g (4oz) dark chocolate
2 cups cream
4 egg yolks, beaten
½ cup castor sugar
1 teaspoon gelatine
1 tablespoon hot water
1 teaspoon vanilla essence

METHOD

Coarsely grate chocolate and place in top of a double saucepan. Stir in cream, egg yolks and castor sugar. Cook over simmering water, stirring constantly until slightly thickened. Remove from heat. Dissolve gelatine in hot water and gradually stir into hot chocolate mixture. Add vanilla essence. Pour mixture into a freezer tray and freeze until almost firm. Remove from freezer and place in a chilled bowl, then beat until fluffy. Spoon into loaf tin lined with foil and freeze until firm. When required for serving, unmould, remove foil and cut into bars. Serve with a sauce of puréed berry fruit.

Serves 8 to 10

PASSIONFRUIT TORTE, Recipe page 180.

An excited child among the Seagulls and Pelicans. The Entrance, NSW.

A pair of Spangled Emperor weighing more than 10 kilos each.

Our Wild West

Take a look at Western Australia on the map and you will see just how massive this State is. With around 2,496,000 square kilometres (975,000 square miles) of land, stretching over 2400 kilometres (1500 miles) from north to south, it is around three and a half times bigger than that most size-conscious of States, Texas.

The variety of sea life from this enormous stretch of coastline is tremendous. From the cooler waters around the old whaling town of Albany in the south, up to the tropical beaches of Broome in the far north, the diversity of the sea's bounty is as great as the stark contrast in landscapes.

The south coast has its huge shoals of Pilchards along with its own peculiar versions of Groper (Giant Blue Groper) and Kingfish (Samson Fish). Around the corner, the southern west coast is quite similar to the east coast, with its Trevally, Mulloway, Snapper, Whiting and Spanish Mackerel. North of the nose of this State's dog-like profile, can be found Blue Groper, Morwong (Queenfish), Parrot and Tusk Fish, Great Trevally and, right at the top, around the Kimberleys, the indomitable Barramundi.

Game fishing is very productive in these waters, with Marlin, Sailfish, Wahoo and the giant Spanish Mackerel all within easy reach of the competent sportsman.

Shellfish, of course, are also abundant, with the Western Rock Lobster, many different Crabs and Prawns, as well as Pipis, Octopus, Squid, Cuttlefish and Mussels.

The freshwater scene is surprisingly luxuriant for a State that has a justifiably strong reputation for aridity. There are a multitude of rivers emptying into the Indian Ocean up and down the west coast. Many of them in the North are raging torrents in the Wet Season and nothing but a series of waterholes in the Dry. These are homes for the Barramundi, as well as Perch and Catfish. In the wetter regions of the southwest, many streams and rivers are now stocked with Rainbow and Brown Trout.

As you can see, the diversity in this large State is quite profound. So it is with the cuisine taken from this marvellous range of seafood. The extent of superb flavours and textures within this selection of recipes is sure to make your next dinner party or barbecue an occasion to remember!

Be sure to try the Grilled Sardines in Fresh Tomato Sauce (page 194) — it's absolutely out of this world — in fact, as straight out of the world of the West as you're likely to get! In fact, all of these recipes are great, which can make menu selection a difficult task.

Across the page we have a fantastic menu suggestion which will knock your guests off their feet! To start, a super sharp soup — the flavours of the Stilton and Onion Soup combine just magnificently! For mains, we have a very quick and easy fish bake, in the form of Stuffed Kingfish Cutlets.- make sure you have a good bottle of WA wine to go with this one! And finally, an exquisitely refreshing iced dessert, the Red Wine Granita, rounds off our ideal Western meal.

So why not let your hair down and enjoy this selection from our very own "Wild West"?

Middle right: RED WINE GRANITA, Recipe page 196. *Middle left*: STILTON & ONION SOUP, Recipe page 188.
Below: STUFFED KINGFISH CUTLETS, Recipe page 194.

This river is brown due to heavy rains from Harkes Head, Kalbarri National Park, W.A.

Stilton and Onion Soup

(Photograph page 185)

INGREDIENTS

1 tablespoon butter or margarine
1 medium onion, finely chopped
250g (8oz) stilton cheese, crumbled
2 tablespoons flour
2L (8 cups) chicken stock
1 bay leaf
salt and pepper to taste
2 medium potatoes, peeled and cubed
1 cup cream

METHOD

Melt butter in a large saucepan, add onion and cook gently until soft. Add cheese, stir until melted, add flour and cook for 1 minute. Gradually add stock, stirring constantly. Add bay leaf, salt, pepper and potatoes. Simmer for 10-15 minutes until potato is tender. Remove bay leaf, add cream, stir until reheated without boiling. Serve immediately.

Serves 6

Marinated Mushrooms

INGREDIENTS

500g (1lb) mushrooms
⅓ cup soy sauce
½ cup good white wine vinegar
2 garlic cloves, crushed
2 tablespoons finely chopped fresh basil
4 tablespoons lemon juice
cracked black pepper to taste
6 lettuce cups, washed and drained

METHOD

Wipe over mushrooms with damp paper towel, trim stems. Slice mushrooms thinly and place in a bowl. Add remaining ingredients, toss and marinate for at least 2 hours before serving.
Spoon mushrooms into the lettuce cups and serve on individual plates.

Serves 6

Kalumburu Aborigines in traditional dance at Napier Broome Bay, W.A.

Fisherman's Omelette

INGREDIENTS

6 Pilchards or Sardines
seasoned flour
1 tablespoon butter
1 tablespoon oil
10 large eggs, separated
1½ cups milk
¼ cup chopped chives
2 tablespoons finely chopped parsley
2 tablespoons finely chopped onion
1 teaspoon French mustard
salt and pepper to taste
¼ teaspoon nutmeg

METHOD

Clean and scale the fish, remove tail, head and backbones. Cut each into 4 pieces and coat with flour. Heat butter and oil in a large frying pan. Add fish pieces and cook on each side until golden.
Beat egg yolks and milk together. Add chives, parsley, onion, French mustard, salt and pepper. Mix well. Beat egg whites until stiff and gently fold through yolk mixture. Pour this over the fish in the pan and cook gently until eggs are fluffy and set. Place pan under a hot grill to cook the top. Invert the omelette onto a platter and cut into wedges for serving. Garnish with salad and serve immediately.

Serves 6

Grilled Devilled Pilchards

INGREDIENTS

12 Pilchards or Sardines
2 cups dry breadcrumbs
good pinch cayenne pepper
¼ teaspoon nutmeg
¼ teaspoon dry mustard
¼ teaspoon salt
flour for coating
1 egg, beaten

METHOD

Scale, clean and remove backbone from fish, leaving the heads and tails on. In a bowl combine breadcrumbs, cayenne pepper, nutmeg, mustard and salt. Mix well. Coat each fish with flour, beaten egg and the crumb mixture. Place on a greased grill plate and cook for 2-3 minutes each side. Serve with lemon wedges.

Serves 6

Tomato and Mozzarella Salad

INGREDIENTS

6 large tomatoes
500g (1lb) mozzarella cheese
12 canned Anchovy fillets
12 black olives, halved
small basil sprigs to garnish

Dressing

3 tablespoons white wine vinegar
1 teaspoon French mustard
¾ cup olive oil
3 tablespoons finely chopped fresh basil
salt and pepper

METHOD

Wash tomatoes. Cut the mozzarella cheese and tomatoes into thin slices. Arrange tomato and mozzarella slices onto 6 appetizer plates, slip the cheese slices in between the tomatoes. Arrange 2 Anchovy fillets crosswise on top of each salad. Place the olive halves on top of the salad. Combine dressing ingredients in a bowl and beat well with a fork. Pour over the salads and garnish each with a sprig of basil. Serve with crusty bread.

Serves 6

PIPIS WITH TOMATO & GARLIC IN RED WINE, Recipe page 189.

Pipis with Tomato and Garlic in Red Wine

(Photograph page 189)

INGREDIENTS

*3kg (6lb) Pipis, in shell
(see page 314)
2 tablespoons oil
2 medium onions, finely
sliced
4-6 garlic cloves, crushed
1½ cups dry red wine
1½ cups water
½ cup finely chopped parsley
4 peppercorns, crushed
2 x 425g (14oz) cans tomatoes
salt to taste
crusty bread*

METHOD

Prepare Pipis as directed. In a large, widebased saucepan heat oil, add onions and garlic. Cook gently for 5-6 minutes until onions are soft. Add red wine, water, parsley, peppercorns, chopped tomatoes and salt. Bring to the boil and boil gently for 10 minutes. Add Pipis, cover and simmer gently until Pipis open, about 8-10 minutes. Remove from heat as soon as all are opened as Pipis can toughen if overcooked. Serve Pipis in their shells in deep plates with the tomato sauce. Provide plenty of crusty bread for mopping up sauce.

Serves 6

Flathead Kebabs with Peanut Sauce

INGREDIENTS

*750g (1½lb) Flathead fillets
kebab skewers*

Peanut Sauce

*1 tablespoon oil
1 small onion, finely chopped
3 garlic cloves, crushed
½ teaspoon dried chili,
crushed
1 teaspoon Blachan (see Note)
1 tablespoon lemon juice
1 tablespoon soy sauce
1½ cups crunchy peanut
butter
1 tablespoon raw sugar*

METHOD

Skin Flathead fillets, removing any bones. Cut into bite-size pieces and thread onto skewers, allowing 2 skewers per serve. Place skewered fish under griller and cook for 2-3 minutes each side or until flesh flakes. Serve hot with Peanut Sauce.
Peanut Sauce: (Prepare before fish). Heat oil and gently fry onion, garlic and chili for 3-4 minutes. Add Blachan, lemon juice, soy sauce, peanut butter and sugar. Gently cook until a sauce consistency. Coconut milk or water may be added to make a more liquid consistency.
Note: Blachan is dried Shrimp paste, available from Asian food stores.

Serves 6

Left: BAR COD. *Right*: FRIED WESTRALIAN JEWFISH (DHU-FISH) & CHIPS, Recipe page 195

Early morning over the Perth skyline and Harbour, W.A.

GRILLED SARDINES WITH FRESH TOMATO SAUCE, Recipe page 194.

Stuffed Kingfish Cutlets

(Photograph page 185)

INGREDIENTS

12 thin Kingfish or Mackerel cutlets
2 cups fresh breadcrumbs
½ cup finely chopped mushrooms
2 shallots, finely chopped
2 tablespoons sour cream
1 tablespoon finely chopped parsley
salt and pepper to taste
½ cup natural yoghurt
½ cup cream

METHOD

Wipe over cutlets with damp kitchen paper. In a bowl combine breadcrumbs, mushrooms, shallots, sour cream, parsley, salt and pepper. Mix well. Place 6 cutlets in a greased baking dish and evenly spread the mixture onto each cutlet. Top each one with a remaining cutlet. Pour over combined yoghurt and cream. Cover and bake at 180ºC (350ºF) for 20-25 minutes until flesh flakes. Serve hot with dish juices.

Serves 6

Grilled Sardines with Fresh Tomato Sauce

(Photograph page 194)

INGREDIENTS

24 fresh Sardines or Pilchards
3 cups peeled and chopped tomatoes
¾ cup white wine
¼ cup finely chopped basil and parsley
1½ cups water
¼ cup tomato paste
salt and pepper

METHOD

Scale, clean and remove backbones of fish. Keep aside.
Place tomatoes, wine, herbs and water in a saucepan and bring to the boil, reduce heat and simmer until liquid has reduced by one-quarter. Add tomato paste and seasonings, simmer. Place fish under grill and cook for 1-2 minutes each side or until flesh flakes. Serve with fresh tomato sauce.

Serves 6

Fried Marinated Pilchards

INGREDIENTS

*24 fresh Pilchards or Sardines
flour for coating
oil for shallow frying
salt and pepper to taste
2 cups white wine vinegar
1 cup water
1 medium onion, finely
chopped
2 garlic cloves, crushed
2 bay leaves
¼ teaspoon ground oregano
6 peppercorns, lightly crushed*

METHOD

Scale, clean and remove backbones of fish. Dry well and coat with flour. Heat oil in frying pan and fry a few fish at a time. Drain fish on paper towels, season with salt and pepper. Place all the cooked fish in a large dish.

Pour vinegar and water into a saucepan, add onion, garlic, bay leaves, oregano and peppercorns. Simmer over a low heat for 10-12 minutes. Cool slightly and then pour over the fish. Cover and refrigerate for 24 hours before serving.

Serve with green salad and crusty bread.

Serves 6

⤸ ⤶

Whole Flathead Baked with Mussels

INGREDIENTS

*3 x 500g (1lb) whole Flathead
500g (1lb) mussels
1 ¼ cups white wine
1 cup fish or chicken stock
2 medium onions, thinly
sliced
2 bay leaves
4 whole black peppercorns
2 x 425g (14oz) cans tomatoes
1 tablespoon finely chopped
fresh basil or 1 teaspoon dried
basil
salt to taste
12 black olives*

METHOD

Scale and clean fish. Trim fins. Wash and scrub Mussels, removing beards. In a large oven-to-table baking dish place fish, pour over wine, stock, add onions, bay leaves, peppercorns, tomatoes, basil, and salt. Bake at 180ºC (350ºF) for 25 minutes or until flesh flakes. Add Mussels to pan during last 10 minutes of cooking time and cook until Mussels are opened. Before serving discard bay leaves and peppercorns. Garnish fish and Mussels with olives.

Serves 6

⤸ ⤶

Red Emperor Poached in Wine Court-Bouillon

INGREDIENTS

*1 x 2kg (4lb) whole Red
Emperor
1 cup dry white wine
3 cups water
½ teaspoon salt
1 large carrot, thinly sliced
1 large onion, thinly sliced
4 whole peppercorns
2 whole cloves
2 bay leaves
½ cup celery tops
6 sprigs parsley*

METHOD

Scale and clean fish. In a fish kettle (poaching pan), combine remaining ingredients. Place fish in pan and cover. Poach for 20-30 minutes or until flesh flakes. Allow fish to cool completely in poaching liquid. Remove fish and chill well before serving with salads. The liquid can be strained and used as a base for aspic or various sauces.

Serves 3 to 4

Stuffed Sardines Baked in Red Wine

INGREDIENTS

*24 Sardines or Pilchards
3 cups fresh breadcrumbs
½ cup tomato paste
1 medium onion, finely
chopped
2 garlic cloves, crushed
2 teaspoons finely chopped
mint
¼ cup lemon juice
salt and pepper to taste
1½ cups red wine*

METHOD

Preheat oven to 180ºC (350ºF). Scale, gut and clean the fish, removing backbones and leaving heads and tails on. In a bowl combine breadcrumbs, tomato paste, onion, garlic, mint, lemon juice, salt and pepper. Mix well. Place spoonfuls of mixture into the cavity of each fish, secure with toothpicks.

Place fish in an ovenproof dish and pour red wine over fish. Bake for 20-25 minutes or until flesh becomes soft.

Serve fish immediately with red wine juices. Accompany with boiled rice.

Serves 6

⤸ ⤶

Baked Trevally with Zucchini and Tomato

INGREDIENTS

*750g (1½lb) Trevally fillets
2 medium zucchini, thinly
sliced
3 medium tomatoes, roughly
chopped
¼ cup fresh basil leaves, finely
chopped
1 teaspoon rosemary leaves
¼ cup lemon juice
salt and pepper to taste
1 cup fresh breadcrumbs
¼ cup grated Parmesan
cheese*

METHOD

Skin the fillets, remove bones. Cut into serving size portions. Place in a greased baking dish and top with zucchini and tomatoes. Sprinkle over basil, rosemary and lemon juice. Season to taste. Cover with combined breadcrumbs and cheese and bake at 180ºC (350ºF) for 20-25 minutes or until flesh flakes and top is golden.

Serves 6

⤸ ⤶

Fried Westralian Jewfish (Dhu-fish) and Chips

(Photograph pages 190 & 191)

INGREDIENTS

*1.5kg (3lb) Dhu-fish or Pearl
Perch fillets
1½ cups self-raising flour
⅓ cup cornflour
½ teaspoon salt
1½ cups water
2 tablespoons lemon juice
2 tablespoons oil
flour for coating
1kg (2lb) frozen chip potatoes
oil for both shallow and deep
frying*

METHOD

Make batter by sifting dry ingredients into a bowl. Make a well in the centre and gradually stir in water, lemon juice and oil. Stand for 30 minutes before using. Coat fish fillets with flour, then in batter and shallow fry for 3-4 minutes on each side, until golden. Drain on kitchen paper and keep warm. Place frozen chip potatoes in a basket and fry in deep oil for approximately 4 minutes. Remove from oil, allow oil to come back to temperature and refry chips for a further 2 minutes until crispy. Drain and serve immediately.

Serves 6

Red Wine Granita

This sweet must be made a day in advance, to allow setting.

(Photograph page 185)

INGREDIENTS

3 cups red wine
1 cup water
1 ¼ cups castor sugar
1 medium orange, juiced and strained
1 medium lemon, juiced and strained
fresh mint leaves

METHOD

Choose a wine that has a good rich flavour and is not too acidic. Combine water and sugar in a saucepan, bring to the boil and simmer for 5 minutes. Make sure the sugar has dissolved. Pour into a bowl and cool. Add the wine, orange and lemon juice. Mix well. Pour the mixture into a shallow freezer tray. During the course of the day, regularly stir the solidifying liquid with a fork. Continue until the mixture is set into a mass of small light crystals. Serve in glass dishes or wine glasses, garnished with mint leaves.

Serves 6 to 8

Rice Mould with Prunes in Port Sauce

(Photograph pages 196 & 197)

INGREDIENTS

½ cup rice
1 cup milk
1 cup water
pinch salt
½ cup sugar
1 tablespoon gelatine
2 tablespoons water
⅓ cup evaporated milk, icy cold
1 teaspoon vanilla essence
500g (1lb) pitted prunes
1 cup port or good red wine
1 cup water
sugar to taste
1 tablespoon lemon juice
whipped cream or natural yoghurt

METHOD

Put rice, milk, water and salt into the top of a double saucepan, cover and cook over gently boiling water for 25-30 minutes, or until rice is cooked, stirring occasionally. Add sugar, stir until dissolved, remove from heat. Dissolve gelatine in water and add to hot rice. Cool rice mixture. Beat the evaporated milk with vanilla until thick, fold into cooled rice mixture and spoon into a greased ring mould, chill until set.
Meanwhile combine prunes in a pan with port and water, cook until prunes plump and liquid is reduced to 1 cup. Stir in sugar and lemon juice. Chill prune mixture.
Unmould the rice ring onto a platter, spoon prunes into centre and trickle a little of the syrup over. Serve with whipped cream or natural yoghurt.

Serves 6

Mandarin Layer Jelly

INGREDIENTS

1 x 310g (11oz) can mandarin segments
water
1 packet orange jelly crystals
250g (8oz) packaged cream cheese, softened at room temperature
1 teaspoon gelatine
2 tablespoons hot water
whipped cream

METHOD

Drain mandarins, reserving syrup. Make syrup up to 1 ¾ cups with water, heat and dissolve jelly crystals in this liquid. Pour half the jelly mixture into a 4-cup mould and place in the freezer to set. Leave only until just set.

Beat the softened cream cheese until smooth. Chop most of the mandarins, reserving a few for decoration. Add chopped mandarins to the cream cheese. Dissolve gelatine in the hot water and cool, then add to the cream cheese, beating thoroughly.

Pour half the cream cheese mixture onto the set jelly and set as before. Repeat the two layers again with remaining jelly and cream cheese mixture, placing mould in refrigerator for final setting. When ready to serve, dip quickly in hot water and invert on a serving plate. Decorate with whipped cream and remaining mandarin segments.

Serves 4 to 6

Sunshine Cassata

INGREDIENTS

1½ cups dry full cream powdered milk
4 tablespoons castor sugar
2½ cups hot water
4 teaspoons gelatine
⅔ cup condensed milk
1 teaspoon vanilla essence
1 teaspoon almond essence
½ cup almonds, toasted and finely chopped
¼ cup red cherries, halved
¼ cup green cherries, halved
½ cup cream, whipped
2 teaspoons instant coffee powder
¼ cup finely chopped walnuts
½ cup dark chocolate, grated
1 tablespoon rum

METHOD

Combine powdered milk with sugar. Mix with 2 cups of the water. Soften gelatine in remaining water and dissolve over hot water, gradually add to mixture. Stir in condensed milk and vanilla essence. Pour into a freezer container and freeze until partially set then beat until light and doubled in bulk. Divide in two. To the first half, add almond essence, almonds, cherries and cream. Pour into a freezer container. To the second half, add coffee, walnuts, chocolate and rum. Mix well and pour over the first half. Freeze until firm. Spoon into dessert glasses and serve.

Serves 6 to 8

RICE WITH PRUNES IN PORT SAUCE, Recipe page 196.

A Vietnamese fishing boat slowly disintegrates in the mangrove mud at Broome, W.A.

Waihope Fishing Village, North Cape, New Zealand.

New Zealand

Well known as a land of great scenic beauty, New Zealand is also renowned for its fantastic fishing. Very much a country for outdoor activities such as skiing, cycling, kayaking and boating, one of the most popular of these activities, and one of the country's most important tourist attractions, is fishing. From the big game fishing haunts of the northland's Bay of Islands to the wild, windswept beaches of the South Island, this land is without doubt the fishing enthusiast's paradise.

Certainly the most famous New Zealand fish is the Trout. The volcanic plateau of the North Island has been called "the world's greatest Trout factory". Aficionados from around the world regularly stream into this area in search of battle with some of the giant Rainbows and Browns that are now legendary.

Lake Taupo is probably the most productive Trout fishing lake in the world, yielding more than 500 tonnes of Rainbow Trout each year. The township of Taupo is a busy year-round resort with new visitors arriving every day.

The South Island also has its well known Trout spots. The southland's three main fishing rivers are the Mataura, the Oreti and the Aparima — all havens for the highly esteemed Brown Trout.

Interestingly enough, it is prohibited to buy or sell Trout in New Zealand — a protection for the sports fishing and tourism industries. Whether or not you are a "Kiwi", one of the best ways to enjoy fresh Trout has to be the way it's done around the fishermen's camp fire; wrap the fish, unscaled and ungutted, in several sheets of wet newspaper. Bury it in hot coals and cook for 30 to 40 minutes. When you unwrap the fish, the paper will pull the skin away from the fish. The guts are easily removed, as they will have formed a hard ball. Best eaten with a squeeze of lemon, and a sprinkle of salt and pepper. There are a number of rather more sophisticated trout recipes to be found in this book, simply by referring to the Index or page 98 of "About the Fish".

The Snapper is probably New Zealand's most plentiful saltwater fish and is commonly caught off the beaches and rocks of the coast. It is a great favourite for the table and once you've tried an exciting dish like the Prawn Stuffed Snapper (page 211), you will understand why!

If it's a large fish you're after, then it's off to the Bay of Islands for you! Many world records have been set in this area for Shark, Marlin and Tuna. Good sized Yellowtail Kingfish are also plentiful and provide good sport.

One of the great advantages of cooking with large fish such as these, is the absence of tiny bones. And don't think for a minute that big means less flavour! One mouthful of the Pan Fried Marlin Cutlets with Olives and Capers (see photo page 212) will convince you of that!

Whitebait is another of New Zealand's better known delicacies. The estuaries of the many swiftly flowing rivers along the west coast of the South Island are the places to be in spring if you would like to try your hand at catching some of these delicious little fish for yourself. If you can't make it there, the next best thing is to try some of our recipes for this famous dish.

The Whitebait Loaf (shown opposite) is the scrumptious centrepiece of this refreshingly natural New Zealand menu which includes Grilled Dory Strips and a delightful dessert of Kiwi Fruit and Orange Slices in Liqueur.

No matter what you choose, you will be enraptured by this fabulous selection of food from New Zealand's waters. So here's to the "land of the long white cloud" and the sensational gourmet seafood it offers!

Top Left: KIWI FRUIT & ORANGE SLICES IN LIQUEUR, Recipe page 216. *Top Right*: GRILLED DORY STRIPS WITH EGG YOLK GLAZE, Recipe page 204. *Below*: WHITEBAIT LOAF, Recipe page 210.

A sweeping view of the East Coast, North Island, New Zealand.

Grilled Dory Strips with Egg Yolk Glaze

(Photograph page 201)

INGREDIENTS

500g (1lb) Dory fillets
2 egg yolks, beaten
2 teaspoons soy sauce
1½ teaspoons dry sherry
fried parsley (page 315)
lemon wedges

METHOD

Cut each fillet into 3 strips. In a bowl, combine egg yolks, soy sauce and sherry. Mix well. Place strips of Dory under grill and brush regularly with egg yolk mixture, turning strips once. Cooking should take 2 minutes each side. Serve immediately with fried parsley and lemon wedges.

Serves 6

Fish Soup

INGREDIENTS

Stock

1 large Snapper head and skeleton
2L (4 pints) water
1 medium onion, peeled and quartered
1 carrot, roughly chopped
6 whole peppercorns

Soup

60g (2oz) butter or margarine
1 large onion, finely chopped
2 carrots, peeled and finely chopped
2 potatoes, peeled and cubed
2 celery stalks, finely chopped
the strained fish stock
salt and pepper to taste

METHOD

Stock:
Wash fish head and skeleton. Place in a saucepan with water, onion, carrot and peppercorns. Simmer gently for 1 hour, remove from heat and strain into a jug. Remove any fish flesh from head and skeleton and keep aside.
Soup:
Melt the butter in a large saucepan, add all the chopped vegetables and fry gently for 5 minutes. Add fish stock, cover and simmer for 30 minutes until vegetables are tender. Cool a little and purée in 3-4 batches in food processor or blender. Return to saucepan, add reserved fish flesh and season to taste. Return to the boil and serve immediately.

Serves 6

Island Fish Salad

INGREDIENTS

750g (1½lb) fish fillets
(Whiting, Flathead or Bream)
2 medium onions, finely chopped
¾ cup lime or lemon juice
4 large tomatoes
1¼ cup mayonnaise
½ cup sour cream
½ cup coconut milk
salt and pepper to taste
6 lettuce cups
fresh coriander for garnish

METHOD

Wash and skin fillets, cut into bite-size pieces. Combine with onions and lime juice. Cover and chill overnight or until flesh turns very white.
Peel tomatoes, remove seeds and dice. Mix mayonnaise with sour cream and coconut milk until smooth and add to fish mixture with tomatoes. Season with salt and pepper. Serve fish salad in lettuce cups. Garnish with coriander.

Serves 6

Cheese and Chive Soufflés

INGREDIENTS

60g (2oz) butter or margarine
1¼ cup flour
1 cup milk
90g (3oz) cheddar cheese, grated
1 tablespoon grated Parmesan cheese
4 large eggs, separated
3 tablespoons chopped chives
salt and pepper to taste

METHOD

Preheat oven to 180ºC (350ºF). Melt butter in a saucepan, stir in flour and cook for 2 minutes. Gradually stir in milk and cook, stirring constantly, until thickened. Remove from heat and add cheeses; stir until melted.
Beat egg yolks into sauce mixture, add chives and season to taste. Beat egg whites until stiff and gently fold through sauce mixture.
Grease and collar 6 small souffle dishes and gradually pour even amounts of mixture into each. Bake for 25-30 minutes or until golden brown, fluffy and firm to touch. Remove collars and serve immediately.

Serves 6

Fresh Asparagus with Hazelnut Sauce

INGREDIENTS

36 fresh asparagus spears
1 tablespoon butter
4 tablespoons hazelnut meal
2 tablespoons hazelnut oil
1 tablespoon white wine vinegar
1/4 teaspoon nutmeg
salt and pepper to taste

METHOD

Melt butter in a small pan, add hazelnut meal and stir over gentle heat until meal turns a pale brown colour. Stir in hazelnut oil, vinegar, nutmeg, salt and pepper. Set aside. Cut any woody ends from asparagus and wash well. Place asparagus in a wide-based saucepan, almost cover with hot water and simmer until just tender. Lift with a slotted spoon onto a warm serving dish. Quickly reheat hazelnut sauce adding a little asparagus water to thin down if necessary and pour over asparagus. Serve immediately

Serves 6

The beautiful, rugged West Coast, New Zealand.

SAVOURY FISH POTS, Recipe page 205.

Savoury Fish Pots

(Photograph page 205)

INGREDIENTS

*500g (1lb) Hapuku or Snapper
fillets
water
250g (8oz) cream cheese,
softened
2 tablespoons milk
1 packet French Onion Soup
Mix
2 tablespoons finely chopped
parsley
2 tablespoons lemon juice
ground black pepper
melba toast, savoury crackers*

METHOD

Skin the fillets. Put fillets in a pan and almost cover with water. Poach gently until flesh flakes. Remove fish from pan and flake, removing all bones. In a bowl combine cheese, milk, soup, parsley, lemon juice and pepper. Mix well. Fold in flaked fish. Spoon mixture evenly into entrée-size pots and chill well before serving. Serve with melba toast or savoury crackers.

Serves 6

Clear Whitebait and Scallop Soup

INGREDIENTS

*50g (8oz) Whitebait
250g (8oz) Scallops
1 egg, beaten
½ cup finely chopped parsley
10 cups fish stock (page 315)
4 shallots, finely sliced
salt and white pepper to taste*

METHOD

Wash Whitebait thoroughly. Remove heads if Whitebait are large. Wash Scallops, remove any black membrane. Place Whitebait and Scallops in a food processor and mince finely.
Place in a bowl and add egg and parsley. Mix well and form into small balls. Put stock into a large saucepan and bring to the boil. Add shallots. Drop fish balls into the hot stock, when they rise they are cooked. Season soup and serve immediately.

Serves 6 to 8

Left: LEMON SOLE WITH GLAZED GRAPES, Recipe page 213. *Right*: SEAFOOD CRÈPES, Recipe page 211.

Church of the Good Shepherd, Lake Tekapo, New Zealand.

SAUTÉD FILLETS OF DORY WITH BLUEBERRIES, Recipe page 210.

Whitebait Loaf

(Photograph page 201)

INGREDIENTS

250g (8oz) Whitebait
1 large horseshoe bread loaf
1 medium onion, finely diced
1 garlic clove, crushed
2 tablespoons tomato paste
2-3 drops Tabasco sauce
salt and pepper to taste
1 cup grated cheddar cheese
2 tablespoons finely chopped parsley

METHOD

Wash Whitebait thoroughly. Remove heads if large in size. Slice bread loaf in half, scoop out soft bread, leaving cavity. Place Whitebait and bread in a food processor and purée. Add onion, garlic, tomato paste, Tabasco sauce, salt and pepper. Mix well. Spoon into bread cavity and replace top. Combine cheese with parsley and sprinkle on top of loaf. Place on a baking tray and bake at 150°C (300°F) for 20-25 minutes or until heated thoroughly. Serve with salad.

Serves 4 to 6

Sautéd Fillets of Dory with Blueberries

(Photograph page 210)

INGREDIENTS

750g (1½lb) Dory fillets
seasoned flour
125g (4oz) fresh or frozen blueberries
1 tablespoon lemon juice
1 teaspoon finely grated lemon rind
1¼ teaspoon sugar
2 tablespoons butter or margarine
1½ tablespoons finely chopped chives
salt and pepper to taste

METHOD

Coat fillets with seasoned flour. In a bowl combine blueberries, lemon juice, rind and sugar. Mix well, slightly softening the blueberries. In a pan melt butter and gently cook fillets for 2-3 minutes each side, add blueberry mixture, chives, salt and pepper, and gently heat through. Serve immediately.

Serves 6

Prawn Stuffed Snapper

INGREDIENTS

1 x 3kg (6lb) Snapper
250g (8oz) cooked Prawn meat, roughly chopped
4 large mushrooms, finely chopped
1¼ cup finely sliced celery
2 tablespoons finely chopped parsley
⅔ cup thick white sauce (page 315)
salt and pepper to taste
pinch cayenne pepper
large sheet of greased foil
½ cup lemon juice

METHOD

Preheat oven to 180ºC (350ºF). Scale, gut and wash Snapper. Trim fins and remove backbone if desired. In a bowl combine Prawn meat, mushrooms, celery, parsley, white sauce, salt, pepper and cayenne pepper. Mix well. Fill the cavity of the Snapper with the mixture and secure with fine skewers. Place fish on greased foil and pour over lemon juice. Wrap like a parcel and place on a baking tray. Bake for 50-60 minutes or until flesh flakes. Open foil carefully and lift Snapper onto a warm serving platter, using 2 egg lifters. Garnish with a few whole Prawns, lemon slices and dill sprigs. Serve hot or chilled.

Serves 6

Baked Marinated Tuna Fillet

INGREDIENTS

1 x 1.5kg (3lb) piece of fresh Tuna
1¼ cup lemon juice
2 tablespoons finely chopped mint
freshly ground black pepper
6 shallots, finely sliced
125g (4oz) mushrooms, finely sliced
3 tablespoons oil
½ cup red wine

METHOD

Remove skin from Tuna, if necessary. In a shallow ovenproof dish, place Tuna with lemon juice, mint, pepper, shallots, mushrooms, oil and wine. Marinate for at least 1 hour before cooking.
Cover dish and bake at 150ºC (300ºF) for 40-50 minutes.
Serve sliced with pan juices poured over.

Serves 6

Whitebait Tempura

INGREDIENTS

500g (1½lb) Whitebait

Batter
½ cup flour
½ cup cornflour
1 teaspoon baking powder
pinch salt
1 cup soda or mineral water
oil for deep frying

METHOD

Wash Whitebait thoroughly. Remove heads if large in size. Pat Whitebait dry with kitchen paper and reserve. In a bowl sift together all the dry ingredients. Gradually stir in soda water until mixture becomes a smooth batter.
Coat Whitebait in batter and deep fry in hot oil until golden—about 1-2 minutes. Drain on crumpled kitchen paper and serve immediately.

Serves 6

Seafood Crèpes

(Photograph pages 206 & 207)

INGREDIENTS

250g (8oz) Snapper fillets
250g (8oz) Mussel meat
250g (8oz) Scallops
30g (2oz) butter
2 garlic cloves, crushed
6 shallots, chopped
1 tablespoon finely chopped parsley
1½ cups White Sauce (page 315)
185g (6oz) cheddar cheese, grated

Crèpe Batter
2 eggs
2 tablespoons brandy
grated rind of 1 lemon
1½ cups milk
pinch salt
1 cup plain flour
butter for frying

METHOD

Cut fillets into 5cm (2 inch) lengths. Melt butter in a large pan, add Snapper, Mussels, Scallops, garlic and shallots and cook gently for 2 minutes. Stir through parsley and white sauce. Fill crèpes with seafood mixture and place in a shallow, lightly buttered ovenproof baking dish, cover with grated cheese and bake at 180ºC (350ºF) for about 15 minutes. Serve with a crisp green salad.
To Make Crèpes:
Place eggs, brandy, lemon rind, most of milk, salt and flour in a food processor and process until smooth. Pour mixture into a jug, cover and stand 1 hour. Check consistency and add more milk if necessary to make a thin batter.
Grease a 20cm (8 inch) crèpe pan with butter and pour a small quantity of batter into the base of the pan. Cook for about 45 seconds each side. Lightly grease the pan with butter before making each crèpe and stack in a pile, with a sheet of grease-proof paper separating each cooked crèpe. Makes 15-18 crèpes. Fill 12 and store remainder in freezer.

Serves 6

Snapper Stuffed with Oysters

INGREDIENTS

2 x 1kg (2lb) whole Snapper
2 dozen Oysters, cut in half
2½ cups fresh breadcrumbs, soaked in ¼ cup white wine
pinch thyme
pinch ground cloves
1 tablespoon grated lemon rind
2 tablespoons finely chopped shallots
salt and pepper to taste
⅔ cup lemon juice
watercress and lemon wedges

METHOD

Scale and clean fish, backbone can be removed if desired. In a bowl combine Oysters, breadcrumbs, thyme, cloves, lemon rind, shallots, salt and pepper. Mix well. Fill the cavity of each fish and secure opening with skewers. Place each fish on a separate piece of greased foil, pour lemon juice over and wrap like a parcel. Bake at 180ºC (350ºF) for 40-45 minutes or until flesh flakes. Garnish with watercress and lemon wedges.

Serves 6

Pan-fried New Zealand Marlin Cutlets with Olives and Capers

(Photograph pages 212 & 213)

INGREDIENTS

6 New Zealand Marlin or
Swordfish cutlets
black pepper
paprika
2 tablespoons butter or
margarine
2 tablespoons oil
12 black olives, halved
12 capers

METHOD

Season cutlets with pepper and paprika.

Heat butter and oil in a heavy based frying pan and gently fry cutlets for 3 minutes each side or until flesh flakes.

Remove cutlets to serving platter and keep warm. To remaining pan juices, add olives and capers. Sauté until hot. Pour over cutlets and serve.

Serves 6

Whitebait Fritters

(Photograph pages 212 & 213)

INGREDIENTS

1kg (2lb) Whitebait
60g (2oz) butter
2 medium onions, finely
chopped
2 garlic cloves, crushed
½ cup plain flour
½ cup self-raising flour
½ teaspoon salt
3 eggs, beaten
1½ cups beer
½ cup finely chopped parsley
oil for shallow frying

METHOD

Rinse Whitebait and drain thoroughly. Melt butter in a large pan, add onion and gently cook for 2 minutes. Remove from heat and add garlic.

Sift dry ingredients into a bowl, make a well in the centre, add eggs, beer, parsley and onion mixture. Whisk gently to combine then add Whitebait. Heat oil in a large shallow pan and fry heaped tablespoons of the mixture for 2 minutes on each side, until golden. Drain on kitchen paper and serve immediately.

Serves 6

Left: PAN-FRIED NEW ZEALAND MARLIN CUTLETS WITH OLIVES & CAPERS, Recipe page 212.
Right: WHITEBAIT FRITTERS, Recipe page 212.

Gingered Hapuku Fillets with Vegetables

INGREDIENTS

750g (1½lb) Hapuku fillets
1 tablespoon oil
6 shallots, finely sliced
2 celery stalks, finely sliced
2 carrots, finely sliced
2 tablespoons finely grated green ginger
2 cups finely chopped spinach
1 tablespoon arrowroot
1½ cups fish or chicken stock (page 315)
2 tablespoons soy sauce
2 teaspoons honey
250g (8oz) green beans, cut diagonally

METHOD

Skin the fillets and wipe over with damp paper towel. In a large wide based saucepan heat oil and gently fry shallots, celery, carrots and ginger for 3 minutes. Add beans and spinach. Blend arrowroot with 2 tablespoons of the fish stock until smooth then stir in remaining stock, soy sauce and honey. Pour over vegetables and stir until thickened. Lay the fillets evenly over the vegetables, cover and cook over a gentle heat for 10-15 minutes or until flesh flakes. Place fillets on plates and spoon around the vegetables.

Serves 6

Lemon Sole with Glazed Grapes

(Photograph pages 206 & 207)

INGREDIENTS

2 whole Lemon Sole or Flounder
salt and pepper
30g (2oz) butter
2 tablespoons lemon juice
½ cup dry white wine
1¼ cup castor sugar
125g (4oz) sultana grapes

METHOD

Clean Sole and wipe dry. Line a large grilling tray with foil and spread liberally with butter. Season prepared Sole with salt and pepper and place dark side up on tray. Spread with remaining butter, pour over lemon juice and grill gently for 3-4 minutes. Turn fish and grill for a further 3-4 minutes until flesh flakes. Place wine and sugar in a medium size saucepan and stir over heat until sugar has dissolved. Increase heat and boil for 2 minutes, add grapes, boil for a further 1 minute and serve immediately, poured over Sole.

Serves 2

Fishing boats moored at Milford Sound, surrounded by majestic mountains. New Zealand.

Kiwi fruit and Orange Slices in Liqueur

(Photograph page 201)

INGREDIENTS

6 kiwi fruit
6 large oranges
6 tablespoons fresh orange juice
6 tablespoons castor sugar
2-3 tablespoons Grand Marnier
whipped cream

METHOD

Peel and thinly slice kiwi fruit. Peel oranges and remove the pith, cut into slices. Place kiwi fruit and orange slices in a bowl. Combine orange juice, sugar and liqueur and mix well. Pour over prepared fruit and refrigerate for at least 1 hour. Serve in dessert glasses with whipped cream.

Serves 6

Bread and Butter Custard

INGREDIENTS

4 slices white bread, buttered
¼ cup sultanas
3 eggs
2 tablespoons sugar
pinch of salt
2 cups milk
ground cinnamon

METHOD

Remove crusts from buttered bread and cut into fingers. Arrange bread fingers, buttered side down, in layers, sprinkling sultanas between layers, in an ovenproof dish.
Beat eggs, sugar and salt together. Mix in milk and stir until sugar is dissolved. Strain over top of bread. Dust with cinnamon.
Stand in a baking dish of hot water. Bake in a moderate oven, 180ºC (350ºF), for 40 minutes or until custard is set, (test by inserting a knife in the centre). The top should be golden brown. Serve hot.
Note: Bread and Butter Custard may be served cold with cream.

Serves 4 to 6

Kiwi Cheese Cake

(Photograph page 217)

INGREDIENTS

Crumb Base

180g (6oz) gingernut biscuits, crushed
100g (4oz) butter, melted

Filling

4 large kiwi fruit
2 teaspoons lemon juice
500g (1lb) fresh ricotta cheese
½ cup castor sugar
1 tablespoon gelatine
4 tablespoons water
1 cup cream, lightly whipped
kiwi fruit slices for garnish

METHOD

Thoroughly mix crushed biscuits and melted butter. Press crumbs into the base of a lightly greased 20cm (8 inch) spring form cake tin. Chill until required.
Peel kiwi fruit, cut into 4, cut out seeds and discard. Purée fruit in a blender or rub through a sieve. Stir lemon juice into purée.
Place ricotta cheese in a large bowl, beat in sugar until smooth. Stir in kiwi fruit purée.
Sprinkle gelatine over water in a small bowl. Stir to dissolve over hot water, allow to cool. Stir gelatine into cheese mixture then fold in whipped cream. Pour into prepared cake tin. Chill several hours until set.
Remove rim from tin and place cheese cake on a flat serving dish. Decorate top with slices of kiwi fruit.

Serves 6

Caramel Banana Tart

INGREDIENTS

Pastry

90g (3oz) butter
2 tablespoons castor sugar
1 egg
1½ cups plain flour
½ teaspoon baking powder

Filling

5 tablespoons plain flour
1 cup brown sugar
2 egg yolks, beaten
2 cups milk
2 tablespoons butter
½ teaspoon vanilla essence
3 bananas
lemon juice
whipped cream for serving

METHOD

Pastry: Beat butter and sugar until light, add egg and beat well. Sift together flour, and baking powder and mix into butter mixture to form a firm dough. Turn onto a floured board and knead lightly. Roll into a circle and line a greased 23cm (9 inch) pie plate. Crimp edge and prick base and sides with a fork. Bake in preheated 190ºC (375ºF) oven for 15 to 20 minutes until cooked and lightly browned. Cool.
Filling: Mix flour and sugar in a saucepan, gradually blend in egg yolks and milk. Add butter and cook over moderate heat, stirring constantly, until thickened and bubbling. Remove from heat, stir in vanilla essence and cool a little. Pour half into pie crust, cover with 2 sliced bananas, top with remaining caramel mixture. Leave until cool. Slice remaining banana and sprinkle with lemon juice. Decorate tart with swirls of whipped cream and banana slices.

A family picnicking on the lake near Queenstown New Zealand.

KIWI CHEESECAKE, Recipe page 216.

Maoris in traditional dress rowing on the beautiful Captain Cook River, New Zealand.

Sunset over the Yarra River, Melbourne, Vic.

Estuarine Delights

As with many cities around the world, the most pleasant aspect of Australian cities has to be down by the waterside. Even the nation's inland capital has its own magnificent waterside down by Lake Burley Griffin.

There are many places of significance along Australia's vast seaboard, and, like thousands of other similar environments, all provide homes for Australia's estuarine fish. These species are probably the most familiar fish to the majority of Australians, given that we're a nation of city dwellers and that the majority of our major cities have been started on estuaries.

Sydneysiders are justifiably very proud of their world famous harbour, but it is not just Sydney that deserves our attention — there are many other harbours, bays and estuaries around the country that are equally spectacular, perhaps even more so, as they don't share the problems that Sydney has with its large population.

Apart from Sydney, we have Perth which spreads itself majestically around the Swan River, Hobart sitting only a little way up from the mouth of the Derwent, Melbourne with its Port Phillip Bay and Brisbane's Moreton Bay. Certainly many Australians have happy memories of sitting on a jetty or wharf as kids, trying hard to catch a Leatherjacket, a Bream or a Yellowtail!

Fishing is certainly a very popular pastime "Downunder" and understandably so — who doesn't enjoy a couple of peaceful hours relaxing by the water, soaking in the sun, perhaps with a "tinny" or two?! And if by chance a fish or two come your way, then there's the unsurpassed pleasure of sharing a really fresh meal with some family or friends.

Of course many people prefer to keep the cooking simple when the fare is so fresh — in this case you should have a look at the easy but delicious Jewfish with Herb Butter (page 229). There are many other tasty ways, though, of preparing these superb fish and here you will find them all!

The photograph on the facing page shows what a little imagination, and a little help from these pages can do. The entrée of Shellfish Baked in Avocado is certain to be very popular and the Grilled Bream is an old favourite that shouldn't be missed. The suggested dessert of Chocolate Orange Mousse is always a great way to finish a meal of super seafood.

So next time you're down by the water, don't forget your fishing line! With a little luck and a little help from this chapter, you may just eat very well that night!

The Great Ocean road, winding itself along the rugged southern coast, Vic.

Top left: SHELLFISH BAKED IN AVOCADO, Recipe page 224. *Top right*: CHOCOLATE ORANGE MOUSSE,
Recipe page 233. *Below*: GRILLED BREAM WITH VERMOUTH, Recipe page 228.

The famous Twelve Apostles at Port Campbell, Vic.

Shellfish Baked in Avocado

(Photograph page 221)

INGREDIENTS

*3 large Balmain or Moreton Bay Bugs, cooked
250g (8oz) cooked King Prawns
125g (4oz) Scallops
1 dozen Oysters
2 tablespoons butter or margarine
3 shallots, finely chopped
2 tablespoons flour
1 cup fish or chicken stock
2 tablespoons finely chopped parsley
1 tablespoon finely chopped capers
1 tablespoon lemon juice
3 tablespoons sour cream or natural yoghurt
salt and pepper to taste
3 large ripe avocados, halved and seeded
6 whole Prawns to garnish*

METHOD

Split underneath tail section of the Bugs and remove meat. Cut each piece of tail meat in half. Wash, shell and devein Prawns and halve if large. Lightly rinse Scallops and remove any dark membrane. Drain Oysters, remove any grit.

In a saucepan, melt butter, sauté shallots, stir in flour and cook for 2 minutes. Gradually pour in stock and stir over heat until thickened and smooth. Stir in parsley, capers, lemon juice and prepared shellfish. Lastly add sour cream (or yoghurt), salt and pepper. Spoon mixture into avocado halves and place in an ovenproof dish. Bake at 180ºC (350ºF) for 10-12 minutes, until avocados are heated through. Serve on individual plates garnished with whole Prawns.

Note: Do not overcook avocados as they develop a strong flavour when overheated.

Serves 6

Smoked Oysters with Cream Cheese

INGREDIENTS

*3 cans Smoked Oysters
250g (8oz) cream cheese
2 garlic cloves, crushed
1 small onion, finely chopped
1 teaspoon Worcestershire sauce
2 teaspoons lemon juice
18 slices white bread, crusts removed
paprika
parsley sprigs*

METHOD

Drain the Oysters. Beat cream cheese until smooth, add garlic, onion, Worcestershire sauce and lemon juice. Mix well. Spread bread with mixture, place 2 Smoked Oysters along one end and roll up from this end. Cream cheese mixture should hold roll in place, otherwise secure with a toothpick. Garnish with a sprinkling of paprika and parsley sprigs.

Serves 6

The grandeur of headlands on the Kimberley Coast near the Prince Regent River, W.A.

Sweet Corn Soup

INGREDIENTS

*250g (8oz) chicken casserole pieces
1½ teaspoons grated green ginger
½ teaspoon salt
water
2 tablespoons cornflour
1 x 440g (16oz) can cream style sweet corn
2 eggs, lightly beaten
⅓ cup finely chopped shallots
salt and pepper to taste*

METHOD

Rinse chicken and place in a pan with ginger, salt and water to cover. Cover and simmer for 1 hour. Strain and measure stock and make up to 8 cups with water. Remove chicken meat and cut into small pieces. Put stock in a saucepan and bring to the boil. Blend cornflour with a little cold water and gradually stir into stock, stir constantly until boiling. Add sweet corn and chicken meat and return to a simmer. Gradually pour in beaten eggs, stirring slowly so that eggs set in shreds. Stir in shallots and add salt and pepper to taste. Serve garnished with chopped shallot tops.

Serves 6

Baked Mushrooms with Cheese Filling

INGREDIENTS

*12 large mushrooms
125g (4oz) blue vein cheese, crumbled
125g (4oz) cheddar cheese, grated
½ cup fresh breadcrumbs
3 shallots, finely chopped
pepper to taste
paprika*

METHOD

Preheat oven to 180ºC (350ºF). Wash and remove stalks from mushrooms, chop stalks finely. In a bowl combine stalks, cheese, breadcrumbs, shallots and pepper. Mix well. Spoon the filling into each mushroom cap and sprinkle with paprika. Place on a baking tray and bake for 10-15 minutes.

Serves 6

Chilled Dory and Potato Salad

INGREDIENTS

*500g (1lb) Dory fillets
½ cup lime or lemon juice
salt and pepper to taste
3 cups cooked, cubed potatoes
3 radishes, thinly sliced
1 tablespoon finely chopped dill
1 tablespoon finely chopped parsley
1 tablespoon finely chopped chives
3 tablespoons good quality mayonnaise
3 tablespoons good quality French dressing
½ teaspoon paprika
salt and pepper to taste
salad greens*

METHOD

Wash and skin fillets. Pat dry with paper towels and cut into very thin strips. In a bowl combine fish, lime juice, salt and pepper, cover and marinate in refrigerator for 3-4 hours, or until flesh turns white.

Meanwhile, in a bowl combine potatoes, radish slices, dill, parsley, chives, mayonnaise, French dressing, paprika, salt and pepper. Mix well. Drain fish and add to potato mixture, gently fold through. Chill well. Serve on a bed of salad greens.

Note: The acidic juice "cooks" the fish.

Serves 6

OYSTER & PRAWN BISQUE, Recipe page 225.

Oyster and Prawn Bisque

(Photograph page 225)

INGREDIENTS

3 dozen Oysters
250g (8oz) cooked Prawn meat
5 cups milk
3 cups fish or chicken stock
(page 315)
1 cup finely sliced celery
1 medium carrot, finely sliced
4 shallots, finely sliced
½ cup flour
1 cup milk, extra
2 teaspoons grated lemon
rind
salt and pepper to taste
3 tablespoons natural yoghurt

METHOD

Check Oysters for grit and remove if present. Wash and devein Prawns and cut into small pieces. In a large saucepan place milk, stock, celery, carrot and shallots. Simmer until vegetables are soft. Put flour in a bowl and gradually blend in extra milk. Pour slowly into pan liquid, stirring constantly until thickened and bubbling. Cool slightly and purée in 3-4 batches in a food processor or blender. Return to saucepan and add lemon rind, salt, pepper, Oysters and Prawns. Heat through over gentle heat. Pour into a soup tureen and fold in yoghurt.

Serves 6

Oysters Teriyaki

INGREDIENTS

6 dozen Oysters
¾ cup teriyaki sauce
¼ cup oil
3 garlic cloves, crushed
2 tablespoons finely grated
green ginger
2 tablespoons dry sherry
1 tablespoon lemon juice
few drops Tabasco sauce
2 tablespoons oil
extra boiled rice

METHOD

Shell Oysters, removing any grit. In a bowl combine teriyaki sauce, oil, garlic, ginger, sherry, lemon juice and Tabasco sauce. Add Oysters and marinate for one hour. Heat extra oil in a frying pan and fry Oysters for 1 minute. Serve on a bed of rice, accompanied by remainder of marinade heated quickly in frying pan after Oysters have been removed.

Serves 6

Scallop boats moored at Mornington Pier, Vic.

JEWFISH WITH GREEN HERB BUTTER, Recipe page 229.

Grilled Bream with Vermouth

(Photograph page 221)

INGREDIENTS

3 medium to large whole Bream
2 tablespoons butter
½ cup vermouth
1 cup fresh breadcrumbs
½ cup grated Parmesan cheese

METHOD

Preheat oven to 180ºC (350ºF). Scale and clean fish. Place fish in a greased ovenproof dish and dot with butter. Pour over vermouth and sprinkle with combined breadcrumbs and cheese. Bake for 20-25 minutes or until flesh flakes. Serve hot.

Serves 6

Teraglin Cutlets with Walnut Oil and Lemon

INGREDIENTS

6 Teraglin or Jewfish cutlets
¾ cup flour, seasoned
1 tablespoon vegetable oil
1 tablespoon walnut oil
4 shallots, finely chopped
⅓ cup lemon juice
2 teaspoons grated lemon rind

METHOD

Wipe cutlets over with damp paper towels. Coat each cutlet in seasoned flour. Heat oils in pan and gently fry two cutlets at a time for 3 minutes each side or until flesh flakes. Remove and keep warm. Add shallots, lemon juice and rind to pan juices and heat thoroughly. Pour this mixture over cutlets. Serve immediately garnished with curled strips of shallot tops and lemon slices.

Serves 6

Jewfish with Green Herb Butter

(Photograph page 228)

INGREDIENTS

1 x 2kg (4lb) Jewfish or Teraglin
6 shallots, chopped finely
2 garlic cloves, crushed
1 tablespoon finely chopped parsley
2 teaspoons finely chopped chervil
2 teaspoons finely chopped chives
60g (2oz) butter or margarine
⅓ cup lemon juice
1 cup white wine
herb sprigs and lemon slices to garnish

METHOD

Scale, clean and wash fish, wipe dry with paper towels. Trim fins. In a mortar or food processor pound or process shallots, garlic, parsley, chervil and chives until puréed. Beat butter until soft and add herbs and lemon juice. Mix well. Spread mixture in cavity of fish. Lay fish in a greased ovenproof dish and pour over wine. Bake at 180⁰C (350⁰F) for 45-50 minutes or until flesh flakes. During cooking time baste fish with wine juices. Lift onto warm serving platter, pour over pan juices and garnish with herb sprigs and lemon slices.

Serves 6 to 8

Curried Blackfish

INGREDIENTS

750g (1½lb) Blackfish or Luderick fillets
2 tablespoons butter or margarine
1 small onion, finely chopped
½ capsicum cut in thin strips
1 celery stalk, finely chopped
2 tablespoons flour
2 teaspoons curry powder
1 cup fish or chicken stock
½ cup white wine
2 drops Tabasco sauce
2 tablespoons finely chopped parsley
1½ teaspoons lemon juice

METHOD

Skin the fish fillets and wipe over with damp paper towels. In a frying pan, melt butter, add onion, capsicum and celery, gently fry for 5 minutes. Add flour and curry powder, stir and gently cook for 2 minutes. Gradually stir in stock and wine, stirring constantly until thickened.
Add fish fillets, cover and gently simmer in curry sauce until flesh flakes, about 5-6 minutes. Add Tabasco sauce, parsley and lemon juice. Serve immediately with fluffy boiled rice and curry accompaniments.

Serves 6

Prawn and Mushroom Casserole

INGREDIENTS

2kg (4lb) medium, green School Prawns
2 teaspoons oil
4 shallots, finely sliced
250g (8oz) mushrooms, thinly sliced
2 large tomatoes, sliced
2 cups thick white sauce (page 315)
buttered breadcrumbs
Parmesan cheese, grated

METHOD

Preheat oven to 180⁰C (350⁰F). Peel and devein Prawns, removing head and tail. Heat oil in a frying pan and gently fry shallots, add Prawns and continue to gently fry for 2-3 minutes.
Remove Prawn mixture and place in ovenproof dish. Place mushrooms and tomatoes on top of Prawns, cover with white sauce, sprinkle with breadcrumbs and cheese and bake for 10-15 minutes or until golden.

Serves 6

Jewfish Chinoise

INGREDIENTS

6 medium size Jewfish or Hairtail cutlets
2 tablespoons oil
¼ cup finely chopped shallots
3 tablespoons soy sauce
3 tablespoons white wine
1 tablespoon finely grated green ginger
1 cup water
500g (1lb) bean sprouts, rinsed
¼ cup water, extra

METHOD

Wipe cutlets with damp paper towels. Heat oil in a large frying pan and gently fry shallots. Add cutlets, soy sauce, wine, ginger and water. Simmer gently until flesh flakes. Remove from heat and keep warm. Put bean sprouts and the ¼ cup water in a saucepan, add one-third cup of sauce from the pan in which the fish was cooked. Simmer for 2 minutes. Arrange the sprouts on a warm serving platter and lay the fish on top with the remaining sauce. Serve immediately.

Serves 6

Leatherjacket Provencale

INGREDIENTS

6 prepared Leatherjackets
1 medium onion, finely sliced
1 garlic clove, crushed
2 tablespoons chopped fresh basil
3 medium tomatoes, peeled and roughly chopped
1 cup thinly sliced mushrooms
½ cup white wine

METHOD

Heads and skin should be removed from fish. Lay fish in a greased ovenproof dish. Place onion slices, garlic, basil, tomatoes and mushrooms on fish. Pour wine over and cover. Bake at 180⁰C (350⁰F) for 30-35 minutes or until flesh flakes.

Serves 6

A wild sunset over a fishing village, off the coast, warns that the wind will be coming in the morning, W.A.

Dory Amandine

INGREDIENTS

750g (1½lb) Dory fillets
flour, seasoned
2 tablespoons butter or
margarine
2 tablespoons oil
½ cup slivered blanched
almonds
⅓ cup lemon juice

METHOD

Coat fillets in seasoned flour. Melt butter in pan, add oil. Fry fillets 2-3 minutes each side or until flesh flakes. Remove and keep warm. Add almonds to pan and gently fry until brown, add lemon juice. Pour over fillets and serve immediately.

Serves 6

Oatmeal Coated Flathead

INGREDIENTS

750g (1½lb) Flathead fillets
seasoned flour
2 eggs, beaten
1½ cups fine oatmeal
oil for shallow frying

METHOD

Skin the fillets. Coat in flour, beaten egg and oatmeal. Rest in refrigerator for 30 minutes. Heat oil in pan and shallow fry fillets, 2-3 minutes each side or until golden and flesh flakes. Drain on kitchen paper and serve immediately with lemon wedges.

Serves 6

Prawn Curry

INGREDIENTS

2kg (4lb) medium, green
School Prawns
1 tablespoon oil
1 medium onion, finely sliced
2 garlic cloves, crushed
1 teaspoon grated green
ginger
½ teaspoon finely chopped
fresh chili
2 tablespoons good curry
powder
1 tablespoon lemon juice
1 cup coconut milk

METHOD

Peel and devein Prawns, leaving tails on.
Heat oil in a pan, add onion, garlic, ginger, chili and curry powder. Fry gently for 1-2 minutes. Add Prawns and cook until Prawns turn orange in colour, 5-6 minutes. Add combined lemon juice and coconut milk. Simmer to heat through.
Serve on a bed of fluffy rice, with diced cucumber, chutney, chopped tomato and natural yoghurt, each served in separate bowls at the table.

Serves 6

Curried Coconut Mullet

INGREDIENTS

750g (1½lb) Mullet fillets
6 tablespoons desiccated
coconut
1½ tablespoons mild curry
powder
2 eggs, lightly beaten
3 large bananas, peeled and
cut in half lengthways
2 tablespoons copha or other
vegetable shortening
lemon wedges
natural yoghurt

METHOD

Clean the fillets and wipe over with damp paper towels. Mix coconut and curry powder on a plate. Dip fillets in egg, then coat with coconut mixture. Heat copha in a pan and fry fish fillets for 2-3 minutes each side or until flesh flakes. Be careful not to let coconut burn. Remove and keep warm.
Add banana halves to pan and cook gently until just tender. Serve fish with banana, lemon wedges and yoghurt.

Serves 6

The Earnslaw, Queenstown, New Zealand.

Divers gather in cheerful congregation at the stern of a wrecked fishing boat far below the surface of the Abrolhos Islands.

MULBERRY ALMOND FLAN, Recipe page 233.

Cherry Strudel

INGREDIENTS

2 x 425g (15oz) cans cherries
1 cup very finely chopped walnuts
¼ cup castor sugar
grated rind of 1 lemon
1 teaspoon cinnamon
3 tablespoons melted butter
1 cup soft white breadcrumbs
375g (12oz) commercial puff pastry
extra melted butter
icing sugar

METHOD

Stone and halve the cherries and drain thoroughly. Mix together walnuts, sugar, lemon rind and cinnamon. Pour melted butter over crumbs, stir to combine.

Put pastry on a well-floured clean tea towel, roll out to a thin rectangle about 35 x 50cm (14 x 20 inch), having the longer side of pastry nearest to you. Brush over with extra melted butter, spread the crumbs over, leaving a 5cm (2 inch) margin of pastry all round. Arrange cherries parallel with longer edge of pastry and near the centre. Fold in sides of pastry, brush folds with melted butter. Roll up and put on a large, greased baking tray. Brush all over with melted butter. Bake in preheated 230ºC (450ºF) oven for 10 minutes, reduce to 190ºC (375ºF) and bake for further 25-30 minutes, or until golden brown, brushing with melted butter every 10 minutes. Dust with sifted icing sugar and serve warm.

Serves 6

Apricot and Apple Cobbler

INGREDIENTS

1 cup dried apricots
hot water
2 cooking apples
½ cup sugar

Topping

90g (3oz) butter
½ cup castor sugar
½ teaspoon vanilla essence
2 eggs
1¼ cups self-raising flour
¼ cup milk

METHOD

Rinse apricots, cover with hot water and leave to soak for 1 hour. Peel, core and slice apples, add to apricots with the sugar and cook until soft. Place fruit and syrup in the base of a greased ovenproof dish, keep hot in oven.

Topping:
Cream together the butter, sugar and vanilla essence, add eggs and beat well. Fold in the sifted flour and milk alternately and spread lightly over the hot fruit. Bake in a preheated 180ºC (190ºF) oven for 30-35 minutes. Serve with custard or cream.

Note: Do not have too much liquid in the stewed fruit when topping goes on top, nor should fruit be over-sweetened as it could scorch. Fruit must be hot when topping is added.

Serves 5 to 6

Chocolate Orange Mousse

(Photograph page 221)

INGREDIENTS

250g (8oz) dark chocolate
¼ cup water
1 tablespoon castor sugar
2 teaspoons butter or margarine
2 tablespoons Cointreau
3 large eggs, separated
300ml (½ pint) cream, lightly whipped
extra whipped cream and orange zest to decorate

METHOD

In the top section of a double saucepan place chocolate, water, sugar and butter. Heat over simmering water until chocolate has melted, stirring until smooth. Pour into a bowl and cool. Stir in Cointreau and beaten egg yolks. Fold in stiffly beaten egg whites and cream. Spoon into individual dessert dishes and refrigerate until set. Decorate with whipped cream and orange zest to serve.

Serves 6

Mulberry Almond Flan

(Photograph page 232)

INGREDIENTS

Pastry

180g (6oz) flour
125g (4oz) butter or margarine, cubed
60g (2oz) marzipan meal
3 tablespoons icing sugar
2 egg yolks, beaten (save whites for meringue)
½ teaspoon vanilla essence
1 tablespoon milk

Filling

500g (1lb) mulberries (fresh or frozen)
2 tablespoons cornflour, blended with a little water or juice

Meringue

2 egg whites
125g (4oz) castor sugar
¼ cup desiccated coconut

METHOD

Pastry:
In a bowl, sift flour and rub in butter until mixture resembles fine breadcrumbs. Add marzipan meal and sugar. Add egg yolks, vanilla and milk and mix to a firm dough. Wrap and chill for 30 minutes. On a lightly floured board roll out pastry to fit a 20cm (8 inch) flan tin.

Filling:
Put mulberries into a saucepan. Add cornflour mixture and stir until thickened. Remove and cool. When cool place mixture into the prepared flan tin.

Meringue:
Beat the egg whites until stiff, gradually beat in sugar. Lightly fold in the coconut and spread over the mulberries.

Bake at 200ºC (400ºF) for 10 minutes, then reduce heat to 180ºC (350ºF) for a further 20-25 minutes. Serve cold.

A Starfish looking like an Indian head dress, Great Barrier Reef, Qld.

An artistic painting by nature. Pindimar near Tea Gardens, NSW.

Kings Cascades in the Prince Regent River,
off the Kimberleys, W.A.

Keeping
it Fresh

Australia is usually thought of as the "dry continent"; thousands and thousands of square miles of hot, arid desert, hard, parched land. Dry and deathly!

It is true that an enormous proportion of the land mass is very dry — something like two-thirds of the country has less than five hundred millimetres (twenty inches) of rain each year. But, of course, Australia is quite a large place, around eight million square kilometres (almost three million square miles). This means that the remaining one-third of the land mass, with over five hundred millimetres of rain per annum, amounts to an area about ten times the size of the United Kingdom!

Given such figures, it should come as no surprise that there are many freshwater fish and shellfish species to be found in Australia. It should also come as no surprise that, as with many things in this vast country, there is a large diversity in freshwater habitats, and hence a large diversity in the species.

Australia's entire coast is heavily indented with a multitude of streams and rivers, all of which carry freshwater fish. From the steamy estuaries of the North to the cool, temperate streams of the "Apple Isle". From the fast flowing mountain streams of the Snowy Mountains, to the tropical mangroves of the "Top End". Even the yellow, languid rivers of outback NSW are laden with fish.

The Snowy Mountains is Australia's "High Country" and is a region of rare beauty. In the rivers, streams and lakes of this area can be found some very fine Trout. There are many other areas throughout NSW, Victoria, Tasmania and, of course, New Zealand (see page 200) where these very tasty members of the Salmonidae family are to be found.

Certainly one of the most impressive freshwater fish to be found anywhere in the world has to be a mature Murray Cod. These fish are found mainly in the Murray-Darling basin, Australia's largest river system. They are also relatively common along the east coast. Fish up to two metres in length have been caught in the past, but unfortunately such specimens are uncommon these days.

The different freshwater Crayfish, the Yabby, the Marron and the Tasmanian Crayfish, are very commonly found across the country in their particular habitats — dams, waterholes, creeks, bore drains, rivers and streams. All are very tasty, and in the case of the Marron, very large — up to 2.5 kg (6 lb); in the case of the Tasmanian Crayfish, absolutely enormous — up to 6 kg (14 lb)!!

Here you will find tantalising recipes for all of these species and more, from the Eel with Apple and Green Peas to the Crayfish Flambé. Or why not enjoy a freshwater meal of Crayfish Bicheno Style and Murray Cod with Chervil and Lemon Butter, followed by Strawberry Chiffon Flans (shown opposite)?

No matter what you choose, the opportunity is here to impress with some unusual and scrumptuous dishes from the often neglected world of the freshwater fish.

Top left: STRAWBERRY CHIFFON FLANS, Recipe page 248. *Top right*: CRAYFISH BINCHENO STYLE, Recipe page 240. *Below*: MURRAY COD WITH CHERVIL & LEMON BUTTER, Recipe page 246.

Lake Tekapo dwarfed by lofty mountains, New Zealand.

Crayfish Bicheno Style

(Photograph page 237)

INGREDIENTS

500g (1lb) cooked Crayfish, Marron or Yabbie meat
2 garlic cloves, crushed
1 teaspoon finely chopped tarragon
1 teaspoon finely chopped parsley
1 teaspoon finely chopped chervil
2 teaspoons finely chopped shallots
1½ cups fresh breadcrumbs
¼ cup melted butter
salt and pepper to taste
¼ cup dry sherry
grated cheddar cheese

METHOD

Cut Crayfish meat into bite-size pieces. Place in a large bowl with garlic, tarragon, parsley, chervil, shallots and breadcrumbs. Add melted butter, salt, pepper and sherry and mix well. Spoon mixture evenly into greased ovenproof ramekins. Sprinkle grated cheese on top and bake in preheated oven for 10-15 minutes, until golden and heated through. Serve hot garnished with fresh herb sprigs.

Serves 6 to 8

Crayfish Corn Squares

INGREDIENTS

500g (1lb) cooked Crayfish, Marron or Yabbie meat
250g (8oz) shortcrust pastry (page 315)
3 eggs, lightly beaten
1 x 300g (10oz) can whole corn kernels, drained
½ cup finely chopped capsicum
⅓ cup milk
salt and pepper to taste

METHOD

Preheat oven at 200ºC (400ºF). Flake Crayfish meat and reserve. Roll pastry to line a 30 x 20cm (12 x 8 inch) slab tin. Separate the egg white from one of the eggs into a small bowl, beat with a fork until frothy and brush onto base and sides of pastry—this prevents pastry becoming soggy. Leave aside to dry. In a bowl beat the eggs, including the yolk of the first egg, and mix in flaked Crayfish, corn, capsicum and milk. Season with salt and pepper and pour into pastry-lined tin. Bake for 10 minutes in preheated oven, reduce heat to 180º (350º) and cook for further 15-20 minutes until set. Serve hot or cold, cut into squares.

Serves 6

White waters at Arthurs Point Queenstown, New Zealand.

Smoked Eel and Pineapple Salad

INGREDIENTS

750g (1½lb) Smoked Eel
1 medium pineapple
2 cups cooked rice
1 cup finely sliced celery
4 shallots, finely sliced
1 tablespoon curry powder
1½ tablespoons honey
2 tablespoons soy sauce
1 tablespoon lime or lemon juice

METHOD

Skin Eel and cut flesh into small pieces, removing all bones. Remove skin from pineapple, halve lengthways and cut out core. Dice the flesh. In a bowl combine Eel, pineapple, rice, celery and shallots, mix well. Put curry powder in a screw-topped jar with the honey, soy sauce and lime juice, seal and shake well to mix. Pour over salad and toss well. Chill before serving.

Serves 6

Tuna and Sweet Corn Soup

INGREDIENTS

250g (8oz) can Tuna
3 tablespoons butter or margarine
4 tablespoons flour
2 teaspoons curry powder
4 cups milk
2 cups chicken stock
2 x 425g (15oz) cans creamed sweet corn

METHOD

Flake Tuna meat. Melt butter in a saucepan, add flour and curry powder and stir, cooking for 1-2 minutes. Gradually stir in milk and stock, simmer until thick and smooth. Add sweet corn, salt, pepper and flaked Tuna. Mix well. Simmer to heat through and serve with chopped parsley.

Serves 6

Smoked Eel and Artichoke Vol-Au-Vents

INGREDIENTS

500g (1lb) Smoked Eel
1 x 400g (13oz) can artichoke hearts
1 tablespoon butter or margarine
½ cup finely sliced mushrooms
1 tablespoon flour
¾ cup milk
1 tablespoon lemon juice
1 tablespoon brandy
pepper to taste
6 pre-cooked vol-au-vent cases (see Note)
finely chopped parsley to garnish

METHOD

Skin Eel and flake flesh finely, removing all bones. Drain artichokes and cut into quarters. Reserve. Melt butter in a pan and gently cook mushrooms. Add flour and stir for 2-3 minutes. Gradually pour in milk, stirring constantly until thickened and bubbling. Reduce heat, boil gently for 1 minute, stir in lemon juice, brandy and pepper. Add Eel flesh and artichokes. Heat through and spoon mixture evenly into hot vol-au-vent cases. Sprinkle with parsley.
Note: Pre-cooked vol-au-vent cases are available in three sizes—small (for appetizers), medium (for entrées) and large. Use medium-sized cases for above recipe and heat at 180ºC (350ºF) for 5-6 minutes before filling.

Serves 6

SPICY MARINATED PERCH, Recipe page 241.

Spicy Marinated Sea Perch

(Photograph page 241)

INGREDIENTS

750g (1½lb) Perch fillets
6 limes, juiced
¼ teaspoon salt
½ teaspoon sugar
sprinkling ground black pepper
3 medium tomatoes, peeled and finely chopped
4 shallots, finely sliced
¾ cup cider vinegar
2 tablespoons finely chopped fresh ginger
2 tablespoons finely chopped coriander
2 tablespoons finely chopped parsley
2 garlic cloves, crushed
⅓ cup olive oil

METHOD

Wash and skin fillets and cut into bite-size pieces. In a bowl combine fish pieces, lime juice, salt, sugar, pepper, tomatoes and shallots. Mix well. In another bowl combine vinegar, ginger, coriander, parsley, garlic and oil. Mix well and pour over fish mixture. Marinate in refrigerator for at least 4-5 hours. Serve well chilled, drained of marinade liquid.

Note: The acidic ingredients in the marinade "cook" the fish.

Serves 6

Chutney Cheese Paté with Mango Slices

INGREDIENTS

250g (8oz) cream cheese, softened
1 cup grated cheddar cheese
2 tablespoons dry sherry
1 teaspoon curry powder
½ cup mango chutney, finely chopped
½ cup finely chopped parsley
3 mangos, thinly sliced

METHOD

In a bowl combine cream cheese, cheddar cheese, sherry, curry and chutney. Mix well and divide into 6 portions. Place each portion on a piece of plastic wrap, form into a log shape. Roll in the plastic wrap, twist ends tightly and reshape. Chill until firm.

Remove plastic wrap and roll each log in parsley. Serve on individual plates with slices of mango and cracker biscuits or melba toast.

Serves 6

Left: RAINBOW TROUT FILLETS IN A CORN CHIP CRUMB, Recipe page 247. *Right*: RIVER & TURF, Recipe page 247.

A magnificent place to sit on a rock listening to the music of nature. McKenzie Falls, Grampians National Park, Vic.

EEL WITH APPLE & GREEN PEAS, Recipe page 246.

Murray Cod with Chervil and Lemon Butter

(Photograph page 237)

INGREDIENTS

1 x 1.5kg (3lb) Murray Cod, cleaned
60g (2oz) butter, softened
grated rind of 1 lemon
2 tablespoons finely chopped fresh chervil

METHOD

Make several cuts along the body of the fish. Combine butter with lemon rind and chervil and pack into cuts. Place fish on a sheet of buttered foil, parcel up, place on a baking tray and bake at 180ºC (350ºF) for 30-40 minutes until flesh flakes.

Serves 4 to 6

Eel with Apple and Green Peas

(Photograph page 246)

INGREDIENTS

1 x 1kg (2lb) Eel
2 large onions, thinly sliced
2 carrots, thinly sliced
3 celery stalks, finely sliced
2½ cups apple cider or juice
2 tablespoons finely chopped parsley
1 cup shelled green peas
½ cup diced apple
salt and pepper to taste

METHOD

Clean and skin Eel. Cut Eel into 5cm (2 inch) cutlets. In an ovenproof dish place onions, carrots, and celery. Lay Eel cutlets on vegetables and pour over cider. Sprinkle parsley, green peas and diced apple on top and season with salt and pepper. Bake at 180ºC (350ºF) for 20-25 minutes or until flesh flakes.

Serves 6

Crayfish with Sweet and Sour Sauce

INGREDIENTS

1kg (2lb) cooked Crayfish, Marron or Yabbie meat

Sauce

1 cup water
4 tablespoons vinegar
2 tablespoons tomato paste
¼ cup brown sugar
1 x 425g (15oz) can lychees
1 tablespoon cornflour
2 tablespoons water

METHOD

Flake Crayfish meat and keep aside. In a saucepan combine water, vinegar, tomato paste, brown sugar and lychee fruit and juice. Blend cornflour with water and add to saucepan, stir over heat until sauce boils and thickens. Gently stir in the Crayfish meat. Serve immediately over boiled rice.

Serves 6

Rainbow Trout fillets in a Corn Chip Crumb

(Photograph pages 242 & 243)

INGREDIENTS

6 large Trout fillets
½ cup plain flour
2 eggs, beaten
2 tablespoons milk
2 large packets plain corn chips, crushed
3 avocados
½ cup sour cream
juice 1 lemon
1 teaspoon finely chopped fresh chili
1 garlic clove, crushed
salt and pepper to taste
oil for shallow frying

METHOD

Coat Trout fillets in flour, then beaten egg and milk mixture and finally crushed corn chips. Place on a tray, cover and refrigerate. Cut avocados in half lengthways and remove stone. Carefully remove avocado from shell and mash with sour cream and lemon juice. Fold in chili and garlic, season with salt and pepper and pile back into avocado shells.
Heat oil in a large frying pan and fry crumbed Trout fillets for approximately 3 minutes on each side. Drain on kitchen paper and serve with avocado halves.

Serves 6

Crayfish Flambé

INGREDIENTS

3 medium size cooked Crayfish
4 tablespoons butter or margarine
4 shallots, finely sliced
1½ tablespoons curry powder
2 tablespoons flour
1 cup fish or chicken stock
½ cup milk
1 tablespoon finely chopped parsley
salt and pepper to taste
pinch paprika
2 tablespoons brandy

METHOD

Split Crayfish in half and wash thoroughly. Remove meat and cut into bite-size pieces. Reserve meat and cleaned shells. Melt butter in pan and gently cook shallots, add curry powder and flour and stir for 2-3 minutes. Gradually stir in stock and milk over a medium heat until sauce thickens and boils gently. Add parsley, salt, pepper and paprika. Add Crayfish meat and heat through. Pour in brandy and flambé. Spoon very carefully into shell halves and serve immediately.

Serves 6

River and Turf

(Photograph pages 242 & 243)

INGREDIENTS

6 x 200g (7oz) boneless sirloin steaks
salt and freshly ground black pepper
1 tablespoon dripping
12 cooked Yabbies, head and shells removed
1 quantity White Sauce (see page 315)

METHOD

Season steaks with salt and pepper. Heat a griddle or barbecue plate and wipe over with dripping. Sear steaks for 2 minutes on each side then continue cooking until cooked to taste. Fold Yabbies through hot white sauce and serve poured over steaks.

Serves 6

Catfish Satay

INGREDIENTS

1 kg (2 lb) Catfish fillets
seasoned flour for coating
2 tablespoons oil
2 tablespoons butter

Sauce

2 tablespoons oil
1 garlic clove, crushed
2 tablespoons grated onion
1 teaspoon chili powder
1 tablespoon lemon juice
1 tablespoon soy sauce
1 cup crunchy peanut butter
1½ teaspoons brown sugar
½ cup coconut milk

Serves 6

METHOD

Coat Catfish fillets with seasoned flour. Heat oil and butter in a large pan. Fry fillets 3-4 minutes or until flesh flakes. Set aside and keep hot.

Sauce
Heat oil and gently cook onion, garlic, chili powder, lemon juice and soy sauce. Stir in peanut butter and brown sugar. Mix well, cool a little. Thin down with coconut milk. If you continue beating the sauce it becomes a paler colour and fluffy. To achieve desired consistency stir in more coconut milk. Serve with fried Catfish fillets.

Sunshine casts a golden glow on old rocks of the Drysdale River, on the North Kimberley Coast, W.A.

Strawberry Chiffon Flans

(Photograph page 237)

INGREDIENTS

2 teaspoons gelatine
1 tablespoon water
1 punnet strawberries
4 tablespoons castor sugar
2 teaspoons lemon juice
2 egg whites
6 x 11cm (4½ inch) cooked sweet pastry flans (page 315)
whipped cream

METHOD

Sprinkle the gelatine over the water in a small bowl, stand over hot water and stir to dissolve. Wash and hull strawberries, reserving 6 for garnish. Purée the remainder. Add dissolved gelatine, half of the sugar and the lemon juice to the strawberry purée. Mix well and refrigerate until just beginning to thicken.

Beat egg whites until stiff and gradually add the remaining sugar to form a meringue. Fold into strawberry mixture and pour into cooked pastry flans. Refrigerate until set. Serve garnished with reserved strawberries and whipped cream.

Serves 6

Spiced Orange Slices

(Photograph pages 248 & 249)

INGREDIENTS

12 medium-large oranges
½ cup castor sugar
1 teaspoon ground ginger
½ teaspoon cinnamon
¼ teaspoon nutmeg
⅓ cup Grand Marnier
whipped cream or ice cream

METHOD

Peel oranges, removing all pith. Slice oranges thinly on a plate to retain juice. Mix sugar with the spices. As oranges are sliced, layer in a bowl with the sugar mixture, pouring juice in as it accumulates. Pour Grand Marnier over oranges, cover and chill well before serving. Serve with whipped cream or ice cream.

Serves 6

Left: FRESH PEACH JELLY, Recipe page 249. *Right*: SPICED ORANGE SLICES, Recipe page 248.

Fresh Peach Jelly

(Photograph pages 248 & 249)

INGREDIENTS

750g (1½lb) fresh peaches
¼ cup sugar, or to taste
2 cups water
½ cup fresh orange juice
2 tablespoons gelatine
¼ cup water, extra
fresh peach slices to decorate

METHOD

Peel peaches and remove stones. Place in a large saucepan, add sugar, water and orange juice. Cover and simmer gently for 15-20 minutes or until peaches are tender. Cool. Put peaches into a blender or food processor and purée. Soak gelatine in the extra water and dissolve over hot water. Add to peach purée. Rinse a jelly mould in cold water, pour in peach purée and place in refrigerator to set. Unmould and serve with fresh peach slices and cream or ice cream.

Serves 6

Golden Syrup Steamed Pudding

INGREDIENTS

125g (4oz) butter
½ cup castor sugar
2 eggs, beaten
5 tablespoons milk
1½ cups self-raising flour
2 tablespoons golden syrup
(approximately)

METHOD

Put water in a large saucepan and bring to the boil for steaming the pudding. Butter the basin to be used.
Cream butter and sugar. Stir in the beaten eggs. Add milk, then lastly fold in flour. Place golden syrup in bottom of basin then add flour mixture. Cover basin with lid or foil, tie on securely.
Place basin in a saucepan of boiling water, cover and steam for 1 ½ hours. Replenish water with boiling water as required. Turn out onto a dish and serve hot, cut in slices, with extra warmed golden syrup and pouring cream or custard.

Serves 6

A lily pool in one of Australia's beautiful rainforests.

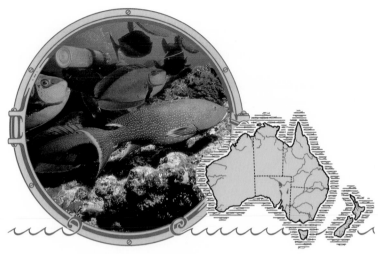

A Lunar-tailed Cod and a bevy of Surgeon Fish.

Exotica from the Deep

*I*n these days of multiculturalism, and in such an ethnically diverse country as Australia, the opportunities to discover the fascinating secrets of the world's wonderful cuisines are not to be missed. Neptune's kingdom is vast, and the bounty it offers us stretches far beyond the delicious, but relatively everyday fare of Bream and Lobster.

Many of the nations of the world have used this knowledge to their great advantage in developing a vast diversity in their seafood cuisine. It has been based on utilising, with a very high degree of efficiency, the resources they have found in the waters around them.

It has been a somewhat sad reflection on the dominance of a conservative Anglo-Celtic tradition in Australia's cuisine, that for many years the fantastic resources of our seas and rivers have gone largely wasted. It used to be the case that Octopus and Squid were once only ever considered good for bait. Whenever a fisherman catches an Eel, chances are it will be thrown back; the same goes for Sharks, Skates and Rays and Catfish. Even Pilchards or Sardines are at best thought of as tinned food and more often as good baitfish.

It is true to say that things are gradually changing The influence of a range of Asian and European cultures has helped us see the light a little better, but still there is much resistance to innovation in the realm of seafood.

In this chapter you will find a fascinating variety of seafoods, all with their own unique character and distinctive taste. One of the problems in introducing many of these sea creatures to the table lies in the presentation. "What exactly are those large, oval-shaped droppings on my plate?" you may hear asked. But once they've tried the Fried Roe (shown opposite), their tune will no doubt change. And the Stuffed Squid Hoods really are magnificent.

One of the most exotic Seafoods has to be the Sea Urchin; as it is eaten raw, no recipe follows, but you can learn how to prepare and eat it on page 314. The thing to understand is that it's all a matter of what we're used to. If you haven't been brought up with the idea of something being a food, then it will take you a little time to get used to it. But once you do, rest assured it will definitely have been worth it!

Be adventurous! Enter the exciting world of exotic seafood. You will be rewarded beyond your wildest dreams!

A fantastic Row boat with Aboriginal crew.

Top Left: FRIED FISH ROE, Recipe page 256. *Top Right*: MELON SALAD, Recipe page 264.
Below: STUFFED SQUID IN TOMATO SAUCE, Recipe page 263.

The beginning of another romantic evening, North Stradbroke Island, Qld.

Fried Fish Roe

(Photograph page 253)

INTRODUCTION

Fresh Roe from a variety of fish is available. The size and flavour of the Roe depends on the type of fish from which it comes. The small white Roe is fried. Its flavour is such that it requires no enhancement from other ingredients; it is a delicacy in itself. The larger yellow Roe is smoked or dried and is used in many ways for hors d'oeuvres.

INGREDIENTS

12 fresh white Roe
½ cup seasoned flour
olive oil for frying
lemon wedges for serving

METHOD

Put oil 5mm (1/4 inch) deep in a heavy based pan, heat to moderate temperature. Coat the Roe with flour, shake off excess. Place immediately into the pan and fry gently on both sides until a pale golden colour. It is important to flour the Roe as you fry. Do not flour all the Roe and allow to stand.

Remove Roe from pan and drain on absorbent paper. Serve on heated plate with lemon wedge. Squeeze lemon over hot Roe before eating. Serve with buttered brown bread triangles.

Serves 6

Tuna and Honeydew Melon Salad

INGREDIENTS

500g (1lb) cooked Tuna (canned may be used)
1 large honeydew melon
1 cup finely sliced celery
1 cup mayonnaise
2 tablespoons lemon juice
2 teaspoons finely grated ginger
½ cup natural yoghurt
fresh coriander leaves and cucumber slices for garnish

METHOD

Flake Tuna, if canned, drain well. Cut melon in half, Vandyke style, discard seeds. Remove flesh from melon by using a melon baller, keeping skins intact. In a bowl combine melon balls, celery, mayonnaise, lemon juice and ginger. Add flaked Tuna and gently fork through. Spoon mixture into melon shells and chill well before serving.

Serves 6

A spotted Reef Eel at the Great Barrier Reef, Qld.

Easy Lobster Mousse

INGREDIENTS

500g (1lb) cooked Lobster meat
salt and pepper to taste
1 tablespoon lemon juice
¾ cup cream
3 egg whites, stiffly beaten
lemon and lime slices
6 cooked King Prawns, shelled and tails left on

METHOD

Preheat oven to 180ºC (350ºF). In a food processor, place Lobster meat, salt, pepper and lemon juice, process until meat is fine. Add cream and mix well. Remove from food processor into a bowl and fold through egg whites. Pour mixture into a greased, ovenproof fish mould. Place mould in waterbath and bake for 20-25 minutes in preheated oven. Unmould the mousse onto a platter and garnish with lemon and lime slices and peeled Prawns. Serve hot.

Serves 4 to 6

Kingfish, Prawn and Pasta Soup

INGREDIENTS

500g (1lb) Kingfish fillets
250g (8oz) cooked Prawn meat
1 teaspoon oil
1 large onion, finely sliced
1 large potato, peeled and diced
1.5L (6 cups) fish stock (page 315)
3 medium tomatoes, peeled and roughly chopped
½ cup pasta shells
4 bacon slices, diced
½ cup parsley, finely chopped
salt and pepper to taste

METHOD

Skin fillets and remove bones. Cut into bite-size pieces. Devein Prawns and cut in half. Reserve. In a large pan heat oil, gently cook onion, add potato, stock, tomatoes, pasta and bacon. Simmer for 10 minutes until potato and pasta are just tender. Add fish, Prawns, parsley, salt and pepper. Cook until fish flesh flakes, about 3-4 minutes.

Serves 6

Pasta and Vegetable Salad

INGREDIENTS

250g (8oz) pasta shells
250g (8oz) mushrooms, finely sliced
4 shallots, finely sliced
1 capsicum, finely chopped
1 cucumber, peeled, seeded and finely chopped
3 tomatoes, finely chopped
6 lettuce cups
½ cup pine nuts, toasted

Dressing

3 tablespoons oil
¼ teaspoon dry mustard
1 garlic clove, crushed
¼ cup white wine vinegar
pinch mixed herbs

METHOD

Cook the pasta shells in boiling water until tender. Drain and rinse in cold water.

In a bowl, combine cooked pasta with mushrooms, shallots, capsicum, cucumber and tomatoes. Combine dressing ingredients, pour over salad, toss well and chill in refrigerator for 1 hour before serving. Place spoonfuls of salad into lettuce cups and sprinkle with toasted pine nuts when serving.

Serves 6

SEAWEED SOUP, Recipe page 257.

Seaweed Soup

(Photograph page 257)

INGREDIENTS

90g (3oz) Iriko (dried Sardines)
1.5L (6 cups) water
125g (4oz) Yaki Nori (roasted Seaweed)
½ cup miso (soy bean paste)
125g (4oz) firm tofu (bean curd) cut in 2cm (¾ inch) cubes
3 shallots, sliced diagonally

METHOD

Place dried Sardines and water in a saucepan, bring to the boil, reduce heat and allow to simmer for 10 minutes. Strain stock, through a muslin lined sieve, into a saucepan and discard Sardines.

Place seaweed in a bowl, cover with cold water, allow to stand for 10 minutes, then drain.

Blend soy bean paste with ½ cup Sardine stock. Bring remaining stock to the boil, stir in blended bean paste, Seaweed and tofu cubes. Add sliced shallots and serve hot, in individual soup bowls.

Note: Iriko, Yaki Nori and miso are available from stores stocking Japanese or Asian ingredients.

Smoked Fish Pâté

INGREDIENTS

500g (1lb) Smoked Fish (Gem, Haddock, Cod or Tailor)
1 cup water
250g (4oz) butter or margarine
2 tablespoons grated lemon rind
½ cup lemon juice
pepper to taste
parsley to garnish

METHOD

Wash Smoked Fish and place in a pan. Add water and bring to the boil. Simmer until flesh flakes. Remove and flake the flesh from the skins, removing the bones. Mash the flesh finely or shred in a food processor. Melt butter and gradually mix with the fish. Add lemon rind and juice. Season with pepper. Place Pâté in a Pâté bowl and chill well until set. Garnish with parsley and serve with toast fingers or savoury crackers.

Note: This will keep for up to 5 days in the refrigerator.

Serves 6

Left: SEAFOOD PASTA, Recipe page 263. *Below right*: RAW KINGFISH AND CORAL LETTUCE SALAD, Recipe page 263.

A cool, fresh morning surrounding the waters of the 'Snowies', South NSW.

ESCALOPES OF SEA SNAILS WITH OYSTER MUSHROOM DRESSING, Recipe page 262.

Escalopes of Sea Snails with Oyster Mushroom Dressing

(Photograph page 262)

INGREDIENTS

6 large Sea Snails
1 cup plain flour
2 eggs, beaten
2 cups very fine soft white breadcrumbs
½ cup finely chopped parsley
2 garlic cloves, crushed
½ cup oil
90g (3oz) butter

Dressing

250g (8oz) oyster mushrooms
2 tablespoons white wine vinegar
2 tablespoons olive oil
2 teaspoons lemon juice
½ teaspoon chopped oregano
salt and pepper

METHOD

Crack Sea Snail shells open and remove meat. Discard soft, lower intestines, scrub body and slice thinly into escalopes. Beat escalopes with a meat mallet to tenderise, then toss lightly in flour, beaten egg then combined breadcrumbs, parsley and garlic. Heat half the oil and butter in a large frying pan and gently fry escalopes for 3 minutes, turning during cooking. Drain on kitchen paper. Add more oil and butter as needed during frying.
Place mushrooms in a bowl. Combine remaining ingredients in a jar, shake well to combine, pour over mushrooms and serve.
Abalone version: See page 314 for preparation and use 750g (1½lb) slices in place of the Sea Snails. *Serves 6*

Stuffed Grilled Lobster

INGREDIENTS

1 cooked Lobster
1 cup buttered fresh breadcrumbs
salt and pepper
2 tablespoons butter or margarine

METHOD

Split the Lobster. Remove digestive tract and discard. Remove the tomalley (liver) and the coral (if present). Mash these well and blend with enough buttered breadcrumbs to bind the mixture. Season with salt, pepper and lemon juice. Fill the Lobster's cavity with this stuffing and dot the flesh with butter.
Place Lobster halves under the griller and cook until golden, approximately 3 minutes. Serve immediately.

Serves 2
(allowing 1 Lobster between 2)

Stuffed Squid in Tomato Sauce

(Photograph page 253)

INGREDIENTS

*1kg (2lb) medium size Squid
2 large onions, finely chopped
½ cup olive oil
½ cup uncooked short grain rice
4 tablespoons pine nuts
4 tablespoons currants
2 tablespoons finely chopped parsley
¼ cup hot water
1 x 425g (15oz) can tomatoes
1 tablespoon tomato paste
¼ cup red wine
salt and pepper*

METHOD

Prepare Squid as directed on page 314. Leave hoods intact and reserve the tentacles for a garnish. Prepare the stuffing. Heat half of the oil in a pan, add half of the onions and cook until transparent. Add rice, pine nuts, currants, parsley and season with salt and pepper. Pour in the water, cover and cook over low heat for 5 minutes only. Partially fill the Squid with the stuffing leaving room for the rice to expand. Close the opening by sewing with thread. Place remaining oil in a widebased saucepan, add remaining onions and cook gently until soft. Add tomatoes plus their juice, tomato paste and wine, bring to the boil then reduce heat. Gently lower the stuffed Squid into the sauce, placing in a neat single layer. Season with salt and pepper.

Cover and simmer gently for 40 minutes. Baste 2 or 3 times with sauce to keep top moist and shake the pan occasionally to prevent sticking. If sauce evaporates, add a little hot water if needed. When cooked, if sauce is thin remove Squid and reduce sauce over high heat to thicken.

Heat a little oil in a small pan. Dip tentacles in flour and fry till golden. They will curl up like rosettes. Arrange Squid on a bed of sauce on a serving platter. Garnish with rosettes of Squid. Serve with a tossed salad and crusty bread.

Seafood Pasta

(Photograph pages 258 & 259)

INGREDIENTS

*250g (8oz) Squid hoods, cut into rings (see page 314)
250g (8oz) Shark fillet, sliced
250g (8oz) Prawns, shells removed
250g (8oz) Scallops, cleaned
12 Mussels, beards removed (see page 314)
60g (2oz) butter
2 onions, sliced
2 garlic cloves, crushed
1 teaspoon each finely chopped fresh oregano and basil
1kg (2lb) ripe tomatoes, peeled and chopped
1 cup dry white wine
salt and pepper to taste
500g (1lb) spaghetti or ribbon pasta, boiled and drained*

METHOD

Prepare seafood and set aside. Melt butter in a large saucepan, add onion and garlic and cook gently for 3 minutes. Add chopped herbs, tomatoes and wine and simmer for 10 minutes. Add Squid and cook for 5 minutes then add Shark, Prawns, Scallops and Mussels and cook for a further 3 minutes until Mussels open. Season with salt and pepper and serve over hot cooked pasta.

Serves 6

Octopus Pie

(This pie is flat and thin)

INGREDIENTS

Pastry

*2 eggs
pinch salt
½ cup milk
¼ cup oil
3 cups flour, sifted
milk for glazing*

Filling

*750g (1½lb) cleaned Octopus (see page 314)
1 cup red wine
2 bay leaves
2 medium onions, finely sliced
4 medium tomatoes, thinly sliced
¼ cup diced capsicum
salt and pepper to taste
1 tablespoon finely chopped fresh basil, or
1 teaspoon dried*

METHOD

Pastry:
In a bowl mix together eggs, salt, milk and oil. Gradually add the flour until a soft dough is formed (the dough should be moist, yet does not stick to your fingers). Knead lightly, wrap in plastic and rest in the refrigerator for 30 minutes.
Filling:
In a saucepan place Octopus, red wine and bay leaves. Cover and simmer for 45-60 minutes or until tender. Drain and remove bay leaves. Cool. Cut Octopus into small pieces.
To Prepare Pie:
Preheat oven to 180°C (350°F). Divide pastry into 2. Roll out half to fit a 30cm (12 inch) pie dish or pizza plate. Cover the plate with the pastry. Place Octopus on pastry, cover with onions, tomatoes and capsicum. Sprinkle with salt, pepper and basil. Roll out remaining dough and cover the dish. Trim the edges and glaze with milk. Bake for 30-40 minutes or until golden.

Serves 6

Squid with Tomato and Rosemary

INGREDIENTS

*750g (1½lb) Squid rings
olive oil
2 medium onions, finely sliced
3 garlic cloves, crushed
2 tablespoons finely chopped parsley
½ teaspoon rosemary sprigs
1½ cups tomato pure
½ cup water*

METHOD

Wash Squid rings thoroughly, removing any skin and grit. If preparing Squid rings from whole Squid, see page 314 for directions. Heat oil in a pan and gently cook onions and garlic. Add parsley, rosemary, tomato purée and water. Lastly add Squid and gently simmer for 3-4 minutes. Do not overcook as the Squid will toughen. Serve with noodles.

Serves 6

Raw Kingfish and Coral Lettuce Salad

(Photograph pages 258 & 259)

INGREDIENTS

*500g (1lb) Kingfish fillets, rinsed and dried
½ cup fresh lime juice
½ cup coconut milk
lettuce leaves (use a variety of lettuce)
1 onion, very finely chopped
½ cup hazelnut oil*

METHOD

Place Kingfish in a shallow dish, pour over lime juice and coconut milk, cover and refrigerate for 24 hours. Remove fish from marinade, slice thinly and arrange on a serving platter. Wash and crisp lettuce and place in a bowl. Heat one-third cup of marinade mixture and boil 2 minutes. Cool and mix with onion and oil, pour over lettuce, toss and serve.

Serves 6

Almond and Orange Torte

INGREDIENTS

2 large oranges
water
6 eggs
1 cup castor sugar
2 cups ground almonds
¼ teaspoon almond essence
julienne strips of peel from 1 orange, extra
¼ cup sugar, extra
1 tablespoon Grand Marnier
1 cup cream, whipped

METHOD

Put whole oranges in a saucepan, cover with water and bring to the boil. Cover and simmer for 1 hour until a skewer penetrates easily. Drain oranges, chop roughly and remove pips. Pure oranges in food processor and cool.

Beat eggs until frothy, gradually beat in sugar. When thick and light, fold in almonds, almond essence and orange pulp. Butter and flour a 23cm (9 inch) spring form tin and pour in batter. Bake in a preheated 190°C (375°F) oven for 55-60 minutes until golden and slightly shrunk from sides of tin. Cool in tin, then remove and place on serving plate.

Meanwhile blanch julienne orange peel (no pith) in water, drain, add ½ cup water with the extra sugar, stir over heat until dissolved, then boil gently 10 minutes. Drain peel. Mix Grand Marnier into whipped cream, pipe onto cake and decorate with the candied strips of peel.

Serves 6

Melon Salad

(Photograph page 253)

INGREDIENTS

1 large ripe honeydew melon
1 pawpaw
1 rockmelon
½ cup Midori (melon) liqueur

METHOD

Cut melons and pawpaw in half, remove seeds and shape into balls and wedges. Place in a bowl, pour over liqueur, cover and refrigerate for approximately 4 hours before serving in individual glasses.

Serves 6

Summer Pavlova Roll

(Photograph page 265)

INGREDIENTS

4 egg whites
¾ cup castor sugar
½ teaspoon vanilla essence
1 tablespoon castor sugar, extra
1 teaspoon cinnamon
½ cup slivered almonds
½ cup cream, lightly whipped
pulp of 3 passionfruit
1 cup sliced fresh summer fruits, (eg. strawberries, pawpaw, peach)
extra whipped cream or ice cream for serving

METHOD

Beat egg whites till stiff, gradually add sugar to form a smooth meringue, add vanilla. Spread mixture over a greased foil-lined 35 x 25cm (14 x 10 inch) Swiss roll tin. Sprinkle with combined extra sugar and cinnamon then almonds. Bake at 180°C (350°F) for about 8-10 minutes till meringue is firm. Turn onto a sheet of greaseproof paper, allow to stand for 3-4 minutes to cool slightly. Quickly spread with cream, top with passionfruit and fruits. Roll up and refrigerate until required. Cut in 2.5cm (1 inch) slices and serve with whipped cream or ice cream.

Serves 6

Almond Custard

INGREDIENTS

4 cups milk
1 cup ground almonds
¼ cup ground rice
pinch salt
¼ cup sugar
4 drops almond essence
pomegranate seeds (optional)
chopped pistachio nuts or toasted almond slivers

METHOD

Put 3½ cups of the milk into a pan, add almonds and gradually bring to the boil. Remove pan from heat and leave aside for 15 minutes to steep. Strain milk through a fine sieve into a heavy-based pan, pressing on almonds with the back of a wooden spoon to extract moisture. Discard almond meal.

Mix remaining ½ cup milk with the ground rice and add to almond milk with salt and sugar. Stir over medium heat until thickened and simmering gently. Stir in almond essence, taste and add more sugar if necessary. Cool a little, then pour into dessert glasses and chill for at least 1 hour. To serve, heap a few pomegranate seeds in the centre of each custard and surround with chopped pistachios or slivered almonds. Fresh raspberries may replace pomegranate seeds if desired.

Serves 6

A giant Groper can become tame and friendly as a dog given the right handling.

SUMMER PAVLOVA ROLL, Recipe page 264.

A versatile camper making a billy of tea with the help of a hot bore, Qld.

Prawns bulging in the net.

The Commercial Catch

*E*very morning, right across the country, from Darwin, to Broome to Fremantle, over to Albany and Esperance, on to Port Lincoln, down to Warrnambool and Wonthaggi, up to Eden, through Sydney, Port Stephens, and up onto the Gold Coast, through Mackay, Townsville, Cairns and up to the Torres Strait, across the Gulf and back to Darwin, the fishing fleets of this vast island called Australia can be seen making their way home.

Some have been out for the night, some for days, some weeks. Some are ageing, small timber boats, others are high-tech juggernauts, but all have a common purpose — the sometimes elusive, sometimes valuable, commercial catch.

As could be expected from a country with an 8 million square kilometre (3 million sq. mls.) landmass, stretching over almost 35 degrees of latitude, there is quite a large amount of variety in Australia's commercial catch. Consequently, there is also a large variety in the styles of commercial fishing — from the giant Prawn trawlers operating in the far north, to the Tuna polers in southern waters. There are various methods of netting, trawling, trapping, lining and farming that are used, depending on the environment and the behaviour of the species that are being sought.

The popular and more important commercial species are of four main types: offshore bottom dwellers such as Gemfish, Redfish, Morwong, Tiger Flathead, John Dory and Snapper; surface swimmers (pelagics) such as Southern Bluefin Tuna; inshore/estuarine species such as Bream, Whiting, Mullet, Jewfish and Luderick and shellfish such as Prawns, Crabs, Rock Lobsters, Scallops, Oysters and Abalone.

In this chapter, you will find recipes for most of these, and also for some of the lesser known species. The Pickled Garfish with Sour Cream (page 273), for example, is a delightfully different way to taste these striking little fish.

Tasmania's famous commercial catch combines exquisitely with fresh Mussells to make the scrumptious Mussell and Scallop Pies, featured on page 277.

The three course meal shown opposite is most definitely a dinner party "must"! The ever popular Gemfish provides the perfect filling for the Potted Rolls, while the Sea Bream with Oysters is an absolute "taste sensation"!! Again, a fruit based dessert — the Chilled Apricot Cream — provides the consumate finishing touch to another superb seafood meal.

Indulge yourself in Australia's seafood harvest. Your choice is most certain to be "commercially sound"!!

A Japanese tuna float catches the glint of the setting sun at Shark Bay, W.A.

Top: CHILLED APRICOT CREAM, Recipe page 278. *Middle*: SEA BREAM WITH OYSTERS, Recipe page 276.
Below: POTTED GEMFISH ROLLS, Recipe page 272.

Fishermen preparing for a new day of fishing at Apollo Bay, Vic.

Potted Gemfish Rolls

(Photograph page 269)

INGREDIENTS

750g (1½lb) Gemfish fillets
¾ cup finely sliced mushrooms
2 tablespoons butter or margarine
2 tablespoons flour
¾ cup cream
salt and pepper to taste
buttered breadcrumbs
button mushrooms and parsley for garnish

METHOD

Skin Gemfish fillets. Cut into 3cm (1 ¼ inch) strips. Grease 6 small custard pots and coil the fillets around the side of the cups. Meanwhile put the mushrooms in a saucepan with the butter and cook gently until the mushrooms soften. Stir in flour and mix for 2 minutes. Gradually add the cream, salt and pepper. Stir until the sauce is thick. Pour the sauce evenly into the pots. Sprinkle buttered breadcrumbs on top of each pot and bake at 150°C (300°F) for 15-20 minutes. Drain off any juice and unmould onto appetizer plates. Garnish with button mushrooms and parsley.

Serves 6

Smoked Oyster Nibblers

INGREDIENTS

4 bacon slices, chopped
1 tablespoon butter or margarine
2 tablespoons flour
1 x 425g (14oz) can Cream of Oyster Soup
2 tablespoons sherry
2 tablespoons lemon juice
2 cans Smoked Oysters, drained
2 tablespoons finely chopped parsley
½ cup cream
pepper to taste
small vol-au-vent cases or breadcases
½ cup grated cheddar cheese

METHOD

In a hot pan sauté bacon until fat runs. Add butter, stir in flour and cook for 2 minutes. Stir in Oyster soup, sherry, lemon juice, Smoked Oysters and parsley and keep stirring until mixture boils and thickens. Add cream; heat gently, do not boil. Season with pepper. Spoon into vol-au-vent cases and sprinke with cheese. Bake in a preheated oven at 180°C (350°F) until cheese is melted and cases are hot. Serve immediately.

Serves 6

Rolled Redfish Fillets with Spinach Purée

INGREDIENTS

750g (1½lb) Redfish fillets
seasoned flour
1 egg, beaten
dry breadcrumbs
toothpicks
oil for deep frying

Filling

4 bacon slices, diced
1 small onion, finely chopped
¼ capsicum, diced
250g (8oz) spinach leaves, roughly chopped
½ cup grated cheddar cheese
2 teaspoons lemon juice
salt and pepper to taste

METHOD

Combine all filling ingredients in a food processor and mince finely. Spread a heaped teaspoon of filling over each fillet and roll up. Secure with toothpicks. Coat with flour, egg and breadcrumbs. Rest rolls in refrigerator for 20 minutes. Heat oil and deep fry rolls until golden for 2-3 minutes. Drain on kitchen paper and serve immediately garnished with herb sprigs and lemon wedges.

Serves 6

Gazpacho

INGREDIENTS

8 medium tomatoes, skinned and quartered
2 medium cucumbers, peeled, seeded and cut into pieces
1 capsicum, seeded and cut into pieces
1 large onion, cut into pieces
3 garlic cloves, skinned
salt and pepper to taste
⅓ cup dry breadcrumbs
3 tablespoons olive oil
⅓ cup good white wine vinegar
water or canned beef consomme, if necessary
finely chopped parsley

METHOD

Place tomatoes, cucumbers, capsicum and onion in a food processor. Process to a coarse or fine purée according to your preference. Keep aside. Crush garlic and work to a soft paste with ½ teaspoon salt. Put garlic in a bowl with pepper to taste and breadcrumbs. Gradually stir in oil until a thick paste is formed, then stir in vinegar. Turn into a soup tureen and mix in puréed vegetables. If a thinner soup is required, add cold water or canned beef consomme. Adjust seasoning and chill well before serving. Serve sprinkled with chopped parsley.

Serves 6

Baked Zucchini with Cheese and Apple Stuffing

INGREDIENTS

6 medium zucchini
2 medium cooking apples
1 tablespoon butter or margarine
1 garlic clove, crushed
2 tablespoons finely chopped parsley
60g (2oz) cream cheese, softened
salt and pepper to taste

METHOD

Wash and trim zucchini. Peel and grate the apples. Melt butter in pan and gently cook the apples until they are soft. Cut the zucchini in half and scoop out the centre of each zucchini to give shells about 5mm (¼ inch) thick. Finely chop scooped out flesh. Combine the apples, zucchini, garlic, parsley, cream cheese, salt and pepper. Mix well. Fill the cavity of each zucchini half, pack firmly and smooth the tops. Place in ovenproof dish and bake at 180°C (350°F) for 15 minutes or until zucchini are tender.
Note: Any mixture left over can be wrapped in foil, placed in the dish and baked alongside the filled zucchini.

Serves 6

Liverwurst Paté

INGREDIENTS

250g (8oz) liverwurst
2 tablespoons butter or margarine, softened
1 tablespoon mayonnaise
1 teaspoon finely grated lemon rind
salt and pepper to taste
finely chopped parsley
endive

METHOD

Combine liverwurst, butter, mayonnaise, lemon rind, salt and pepper. Mix until smooth. Shape into a log and roll in chopped parsley. Chill well before serving. Serve on a bed of endive with crispy bread or cracker biscuits.

Serves 6

PICKLED GARFISH WITH SOUR CREAM, Recipe page 273.

Pickled Garfish with Sour Cream

(Photograph page 273)

INGREDIENTS

12 Garfish
2 tablespoons pickling spice tied in a cheesecloth bag
¾ cup water
½ cup brown sugar
1½ cups white wine vinegar
3 medium onions, thinly sliced
1 lemon, thinly sliced
2 cups sour cream
caviar for garnish

METHOD

Scale and fillet Garfish, rinse and refrigerate until required. Combine pickling spice, water, brown sugar and vinegar in a saucepan and boil for 5 minutes. Cool.
Layer Garfish fillets in a large casserole dish with onions and lemon. Cover with vinegar mixture and refrigerate for 12-24 hours before serving. Serve drained fillets with sour cream and caviar.
Note: This will keep for up to 1 week in the refrigerator.

Serves 6

Capsicums Filled with Redfish

INGREDIENTS

750g (1½lb) Redfish fillets
6 capsicums
⅓ cup sour cream
2 tablespoons mayonnaise
1 cup cooked rice
¼ teaspoon nutmeg
¼ teaspoon paprika
salt and pepper to taste
2 teaspoons lemon juice

METHOD

Put fillets in a food processor and mince finely. Cut tops off capsicums and remove seeds. Wash thoroughly. In a bowl combine minced fish, sour cream, mayonnaise, rice, nutmeg, paprika, salt, pepper and lemon juice. Mix well. Spoon mixture evenly into capsicums, top with capsicum lids, and place in a greased baking dish. Bake at 180ºC (350ºF) for 25-30 minutes or until capsicums are tender.

Serves 6

Left: BUGS IN CREAM & TOMATO SAUCE, Recipe page 277.
Right: INDIVIDUAL MUSSEL & SCALLOP PIES, Recipe page 277.

PRAWN NEWBERG WITH GREEN RICE, Recipe page 276.

Prawn Newberg with Green Rice

(Photograph page 276)

INGREDIENTS

2kg (4lb) medium King Prawns
3 tablespoons butter or margarine
5 tablespoons flour
2 cups milk
1 cup fish or chicken stock
½ teaspoon dry mustard
pinch cayenne pepper
2 tablespoons sherry
½ cup cream
salt and pepper to taste

METHOD

Peel and devein Prawns, removing heads and tails.

Melt butter in a large saucepan, stir in flour and cook gently for 2 minutes. Gradually stir in milk and stock stirring constantly until thick and smooth. Boil gently for 2 minutes, add mustard, cayenne pepper, sherry, cream and cooked Prawns. Simmer for 3-4 minutes, just enough to allow the Prawns to heat through. Do not boil. Season to taste and serve with the green rice.

Green rice

3 cups cooked white rice
½ cup finely chopped parsley
3 tablespoons chopped chives
2 eggs, lightly beaten
salt and pepper to taste

Green Rice:
Combine all ingredients and mix well. Spoon into a greased ring tin and bake for 20-25 minutes or until set. Unmould onto a warm serving platter and serve Prawn Newberg in the centre of ring.

Serves 6

Sea Bream with Oysters

(Photograph page 269)

INGREDIENTS

750g (1½lb) Sea Bream (Morwong) fillets
2 dozen Oysters
½ cup white wine
2 teaspoons grated lemon rind
2 tablespoons finely chopped parsley
1 teaspoon grated ginger

METHOD

Preheat oven to 180ºC (350ºF).
Skin the fillets. Lay fillets in a greased ovenproof dish. Arrange Oysters on top of fish. Pour over wine and sprinkle with lemon rind, parsley and ginger. Bake for 20-25 minutes or until flesh flakes. Serve hot.

Serves 6

Baked Stuffed Garfish

INGREDIENTS

12 Garfish
4 canned Anchovies
1 garlic clove, crushed
2 tablespoons finely chopped parsley
1 cup fresh breadcrumbs
½ cup grated Parmesan cheese
2 tablespoons lemon juice
salt and pepper to taste
½ cup white wine

METHOD

Preheat oven to 180ºC (350ºF). Scale and clean Garfish, trim fins and remove backbones. In a bowl, mash Anchovies well, mix in garlic, parsley, breadcrumbs, Parmesan cheese, lemon juice, salt and pepper. If mixture is too dry, moisten with a little water to bring together. Fill the cavity of each fish and secure with toothpicks. Place all fish in a greased ovenproof baking dish and pour over white wine. Bake for 15-20 minutes or until flesh flakes.

Serves 6

Bugs in Cream and Tomato Sauce

(Photograph pages 274 & 275)

INGREDIENTS

1kg (2lb) green Balmain Bug tail meat
30g (2oz) butter
3 garlic cloves, crushed
1 cup finely chopped parsley
salt and pepper
2 tablespoons lemon juice
2 tablespoons tomato paste
1 cup thin cream

METHOD

Melt butter in a large shallow pan, add Bug tails, garlic and parsley and gently fry for 2-3 minutes. Season with salt and pepper, stir in lemon juice, tomato paste and cream, heat gently and serve on a bed of boiled rice.

Serves 4 to 6

Individual Mussel and Scallop Pies

(Photograph pages 274 & 275)

INGREDIENTS

250g (8oz) Mussel meat
250g (8oz) Scallops
3 tablespoons butter or margarine
6 shallots, finely chopped
2 teaspoons finely chopped fresh tarragon
½ capsicum, finely diced
2 teaspoons finely chopped pimento
½ teaspoon nutmeg
salt and pepper
1 quantity shortcrust pastry (page 315)
milk for glazing
6 small ovenproof pie plates

METHOD

Wash Mussels and Scallops, removing any hard pieces and grit. Cut Mussels and Scallops in half. Melt butter in pan, add shallots, tarragon, capsicum and pimento. Gently cook for 2-3 minutes. Add Mussels, Scallops and seasoning, cook 2 minutes, just allowing enough time for seafood to exude any liquid. Line the bases of the pie plates with pastry and prick with a fork. Blind bake for 5-8 minutes. Remove. Strain seafood mixture and place evenly into the pie shells. Cover with remaining pastry, pinch edges and glaze with milk. Bake at 180ºC (350ºF) for 10 minutes or until golden. Serve hot or cold.

Serves 6

Gemfish Florentine

INGREDIENTS

750g (1½lb) Gemfish fillets
1 egg, lightly beaten
½ cup milk
1 cup flour
oil for frying
24 spinach leaves, cut into pieces
125g (4oz) ricotta cheese, crumbled
⅓ cup sour cream
¼ teaspoon nutmeg
2 tablespoons lemon juice
salt and pepper to taste

METHOD

Wash and skin fillets and cut into 6 serving portions. Mix egg and milk together in a bowl. Dip fillets into this mixture and then dredge with flour. Heat enough oil in a pan for shallow frying. Add fillets and cook for 3 minutes on each side or until flesh flakes. Remove fillets and keep warm. In a saucepan, place spinach and cook gently for 3-4 minutes. Mix in ricotta cheese, cream, nutmeg, lemon juice, salt and pepper. Cook for 2-3 minutes over a medium heat. Arrange fillets on a serving platter and spoon over spinach mixture. Serve immediately.
Note: English spinach should be used for this recipe. If using silverbeet, 12 leaves would be sufficient—remove stems and white rib.

Serves 6

Redfish Fillets with Hollandaise Sauce

INGREDIENTS

4 tablespoons white wine vinegar
1 bay leaf
1 small onion, finely sliced
3 peppercorns
3 egg yolks
175g (6oz) butter, cut into small cubes
750g (1½lb) Redfish fillets
seasoned flour
oil for shallow frying

METHOD

Put the vinegar, bay leaf, onion slices and peppercorns into a saucepan and boil until vinegar has reduced by about two-thirds. Strain and cool. In a bowl put egg yolks, whisk in vinegar, then put into either a double saucepan or a bowl over a saucepan of gently simmering water. Add cubes of butter, one at a time, whisk until melted and incorporated into the yolk mixture before adding the next piece. Stir until thickened. Keep warm. Coat fillets in flour, heat oil and shallow fry 2-3 minutes each side or until flesh flakes. Place fillets on platter and mask with sauce. Garnish with lemon butterflies and parsley.
Note: Should sauce show signs of separating, pour in a drop of boiling water and whisk.

Serves 6

Chocolate Self-Saucing Pudding

INGREDIENTS

1 cup self-raising flour
2 teaspoons cocoa
60g (2oz) butter
½ cup castor sugar
1 egg, beaten
½ cup milk

Sauce

½ cup brown sugar
1 tablespoon cocoa
1 ¼ cups boiling water

METHOD

Sift flour and cocoa. Cream butter and castor sugar, add egg, mix well. Stir in flour and milk alternately, pour into flameproof 6-cup casserole.
Sauce: Combine brown sugar and cocoa, sprinkle on top of mixture in dish and pour boiling water gently on top.
Bake uncovered in preheated 180°C (350°F) oven for 30-35 minutes. Serve hot or warm with cream.

Chilled Apricot Cream

(Photograph page 269)

INGREDIENTS

500g (1lb) dried apricots
1½ cups water
2 egg yolks, lightly beaten
½ cup sugar
1 tablespoon arrowroot
1¼ cups milk
½ teaspoon vanilla essence
¾ cup cream, whipped

METHOD

Wash apricots, place in a saucepan, add water. Cover and simmer gently for 15-20 minutes, until soft. Cool, then purée in food processor. In a saucepan stir egg yolks with sugar and arrowroot, add milk. Place over heat and stir until custard thickens. Cool, then fold in apricot purée and vanilla essence. Chill for 30 minutes then fold through whipped cream. Pour into dessert glasses and chill well before serving.

Serves 6

Toffee Dipped Grapes

INGREDIENTS

2kg (4lb) seedless grapes
4 cups sugar
2 cups water
2 teaspoons lemon juice
cream, lightly whipped

METHOD

Wash grapes. Snip with scissors into small bunches. Pat dry with paper towels. Combine sugar, water and lemon juice in a saucepan, stir over a low heat until sugar dissolves. Bring to the boil and boil briskly, without stirring, for 10 minutes or until toffee is light brown. Allow bubbles to subside, quickly dip grapes into toffee using tongs. Place on a lightly greased aluminium tray to set. Place toffee grapes on individual sweet plates and serve with whipped cream.

Note: Toffee can harden before all grapes are dipped. Either stand pan of toffee in a dish of simmering water while dipping, or make toffee in 2 smaller batches.

Serves 6

Aussie Dried Fruit Slice

(Photograph page 279)

INGREDIENTS

1 egg
½ cup castor sugar
125g (4oz) butter or margarine, softened
2½ cups self-raising flour, sifted
4 tablespoons lemon juice
2 teaspoons grated lemon rind
1 cup dried currants
2 cups dried dates
½ cup water
milk for glazing
extra castor sugar

METHOD

Preheat oven at 180°C (350°F). In a bowl beat egg and sugar until thick, add butter, beat until smooth. Add flour and 1 tablespoon of the lemon juice. Mix together, knead lightly and chill. In a saucepan combine the remaining lemon juice, lemon rind, currants, dates and water. Cook gently till mixture is soft and forms a pulp — about 10 minutes. Cool. Divide pastry in half and roll one half to fit base of 23cm (9 inch) sandwich tin. Spread fruit filling over pastry and roll remaining pastry to cover fruit. Glaze with milk and sprinkle with castor sugar. Bake in preheated oven for 30-40 minutes. Serve warm or cold with cream or ice cream. *Serves 6*

The great White Shark deserves its dreaded reputation. The serrated triangular teeth have cutting edges sharper than any steak knife. They can grow to six metres and two tonnes in weight.

AUSSIE DRIED FRUIT SLICE, Recipe page 278.

The always colourful, blessing of the fleet at Ulladulla, NSW.

Toasting bread in the bush.

Sizzling Seafood

O ne of the great "Aussie" pastimes is the barbecue, and not without good reason. In a country blessed with summers that are "beautiful one day and perfect the next" — to borrow a phrase from Queensland — what better way to take advantage of the glorious blue skies than by spending it outdoors with a couple of friends, some fine food and perhaps a few drinks.

Whether it be in the good old backyard, over at the local park, out in the "bush" or down on a beach or river, a barbecue is always a convivial and enjoyable occasion. The enjoyment is always enhanced, of course, if the food is good! What better way to ensure that, than by ensuring that seafood gets a fair representation on the hotplate!

In these days of high health awareness, it is becoming more and more common for people to eat less meat. When it comes to the "barbie", there's no better alternative to meat than some fish and shellfish; a few King Prawns, a Tuna steak or two, some Kingfish cutlets, perhaps a dozen Garfish, some marinated Octopus, a specially prepared whole Mullet wrapped in banana leaves . . . . the possibilities are endless.

Quite often the best seafood for the barbecue is some of the cheapest: Octopus, Squid, Mullet, Garfish are all at the bottom end of the price range, but certainly not at the bottom when it comes to flavour!

Very important, naturally, is the preparation and cooking of these tender delicacies. You will be surprised to learn in this chapter just how easy it is to achieve superb results when you're barbecuing seafood.

The meal shown across the page, for example, is extremely easy and fast to prepare. Provided you're organised in planning a couple of hours ahead and popped the Octopus in the marinade, it is all very straight forward and I'm sure you will find the results most impressive!

So next time you are planning a barbecue, make sure you include some of these marvellous dishes on the menu. Or why not go the whole way and plan an entirely seafood barbecue? Your friends will most surely be very impressed!!

Mangrove creeks and tidal flats at Wyndham form shining patterns. A close inspection would show other regular imprints — the claw-tracks of a salt-water Crocodile. Far North of Western Australia.

Left: PEPPERED PINEAPPLE WITH WHISKY CREAM, Recipe page 294. *Right*: BARBECUED OCTOPUS WITH PEPPER SALAD, Recipe page 286.
Bottom: BARBECUED MULLET IN BANANA LEAVES, Recipe page 291.

Catching some fish for the 'barbie' on Wallace Lakes, near Foster, NSW.

Barbecued Octopus with Pepper Salad

(Photograph page 283)

INGREDIENTS

500g (1lb) small Octopus (page 314)
¼ cup olive oil
½ cup lemon juice
1 teaspoon dried oregano or marjoram
1 garlic clove, crushed
1 medium size green capsicum
1 medium size red capsicum
1 medium size yellow capsicum or pepper (optional)

Dressing

½ cup olive oil
1 tablespoon lemon juice
1 tablespoon red wine vinegar
1 garlic clove, crushed
1 tablespoon finely chopped parsley
½ teaspoon salt
freshly ground pepper

METHOD

Cut Octopus hood into strips. Cut tentacles into 2.5cm (1 inch) pieces. If Octopus is very small they may be left whole. Wash well, pat dry and place in a glass bowl. Add oil, lemon juice, herbs and garlic. Cover and place in the refrigerator and allow to marinate for 24 hours. Turn in the marinade occasionally.

Cut capsicums into four lengthways, remove seeds and white membrane. Brush outer skin with oil and place skin side down on hot barbecue until skins are well blistered, rub off skins with a towel. Arrange on a platter or individual plates, alternating the colours. Drizzle with half of the dressing and set aside. Heat barbecue to medium heat. Place Octopus on the barbecue plate and cook for 15-20 minutes, turning frequently and splashing on a little marinade as they cook. Remove and pile into the centre of the pepper salad. Pour over remaining dressing and serve.

Serves 4 to 6

Egg and Mustard Crudites

INGREDIENTS

250g (8oz) cream cheese
¾ cup mayonnaise
¾ cup natural yoghurt
250g (8oz) grated cheddar cheese
2 teaspoons French mustard
6 hard boiled eggs
1½ tablespoons finely chopped chives
1½ tablespoons finely chopped parsley
salt and pepper to taste
raw vegetables (see below)

METHOD

Place all ingredients except raw vegetables into a food processor and blend until smooth. If mixture is too thick add some cream to thin a little. Serve in a bowl on a large platter surrounded by prepared raw vegetables.

Raw vegetables (Crudites): Choose some of the following and prepare as indicated—carrot, zucchini, capsicum, celery and crisp cucumber, cut in sticks; asparagus spears, snow peas, cauliflower and broccoli florets, lightly blanched; small mushroom caps and radishes, trimmed and left whole. Make selection according to seasonal availability and shape and colour variation. Group the various vegetables on the platter.

Serves 6

Barbecued Garlic Clams

(Photograph page 287)

INGREDIENTS

36 Tasmanian Clams in shells
3 garlic cloves, crushed
¼ cup olive oil
¼ cup bland vegetable oil
2 tablespoons finely chopped parsley
½ teaspoon salt

METHOD

Place Clams on a hot barbecue griddle plate. Combine garlic, oils, parsley and salt. Place mixture in each Clam as it opens and cook over a hot barbecue for 2-3 minutes. Serve immediately.

Serves 6

Prawn and Bread Soup

INGREDIENTS

1kg (2lb) green King Prawns
2L (8 cups) water
2 teaspoons salt
3 large tomatoes, skinned and roughly chopped
1 capsicum, seeded and diced
2 onions, sliced thinly
2 garlic cloves, crushed
pinch saffron
salt and pepper to taste
12 thin slices of bread, crusts removed and cut into 2.5cm (1 inch) squares

METHOD

Wash Prawns thoroughly. Put water into a large saucepan, add salt and bring to the boil. Add Prawns, return to boil, then simmer until Prawns turn orange, about 2-3 minutes. Remove Prawns with slotted spoon and cool under running water. Shell Prawns, return heads and shells to pan and boil briskly for 10 minutes. Devein Prawns, cut each in 2-3 pieces and set aside. Strain Prawn stock into a bowl, clean pan, return stock and add tomatoes, capsicum, onions and garlic. Cook until vegetables are tender. Add saffron, salt, pepper, and Prawn meat. Lastly, add the bread squares. Refrigerate if not being used immediately. To serve at a barbecue meal, place the pan of soup on the barbecue and heat well.

Serves 6

Potato Salad Roll

INGREDIENTS

4 cups cooked, mashed potato
1 cup finely sliced celery
½ cup finely chopped pickled cucumber
1 small onion, finely chopped
2 tablespoons mayonnaise
2 tablespoons lemon juice
salt and pepper to taste
1 cup finely chopped parsley
4 eggs, hard boiled

METHOD

In a bowl combine potato, celery, cucumber, onion, mayonnaise, lemon juice, salt and pepper. Mix well. Sprinkle parsley over a large sheet of greaseproof paper. Spread or pipe potato mixture over paper, into a large rectangle shape. Place eggs along the long side of potato. Using the paper as a lever, roll like a swiss roll, keeping the paper to the outside.

Chill well, cut into slices, and serve with a green salad.

Serves 6

BARBECUED GARLIC CLAMS, Recipe page 286.

Tomatoes Stuffed with Sea Perch

INGREDIENTS

250g (8oz) Sea Perch or Red Emperor fillets
water
6 large tomatoes
½ cup cooked rice
3 tablespoons mayonnaise
1 tablespoon finely chopped parsley
salt and pepper to taste
parsley and lemon slices for garnishing

METHOD

Skin the fillets. Place fillets in a pan and just cover with water. Poach until flesh flakes, 2-3 minutes. Remove fish from pan and flake flesh finely, removing any bones. Cut a thick slice from the top of each tomato; reserve. Scoop out flesh from the inside, trying not to break the skin. In a bowl combine fish, chopped tomato flesh, rice, mayonnaise, parsley, salt and pepper. Evenly spoon mixture into each tomato and replace tops. Chill well before serving. Garnish with parsley and lemon. Any remaining mixture can be served in lettuce cups.

Serves 6

Anchovy, Tomato and Onion Tart

INGREDIENTS

1 quantity shortcrust pastry (page 315)
250g (8oz) canned Anchovy fillets
4 tablespoons olive oil
500g (1lb) white onions, finely sliced
3 garlic cloves, crushed
4 medium tomatoes, roughly chopped
2 tablespoons tomato paste
¼ teaspoon sugar
salt and pepper to taste
6 black olives, halved

METHOD

Roll out pastry and line a 30cm (12 inch) flan tin. Prick base and sides and blind bake in preheated 200ºC (400ºF) oven.
Drain Anchovies. Heat oil in a pan, add onions and garlic. Cook until soft. Add tomatoes, tomato paste, sugar, salt and pepper. Spread the tomato and onion mixture evenly over the baked pastry case. Cut Anchovies in half lengthways and arrange in a lattice design over the tomato. Garnish with olives and bake for 20 minutes or until pastry is properly cooked and the filling is hot. Serve hot or warm.

Serves 6 to 8

GARLIC LOBSTER TAILS WITH JACKET POTATOES & ROE, Recipe page 291.

CARPETBAG STEAKS WITH HERB AND BACON BREAD, Recipe page 290.

Island Luau Fish

INGREDIENTS

1 x 1.5kg (3lb) whole Snapper
3 tablespoons butter
½ teaspoon salt
1 tablespoon lime juice
1 teaspoon ground cumin
2 teaspoons ground coriander
fresh banana leaves

METHOD

Clean and scale the fish, rinse and wipe dry with a paper towel. Make 3 or 4 deep slashes on each side of the fish. Mix together butter, salt, lime juice, cumin and coriander and spread into the slashes on each side. Cut centre rib from banana leaves, pour boiling water over leaves to soften. Wrap fish in the leaves and then in heavy foil. Place on heated barbecue and cook for approximately 25 minutes turning every 5 minutes. Unwrap and test by placing a round bladed knife into the cavity and lifting the flesh from the bone. If flesh comes away from the bone the fish is cooked. Remove foil.
Serve fish on the banana leaves, garnished with lime slices.

Carpetbag Steaks with Herb and Bacon Bread

(Photograph page 290)

INGREDIENTS

6 x 250g (8oz) tail-end Eye Fillets of Beef
1 large jar (20) fresh Oysters
salt and cracked black pepper
oil for glazing
1 loaf fresh white plaited bread
125g (4oz) butter, softened
3 slices bacon, finely chopped and lightly fried
3 garlic cloves, crushed
½ cup finely chopped parsley

METHOD

Make a pocket in broad end of each beef fillet, stuff with Oysters and tie with string. Dust with salt and pepper and barbecue over a hot flame for approximately 10-15 minutes, brushing with oil, until cooked. Meanwhile combine butter with fried bacon, garlic and chopped parsley, stuff into 'plaits' of bread, wrap in foil and heat on barbecue plate. Serve with a tomato and lettuce salad.

Serves 6

Barbecued Sole with Crab meat Stuffing

INGREDIENTS

6 plate-size whole Sole or
Flounder
2 cups cooked Crab meat
1 tablespoon oil
1 small onion, chopped
1 garlic clove, crushed
1 tablespoon finely chopped
parsley
salt and pepper to taste
½ cup lemon juice

METHOD

Preheat oven to 180°C (350°F). Scale and clean fish. Shred Crab meat finely. In a saucepan heat oil and gently cook onion and garlic. Add parsley, Crab meat, salt and pepper. Mix and allow to cool. Debone fish and place one-third cup crab meat mixture into the cavity of each fish. Secure fish with skewers. Place each fish onto a sheet of greased foil and baste with lemon juice. Wrap like a parcel. Place parcels of fish over medium barbecue heat and cook for 8-10 minutes each side.

Serves 6

Hot Spiced Barramundi

INGREDIENTS

750g (1½lb) Barramundi or
Ling fillets or cutlets
½ teaspoon salt
¼ teaspoon pepper
2 garlic cloves, crushed
¼ cup oil
2 tablespoons soy sauce
4 tablespoons lemon or lime
juice
¼ hot red chili pepper,
crushed

METHOD

Wipe over the fish with damp paper towels. Mix salt, pepper and garlic together and rub into fish. Combine oil, soy sauce, lemon juice and crushed chili. Brush fish with mixture and barbecue over glowing coals, basting often with oil mixture. Cook only until flesh flakes.

Serves 6

Barbecued Mullet in Banana Leaves

(Photograph page 283)

INGREDIENTS

2 x 750g (1½lb) Mullet
1 lemon, thinly sliced
2 garlic cloves, crushed
1 teaspoon salt
banana leaves, scalded and
trimmed
water

METHOD

Scale and clean fish. Cut each fish diagonally twice on each side about 5mm (1/4 inch) deep. Place lemon slices in each cut and in the cavity of the fish. Combine garlic and salt and rub fish with the mixture. Lay each fish onto individual banana leaves, sprinkle with water and wrap firmly. Place on barbecue and cook for 35-40 minutes, or until flesh flakes and skin lifts easily. You may have to open parcels during cooking time to check if fish is cooked. When ready to serve, open up and present fish on leaves.

Serves 2 to 4

Red Emperor Fillets with Horseradish Marinade

INGREDIENTS

750g (1½lb) Red Emperor fillets

Marinade

1 teaspoon prepared
horseradish
½ cup olive oil
1 tablespoon white wine
vinegar
1 garlic clove, crushed
¼ teaspoon paprika

METHOD

Skin the fillets. In a shallow dish combine all marinade ingredients. Place fillets in marinade and let stand in refrigerator for at least 30 minutes, baste occasionally. Drain fillets and cook on heated barbecue plate, basting often with marinade. Turn once during cooking.

Serves 6

Garlic Lobster with Jacket Potatoes and Roe

(Photograph pages 288 & 289)

INGREDIENTS

6 medium potatoes, scrubbed
6 x 250g (8oz) green Lobster
tails
90g (3oz) butter, softened
3 garlic cloves, crushed
2 tablespoons finely chopped
coriander leaves
1 cup sour cream
30g (1oz) Atlantic Salmon Roe

METHOD

Wrap potatoes in aluminium foil, bury in hot barbecue coals and cook for 45-60 minutes, until tender. Remove membrane-like skin along the under side of each Lobster tail. Combine butter and coriander. Spread evenly on exposed Lobster meat. Place on barbecue grid and cook over hot coals for approximately 10 minutes, turning during cooking. Remove foil from potatoes, top with sour cream and Salmon Roe and serve with Lobsters.

Serves 6

Nature occupying an old boat at Kingston Jetty, Norfolk Island.

Char-Grilled Atlantic Salmon

INGREDIENTS

6 Atlantic Salmon cutlets
½ cup dry sherry
⅓ cup soy sauce
⅓ cup peanut oil
1 tablespoon sesame oil
1 teaspoon grated fresh ginger
2 tablespoons lemon juice
1 tablespoon brown sugar
salt and pepper to taste

METHOD

Wipe over Salmon and place in a shallow dish in a single layer. Mix remaining ingredients and pour over Salmon. Cover and refrigerate for 2 hours. Turn cutlets occasionally. To barbecue, drain Salmon and place marinade in a small pan at the side of the barbecue to boil gently. Barbecue Salmon over glowing coals, for 3-4 minutes each side, basting frequently with the simmering marinade. Serve the Salmon with a little of the reduced marinade on each cutlet.

Serves 6

Barbecued Stuffed Fish

INGREDIENTS

1.5kg (3lb) Snapper or other suitable fish
3 bacon slices, rind removed
freshly ground pepper

Stuffing

60g (2oz) butter or margarine
1 medium onion, finely chopped
½ cup chopped celery
2 tablespoons finely chopped parsley
grated rind and juice of ½ lemon
½ teaspoon salt
½ teaspoon dried thyme
1 cup soft white breadcrumbs

METHOD

Scale and clean fish, wash and dry thoroughly. Place stuffing in cavity of fish, close opening with fine skewers or toothpicks. Place on a large piece of greased, heavy-duty foil, place bacon slices over top and sprinkle with pepper. Wrap fish securely in foil and cook over medium hot coals for about 40-45 minutes or until flesh flakes easily with a fork. Turn occasionally while cooking. Serve with lemon wedges.
Stuffing: Melt butter and place in a bowl with remaining ingredients. Mix together thoroughly.

Herbed Barbecued Bream

INGREDIENTS

750g-1kg (1½-2lb) whole Bream
fresh fennel, dill or thyme sprigs

Sauce

125g (4oz) butter, melted
1 teaspoon salt
freshly ground pepper
1 teaspoon ground coriander seed
¼ teaspoon cardamom
2 tablespoons lemon juice
1 cup yoghurt

METHOD

Scale, clean and rinse fish, dry thoroughly. Brush fish inside and out with the sauce. Place on a greased barbecue grill.
Barbecue over medium coals for about 15-20 minutes or until fish is lightly brown on both sides and flakes easily with a fork. Turn frequently and baste occasionally with the sauce while cooking. Before removing fish from barbecue, place fresh herbs on coals, the smouldering herbs will flavour the fish. Heat any remaining sauce and serve with the fish.
Sauce: Combine all ingredients and mix together thoroughly.

Serves 6

Barbecued Fish with Watercress-Mustard Butter

INGREDIENTS

6 fish cutlets or 1kg (2lb) fish fillets
oil
lemon juice
salt and pepper to taste

Watercress–Mustard Butter

185g (6oz) butter
1 cup washed and chopped watercress (packed)
¼ cup mustard cress sprigs (packed)
2 tablespoons chopped parsley
2 shallots, roughly chopped
2 tablespoons Dijon or French mustard
1 tablespoon lemon juice
salt and freshly ground pepper

METHOD

Choose fish cutlets or steaks suitable for barbecuing. Brush with a mixture of equal parts oil and lemon juice with salt and pepper added. Barbecue over hot coals, turning once, and brushing often with oil mixture. Serve hot with a scoop of Watercress-Mustard Butter on each serving.
Watercress-Mustard Butter: Put butter in food processor with remaining ingredients and process until herbs are finely chopped and butter is softened. Turn into a butter crock, smooth top, cover and chill until firm. Serve with barbecued fish.

Serves 6

Garfish with Pineapple Marinade

INGREDIENTS

12 Garfish
2 cups pineapple juice
2 teaspoons grated fresh ginger
2 teaspoons lime or lemon juice
1 teaspoon ground coriander
¼ teaspoon cinnamon

METHOD

Scale and clean Garfish, trim fins and remove back bone if desired. Combine all other ingredients in a shallow dish, add Garfish and marinate in the refrigerator for at least 1 hour. Drain and barbecue over glowing coals 2-3 minutes each side, basting frequently with marinade.

Serves 6

Honeyed Prawns on Skewers

INGREDIENTS

1.5kg (3lb) green King Prawns
2 teaspoons finely chopped fresh ginger
2 garlic cloves, crushed
2 tablespoons honey
½ cup soy sauce
¼ cup lemon juice
2 tablespoons oil
freshly ground pepper

METHOD

Shell Prawns, leaving tail intact. Devein, rinse and drain well. Mix remaining ingredients in a plastic container, add Prawns and toss lightly. Seal and leave to marinate in refrigerator for 3-4 hours or overnight, shaking container occasionally to distribute marinade. When required to barbecue, thread Prawns onto 6 long, flat metal skewers. Pour remaining marinade into a small pan. Barbecue Prawns over glowing coals for about 3 minutes, turning skewers and basting with marinade. Serve hot with a rice salad and with any left-over marinade, heated thoroughly and served separately.

Serves 6

A thirsty kangaroo approaches a Kimberley Creek with caution.

Swordfish Steaks with Orange-Currant Butter

INGREDIENTS

6 x 250g (8oz) Swordfish, Sailfish or Tuna steaks
oil
salt and freshly ground pepper

METHOD

Wipe Swordfish with damp kitchen paper. Brush on both sides with oil and season with salt and pepper. Barbecue over glowing coals for 5-6 minutes on one side, turn and cook for further 2-3 minutes until flesh is just firm and turns white. Take care not to overcook. Fish can be brushed with oil during cooking. Serve immediately with a scoop of Orange-Currant Butter placed on each steak.

Orange–Currant Butter

185g (6oz) butter
1 garlic clove, crushed
2 tablespoons fresh rosemary leaves
grated rind of 1 orange
2 tablespoons orange juice
1 tablespoon cider vinegar
¼ cup currants, soaked in warm water for 10 minutes

Orange-Currant Butter: Put butter, garlic, rosemary leaves and orange rind in food processor and process until creamy. While processing, add orange juice and vinegar. Add currants and process briefly just to mix. Turn into a butter crock, smooth top, cover and chill until required. Excellent served on barbecued Barramundi, Ling and Snapper as well as Swordfish and Tuna.

Serves 6

Peppered Pineapple with Whisky Cream

(Photograph page 283)

INGREDIENTS

1 large ripe pineapple
2 tablespoons butter, melted
freshly ground pepper
glacé cherries
300ml (½ pint) thickened cream
1 tablespoon whisky

METHOD

Cut top from pineapple and remove skin. Cut pineapple into thick slices and cut out core. Brush each slice with melted butter and sprinkle with pepper on both sides. Place on barbecue and cook 2 minutes on each side. Remove to serving plate and place a cherry in the centre of each slice. Serve with whisky cream.
Whisky Cream: Whip the cream to soft peak stage, add the whisky and continue to beat until stiff.

Serves 6

Chocolate Fondue

INGREDIENTS

250g (8oz) dark chocolate
¾ cup cream
¼ teaspoon cinnamon
¼ teaspoon nutmeg

METHOD

Grate chocolate, place in a heavy based saucepan. Add cream and spices, blend well. Heat gently, stirring with a wooden spoon until smooth and blended. This can be done on the stove ahead of time, and

fresh fruit: peaches, apricots, strawberries, cherries, pawpaws, bananas
marshmallows

transferred to an earthenware fondue pot or a flameproof casserole dish.

Arrange your selection of fruits on a platter—whole, cubed or sliced into bite-size portions. Place marshmallows in a bowl.

Ten minutes before required for serving, place pot of fondue on cooler part of barbecue and heat gently, stirring occasionally with a wooden spoon. Take to table and place over a spirit burner; alternatively the pot can be replaced on the barbecue if necessary when fondue cools too much.

Desired fruit, etc., is speared onto fondue forks by diners, dipped into chocolate, then transferred to dessert fork. Provide dessert plates also.

Serves 6

CUSTARD APPLES IN PORT, Recipe page 295.

Custard Apples in Port

(Photograph pages 294 & 295)

INGREDIENTS

*3 ripe custard apples
6 tablespoons castor sugar
½ cup port
1 tablespoon lime juice
1½ teaspoons grated lime rind
whipped cream*

METHOD

Halve the custard apples and remove seeds from cut surfaces. Mix sugar, port, lime juice and rind. Place each custard apple half on a large square of greased foil, turn up edges and sprinkle generously with port mixture. Wrap securely. Cook on barbecue for 5 minutes or until heated through. Serve with cream. With Barbecued Bananas: Place whole bananas on the barbecue for 5 minutes on each side. Bananas should discolour and become soft. Serve with the custard apples—slit skin and fork out flesh.

Carrot Cake

INGREDIENTS

*2 cups castor sugar
1½ cups oil
4 eggs
2 cups plain flour
3 teaspoons baking powder
pinch of salt
2 teaspoons cinnamon
3 cups grated carrot
½ cup finely chopped pecan nuts*

Frosting

*250g (8oz) packaged cream cheese
4 tablespoons butter
500g (1lb) icing sugar
1 teaspoon vanilla essence*

METHOD

Grease and flour 2 x 23cm (9 inch) round cake tins, lining bases with greased greaseproof paper. Preheat oven to 160ºC (325ºF).
In a small bowl, beat together sugar, oil and eggs. Sift flour, baking powder, salt and cinnamon into a large bowl. Stir in egg mixture, carrot and pecans. Mix well. Spread evenly in prepared cake tins and bake in heated oven for 40-45 minutes until cooked when tested. Turn out onto racks to cool.
To make frosting, beat together cream cheese and butter until light, gradually add icing sugar and vanilla, beating until smooth. Join cakes together with frosting, spread remainder on top and decorate with pecan nut halves.

Hot air balloons taking off for a beautiful day, viewed from Mt. Ainslie, Canberra, ACT.

Friendly Dolphins roll in the shallows.

Faster Fish

Microwave ovens are one of the great time savers of our modern age. An extremely useful tool in the kitchen, they are very easy to use and to keep clean, as well as being compact and relatively inexpensive to purchase and run. Why is it then, that so many people use them only for simple chores such as defrosting and warming up food?

It certainly is true that old habits die hard, and so perhaps it is that some newer habits, such as cooking with a microwave oven, are slower to be accepted. Whether you have been a regular user of a microwave or not, this chapter will no doubt help to broaden your microwaving horizons!

Seafood is well suited to the world of the microwave; cooking times are short, and overcooking, which can ruin the best seafood, is easily prevented if you follow the guidelines given in recipes. Best of all, it's fast! It doesn't matter that the kids were late out of school, that the check-out queue was dead slow, that the car ran out of petrol and the dog escaped! You still have time to prepare that special meal, as it literally only takes minutes!

Speed is the essence of the microwave, and as you will discover when you cook for yourself from this chapter, there is absolutely no sacrifice made to the quality or flavour of the food.

Flick through these pages and you will find some truly delightful recipes from a broad range of seafood; whole fish, fish fillets, crab, mussels, oysters, prawns and more. The recipes themselves cover entres, main meals and desserts — so you can microwave yourself an entire meal with no fuss!

Direct your gaze for a second across the page, and you will see the perfect example of a meal " la microwave". The entre is an old favourite, and Oysters Kilpatrick have never tasted so good! A taste of the tropics follows for the main meal, and this dish of Sea Bream Cutlets with Mango Sauce will melt in your mouth. To finish, we have a fantastic dessert of Fruit Pizza, another scrumptiously rapid delight!

You will have a lot of fun preparing these dishes and a whole lot more fun in eating them! Give yourself a break, fire off a quick meal or two and enjoy the time you've saved in the kitchen. The world of "faster fish" is at your fingertips!

A stark scene at Wilsons Promenade, Vic.

Top: SEA BREAM CUTLETS WITH MANGO SAUCE, Recipe page 307. *Left*: OYSTERS KILPATRICK, Recipe page 302.
Right: FRUIT PIZZA, Recipe page 308.

A sweeping sky is announcing another tropical night in Cairns, Qld.

Oysters Kilpatrick

(Photograph page 299)

INGREDIENTS

12 Oysters in shell
2 bacon slices, finely chopped
2 tablespoons Worcestershire sauce
pepper to taste

METHOD

Remove Oysters from their shells. Wash shells to remove grit and replace Oysters in shells, prick Oysters once with a fine skewer. Place bacon between sheets of absorbent paper on a glass or china plate. Cook on High power for 3 minutes. Drain on clean absorbent paper. Combine bacon and sauce, sprinkle over each Oyster, sprinkle with pepper.

Arrange Oysters around the outside edge of a large round glass or china microproof serving plate. Microwave on Medium High power for 2 minutes. Stand covered 1 minute then serve immediately.

Note: If double quantity is needed cook in lots of 12 at a time.

Serves 2 to 3

Fish Chowder

INGREDIENTS

1 large onion, finely chopped
1 large potato, peeled and diced
2 celery stalks, diced
1 tablespoon butter
2 cups water
2 chicken stock cubes
2 cups milk
250g (8oz) Cod fillets
250g (8oz) mushrooms, sliced
1 x 360g (12oz) can creamed sweet corn
1/8 teaspoon nutmeg
salt and pepper

METHOD

Place onion, potato, celery and butter in a 3L (12 cup) microproof casserole dish and microwave on High power for 6 minutes, stir twice during cooking. Add water, stock cubes and milk and microwave on High power for 6 minutes.

Remove skin and bones from fish fillets and cut into 1cm (1/2 inch) cubes. Add fish, mushrooms and sweet corn to the casserole dish and microwave on Medium High power for 8 minutes or until fish is tender. Season to taste with nutmeg, salt and pepper and serve immediately.

Serves 5 to 6

A Cardinal fish and two Sweetlips.

Prawn and Fetta Appetizer

INGREDIENTS

750g (1½lb) medium size Green Prawns
4 medium ripe tomatoes
1 medium onion, finely sliced
2 garlic cloves, crushed
½ teaspoon dried marjoram
salt and pepper
½ teaspoon sugar
1 teaspoon tomato paste
2 tablespoons olive oil
125g (4oz) fetta cheese, crumbled

METHOD

Shell Prawns and devein. Skin tomatoes, chop and place in a bowl. Stir in onion, garlic, seasonings, sugar, tomato paste and oil. Cover and microwave on High power for 4 minutes.

Place half of the tomato mixture on the base of 4 or 6 individual microproof dishes or plates. Place Prawns on dishes and cover with remaining tomato mixture. Sprinkle evenly with crumbled fetta cheese. Cover and microwave 2 individual dishes at a time on Medium power of 1½ minutes, just until Prawns turn pink. Stand 1 minute. Repeat with remaining dishes. Serve immediately with crusty bread.

Serves 4 to 6

Prawn and Pumpkin Soup

INGREDIENTS

500g (1lb) pumpkin
1 medium onion, finely chopped
3 cups chicken stock
¾ cup cream
125g (4oz) cooked, shelled School Prawns
¼ cup lemon juice
salt and pepper
chopped parsley

METHOD

Peel pumpkin, cut into small pieces. Put pumpkin and onion in a freezer bag, place on a plate and microwave on High power for 7 minutes until soft. Stand 2 minutes then purée in a food processor or blender.

Place purée and chicken stock in an 8-cup casserole and microwave on High power until boiling, about 7 minutes. Finely chop the Prawns and mix with lemon juice. Stir into the hot soup with the cream. Reheat if necessary on Medium power for 5 minutes. Season to taste with salt and pepper, sprinkle with parsley and serve.

Avocado Trout

INGREDIENTS

4 small Trout, about 800g (1lb 10oz) in all
salt and pepper
lemon juice
1 ripe avocado
1 teaspoon lemon juice, extra
½ cup sour cream
¼ teaspoon Tabasco

METHOD

Prepare fish, pierce eyes, sprinkle cavity with salt, pepper and lemon juice. Place on a shallow microproof plate. Shield head and tail with foil. Cover fish with paper towel and Microwave on High power for 7-8 minutes or until flesh flakes. Turn after 3½ minutes and remove foil shields. Stand covered for 4 minutes. Mash avocado, add lemon juice, sour cream, Tabasco sauce and season to taste. Remove skin from fish, mask fish with avocado cream and serve.

Serves 4

GREEN LIP MUSSELS FLORENTINE, Recipe page 303.

Green Lip Mussels Florentine

(Photograph page 303)

INGREDIENTS

24 Green Lip Mussels in the shell
1 bunch English spinach, washed, shredded
2 shallots, finely sliced
2 garlic cloves, crushed
60g (2oz) butter
1 cup soft white breadcrumbs
¼ cup grated Parmesan cheese
salt and pepper

METHOD

Scrub and remove beards from Mussels. Open by forcing the sharp edge of a knife through the curved edge of the shell.

Place prepared spinach, shallots and garlic in a microproof bowl, cover and microwave on High power for 3 minutes. Allow to stand for 3 minutes then drain off excess liquid. Add butter, breadcrumbs, Parmesan cheese, salt and pepper.

Pack the spinach mixture into the opened Mussels and tie securely with string if desired. Place Mussel packages on a microwave platter and microwave on High power for 3 minutes. Allow to stand for 3 minutes then serve.

Note: The Mussels spring open as the string is cut. If not tied with string, Mussels remain open during cooking.

Serves 4

Mussels with Garlic Butter Sauce

INGREDIENTS

24 Mussels in shells
2 tablespoons finely chopped onion
1 garlic clove, crushed
2 tablespoons dry white wine
salt and pepper
125g (4oz) butter, chilled and cut into 8 cubes

METHOD

Scrub Mussels well and remove beards. Arrange half in a wide circle on a large plate with hinge side towards the outside. Microwave on High power for approximately 7 minutes. After 5 minutes open door every 30 seconds and remove each Mussel as it opens. Repeat with remaining mussels. Break off top shell and discard. Arrange Mussels on a serving platter and cover with foil. Set aside.

In a large 4-cup microproof jug or bowl place onion, garlic, wine, salt and pepper. Microwave on High power for 3 minutes. Quickly whisk in a cube of butter and microwave for 30 seconds. Repeat until all butter has been added. Spoon butter sauce over each Mussel and serve immediately.

Left: FLOUNDER WITH HOLLANDAISE SAUCE, Recipe page 307. *Right*: CRAB & CORN OMELETTE, Recipe page 306.

HONEYED TROUT & ALMONDS, Recipe page 306.

Honeyed Trout and Almonds

(Photograph page 306)

INGREDIENTS

2 x 375g (12oz) Rainbow Trout
salt and pepper
60g (2oz) butter
1 tablespoon lemon juice
2 tablespoons honey
¼ cup flaked blanched
almonds

METHOD

Pierce or remove eyes of Trout, sprinkle cavity with salt and pepper and place in a well buttered, shallow microproof dish. Spread remaining butter on top of Trout, pour over lemon juice and honey, cover loosely with greaseproof paper and microwave on Medium high power for 3 ½ minutes.

Remove from oven, turn Trout over, baste with butter and honey mixture, sprinkle with flaked almonds, cover with paper and microwave on Medium High power for a further 3 ½ minutes. Allow to stand for 4 minutes before serving.

Serves 2

Crab and Corn Omelette

(Photograph pages 304 & 305)

INGREDIENTS

6 eggs
salt and pepper to taste
6 tablespoons water
250g (8oz) Crab meat
6 ears canned baby corn
90g (3oz) cheddar cheese,
grated

METHOD

Make omelettes, one at a time by beating 3 eggs with salt, pepper and 3 tablespoons water. Pour mixture into a lightly buttered 23cm (9 inch) microproof pie plate and microwave on Medium power for 4-5 minutes. When egg sets around edge of dish, push into centre to allow uncooked egg to flow over dish. Continue to microwave until top is almost set. Spread half of the Crab meat, corn and cheese over half of the omelette, fold over and serve immediately.
Note: Omelettes can be browned briefly under a hot grill. Also creamed corn or corn kernels may be used in place of baby corn.

Serves 2

Flounder with Hollandaise Sauce

(Photograph pages 304 & 305)

INGREDIENTS

2 x 500g (1lb) whole Flounder, cleaned
30g (1oz) butter
2 tablespoons lemon juice

Sauce

90g (3oz) butter
4 tablespoons lemon juice
4 egg yolks, beaten

METHOD

Remove or pierce eyes of Flounder. Microwave Flounder, one at a time. Place each Flounder on a lightly buttered microproof platter, sprinkle with lemon juice, and shield tail section with foil. Cover with plastic wrap and microwave on Medium High power for 5 minutes, until flesh flakes on testing. Cover fish and keep warm. Make sauce by placing butter in a bowl. Microwave on Medium High power for 45 seconds or until melted and hot. Whisk in lemon juice and egg yolks and continue to microwave on Medium High power for 1 minute, whisking at 15 second intervals, until thick and smooth. Whisk for a few seconds after sauce has been removed, then serve.

Serves 2

Sea Bream Cutlets with Mango Sauce

(Photograph page 299)

INGREDIENTS

4 Sea Bream cutlets, about 750g (1½lb) in all
lime or lemon juice
freshly ground pepper
1 fresh mango
¼ cup water
2 teaspoons brown sugar
1 tablespoon malt vinegar
2 teaspoons cornflour, blended with a little water
2 teaspoons lime or lemon zest

METHOD

Arrange fish around the outside edge of a large shallow microproof dish or dinner plate. Sprinkle with lime or lemon juice and pepper, cover with plastic wrap leaving a vent at the side. Microwave on Medium High power for 7 minutes, turning once during cooking. Stand covered while sauce is being made.
Peel mango and cut into slices. Place half of the mango slices in a blender with water, sugar and vinegar and blend to a puré. Pour purée into a bowl, stir in blended cornflour and lime zest. Microwave on Medium power for 2 minutes, stirring after 1 minute until sauce boils and thickens.
Pour sauce over fish cutlets and garnish with remaining mango slices. Serve immediately with vegetable accompaniments.

Serves 4

Sweet and Sour Fish

INGREDIENTS

1 x 1kg whole Bream or Snapper
½ lemon
salt and pepper

Sauce

1 x 225g (7oz) can pineapple pieces
½ cup brown vinegar
1 tablespoon brown sugar
1 tablespoon tomato sauce
1 teaspoon soy sauce
¼ teaspoon ground ginger
1 small onion, sliced lengthways
½ each green and red pepper, chopped
2 teaspoons cornflour
2 tablespoons water

METHOD

Clean fish, wipe over with damp paper towels, remove or pierce the eyes. Rub the fish inside and out with the cut lemon, squeezing juice as you rub. Sprinkle inside with salt and pepper. Place on a shallow microproof platter or large plate, cover with a paper towel and microwave on Medium power for 10-12 minutes. Cover with foil and stand while making sauce. Combine all sauce ingredients, except the cornflour, in a bowl and microwave on High power for 2 minutes. Blend cornflour with water, stir into sauce and cook 1 ½ minutes more; stir during cooking. Pour sauce over fish and serve immediately with boiled rice.

Serves 2

Crumbed Fish Fillets

INGREDIENTS

500g (1lb) Bream or Flathead fillets
½ cup cornflake crumbs
2 tablespoons grated Parmesan cheese
1 tablespoon chopped parsley
¼ teaspoon finely chopped garlic
salt and pepper
1 egg white, lightly beaten
Tartare Sauce or lemon slices for serving

METHOD

Skin fillets, wipe over with damp paper towels.
On a flat plate combine cornflake crumbs, cheese, parsley, garlic and seasoning. Dip fish fillets in the egg white, then into the crumbs, press crumbs on firmly to coat well. Arrange fillets in a shallow microproof dish, thickest part to the outside. Cover with paper towels and microwave on High power for 3 minutes. Stand, covered for 1 minute then serve with Tartare Sauce and/or lemon wedges.

Serves 4

Sole Fillets in Mushroom Cream

INGREDIENTS

4 Sole fillets
4 shallots, finely chopped
185g (6oz) mushrooms, finely chopped
2 teaspoons butter
¼ cup dry sherry
½ teaspoon dried rosemary
salt, pepper
1 tablespoon lemon juice
2 teaspoons cornflour
½ cup cream
2 tablespoons toasted flaked almonds

METHOD

Arrange fish fillets in a shallow microproof casserole dish with thickest part to the outside. Place shallots, mushrooms, butter, sherry, seasonings, and lemon juice in a glass bowl, stir to mix then microwave on High power for 3 minutes. Sprinkle in the cornflour and stir well to blend then stir in the cream. Pour sauce over the fish fillets and microwave on Medium power for 7 minutes. Stand covered for 3 minutes. Sprinkle with toasted flaked almonds and serve immediately with vegetable accompaniments.

Fruit Pizza

(Photograph page 299)

INGREDIENTS

125g (4oz) butter
2 tablespoons icing sugar
2 teaspoons brandy
¼ teaspoon baking powder
1¾ cups plain flour, sifted
250g Neufchatel or cream cheese
2 tablespoons sugar
¼ teaspoon almond or rum essence
assorted fresh fruits (strawberries, kiwi fruit, peach slices, melon, mandarin segments)

METHOD

Beat butter with an electric mixer until white and fluffy. Add icing sugar and continue beating. Dissolve baking powder in the brandy and add to the butter. Turn mixer to low speed and add half the flour. Stop mixer and remove beaters, then add remaining flour gradually while kneading with one hand. Knead until mixture all comes together into a stiff dough.

Line a 23cm (9 inch) glass pizza plate with non-stick baking paper, cut to fit. Shape dough into a ball, flatten with palm of hand and place on pizza plate, continue to press out with fingers to cover the plate. Pinch a border around the edge and prick evenly all over with a fork. Microwave on High power for 3 minutes. Shield outer edge with a foil shield (see Note), and cook for 1 minute more. Allow to cool then slide paper out from under pizza base.

Place cheese in a small heatproof bowl and soften if necessary on Medium Low power for 1 minute. Beat in sugar and essence until smooth. Spread over pizza base and refrigerate until cold. Just before serving arrange fruit attractively over cheese.

Note: To make shield, cut a circle of foil the same diameter as the pizza plate, then cut a 12cm (5 inch) circle from the centre to form a doughnut shape.

LIQUEUR CREAM CHEESE SLICE, Recipe page 309.

Liqueur Cream Cheese Slice

(Photograph pages 308 & 309)

INGREDIENTS

Base

250g (8oz) plain sweet biscuits
60g (2oz) walnut pieces
125g (4oz) butter or margarine, melted

Filling

500g (1lb) cream cheese
1 cup castor sugar
2 eggs separated
¼ cup kirsch or brandy
1 cup sultanas
½ teaspoon cinnamon

Topping

300ml (½ pint) sour cream
1 tablespoon brown sugar

METHOD

Base:
In a food processor or blender put biscuits and walnut pieces, mix till fine crumbs are formed. Add melted butter and press mixture into a 20cm (8 inch) microproof square dish.
Filling:
Put cream cheese in a large microproof bowl. Soften for 2 minutes on Medium power. Remove from microwave, add sugar and beat until light. Add egg yolks, kirsch, sultanas and cinnamon, mix well. Beat egg whites till stiff and fold into cream mixture. Spoon onto base, spread evenly and cook 8 minutes on Medium power. Shield edges with foil and microwave a further 4 minutes. Stand 4 minutes.
Topping:
Combine topping ingredients, spread on hot slice, sprinkle with cinnamon. Cook a further 3 minutes on High power. Leave till cool to cut.

Chocolate Walnut Cake

INGREDIENTS

175g (6oz) butter
¾ cup sugar
3 eggs
1½ cups self-raising flour
2½ tablespoons cocoa powder
½ cup chopped walnuts
¾ cup milk

Chocolate Frosting

200g (7oz) dark chocolate
¾ cup sour cream
½ cup icing sugar

METHOD

Cream butter and sugar well together. Add eggs one at a time, beat well after each addition. Sift flour and cocoa together, fold into mixture alternately with milk and nuts. Pour into a greased microproof ring mould. Cook on High power for 8 ½ minutes. Stand 10 minutes before turning out. Cool completely.
Chocolate Frosting:
Break chocolate into small pieces, place in a bowl and microwave on Medium power for 2 or 3 minutes until melted, stir each minute. Stir in the sour cream and icing sugar, beat as it cools to a fluffy consistency. Spread over cake.

A fisherman's antics at Batemans Bay, NSW.

Strict regulations are in force on the size of Crayfish that may be taken.

Seafood Preparation Guide

*T*he preparation of seafood is an important task — it can make or break your meal. How to shuck an oyster; how to cut a lobster; how to fillet a fish; all of this information and much more follows in this vital guide.

Are you prepared?

Recommended Equipment

CHEF'S KNIFE

A heavy-bladed knife with a sharp point, straight-edged with a slight curve at the tip, and about 4cm (1 1/2 inches) wide at the handle. Length of blade and width at handle can vary. Use for heavy jobs such as cutting off fish heads, halving Lobsters and slicing fish through the backbone into cutlets. It is also good for skinning fillets.

BONING KNIFE

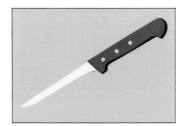

A thin-bladed knife with a sharp point, with the blade curved and widening where it joins the handle. Use for gutting, removing gills, separating flesh from skeleton when boning whole fish and removing rib bones from cavity.

FILLETING KNIFE

A thin-bladed knife with a sharp point; the blade is about 20cm (8 inches) long, slightly curved at the tip, and only 2cm (3/4 inch) wide at the handle. Use for filleting fish and for skinning fillets.

FISH SCALER

A flat metal hoop fastened onto a handle, with one side of the hoop serrated. The dull side of a knife can also be used to scale fish.

PARING KNIFE

A small version of a chef's knife with a light blade. Use for boning small fish, deveining Prawns, removing soft shells from small crustaceans such as Balmain Bugs.

KITCHEN SCISSORS

For cutting off fish fins, snipping backbones in small and medium-sized fish and snipping soft shell of Lobster and Crayfish tails.

OYSTER KNIFE

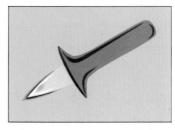

A short knife with a rigid blade, pointed at the tip and set in a short, rounded handle easily enclosed in the hand. Only the tip is sharp.

Fish

Gutting and Cleaning

Slit the belly to expose gut and ease out the contents with a knife. Remove gills. Rinse well, removing any dark matter with salt and a brush.

Scaling

Wet fish; soak in cold water if fish is dry, so that scales can be removed easily. Hold fish firmly by the tail and run fish scaler or the blunt edge of a knife at a right angle towards the head. To prevent fish scales flying around, scale the fish in a sink of cold water. Do not scale if skinless fillets are required. Scales from small fish such as Anchovies and Sardines can be rubbed off with fingers under running water.

Trimming

If desired, head and fins can be removed. To remove head, cut behind gills through backbone and cut out pectoral fins and underlying bone. Snip off dorsal fins close to body.

Cutlet Preparation

For large round fish (Kingfish, Jewfish, Mackerel, Salmon etc.).

Gut, scale, remove fins and cut off head. Use a sharp, heavy chef's knife and cut in 2cm (3/4 inch) slices through the backbone. It may be necessary to tap the back of the knife blade with a mallet to get through the backbone. A saw may be necessary for very large fish.

Filleting

ROUND FISH
Hold fish firmly on board and cut into back along dorsal fin from head to tail. Cut just below the pectoral fin across the body to the backbone and slide the knife along the backbone and ribs to the tail. Remove fillet, turn fish over and repeat on other side.

FLATFISH
(Such as Sole and Flounder).

Cut along the centre (spine) of the fish from head to tail to the backbone. Carefully cut away flesh, keeping knife close to the rib bones and remove first fillet. Repeat on other side of spine, turn fish over and remove another two fillets in the same way.

Skinning Fillets

Beginning at the tail end of the fillet, cut a little of the flesh to the skin. Hold the tail skin firmly with salt-coated fingers, run the knife between the skin and the flesh, keeping the knife flat against the skin.

Skinning Whole Flatfish and Leatherjacket

Nick skin at tail end and with salt-coated fingers, hold tail firmly with one hand and pull skin towards head with other hand. When top of head is reached, leave skin attached, turn fish over and pull from head to tail on other side. However, it is better to retain skin on one side if fish is to be grilled whole; grill skin side first, then skinless side which is uppermost when served.

For Leatherjacket, cut off head and pull off skin from head to tail on both sides.

Boning Whole Fish

Bream, Snapper, Sole, Flounder, etc

Scale and clean fish, remove all fins, removing bone attached to pectoral fins. Rinse and dry with paper towels. Extend body slit to tail. With a boning knife, cut through membrane covering rib bones in cavity, ease out rib bones and break them off from the backbone. Run knife along top of backbone, gently easing flesh from the bones; take care not to cut through the skin on the dorsal fin side. Repeat on other side of backbone. Cut backbone as close to the head as possible with kitchen scissors, lift away, snipping it free from the flesh. Snip off backbone at tail.

Removing Backbone from Small Fish

Anchovies, Garfish, Pilchards, Sardines

Scale the fish, gut, leave head on, rinse well and drain. Cut from body cavity to tail. Pinch or snip backbone away from tail, pull toward head and snip it off. Garfish should have the flesh eased away from backbone with the blunt edge of a knife.

Crustaceans

Balmain or Moreton Bay Bug Preparation

See page 315 re dispatching live crab, lobster and crayfish painlessly.

Green (uncooked) or cooked

Break tail carefully away from body. With scissors, snip down centre of soft shell on underside, pull apart and gently ease out soft tail meat. Discard head and shells.

Crab Preparation

Green (uncooked)

To prepare green Crab pieces for Asian-type dishes, drown first in freshwater. Scrub well to clean thoroughly. Chop in half with a cleaver or heavy knife, pull out grey fibrous gills and stomach bag and discard. Rinse and chop each half into 2-3 pieces, leaving legs attached. Remove large claws and crack with a mallet or the side of a cleaver. Crack legs lightly. Crab is now ready for stir-frying.

Cooked Crab

Hold Crab firmly and slide the point of a heavy knife under the top of the shell at the back and lever it off. Pull out white fibrous gills from bottom section and discard. Rinse top shell if to be used for serving Crab. Rinse bottom section and twist off legs and claws. Remove meat from between body partitions using a small knife. Put meat in a bowl. Crack legs and claws and remove meat.

Lobster and Crayfish Preparation

Green (uncooked) or cooked

Place on board with back down. Beginning at the chest, insert point of knife and cut down through the centre of the tail. Turn around and cut in opposite direction through head. Separate the two halves.

Discard white gills in head section, remove and discard intestine running down centre of tail. The creamy green liver (tomalley) and the coral if present, can be removed and used in a Lobster sauce; must be heated well if taken from green (uncooked) Crustaceans. Rinse halves.

Lift out tail meat, slice and return to shell or use according to recipe. Twist off legs, crack shells and remove meat if not to be left on for serving.

Prawn Preparation

Green (uncooked) or cooked

Remove head and peel off shell and legs, leaving on tail shell if desired. Using a small, sharp knife, make a shallow incision along back of prawn to the tail, open out and pull out dark vein. Rinse and drain well.

To Butterfly Prawns

Cut along curve of back where vein was removed, taking care not to cut right through. Gently press flat with hands.

A sensational Prawn catch offloading from the 'Sensation'.

Feeding the Trout on a Trout farm, near Tumut, Snowy Mountains, NSW.

Molluscs

Abalone Preparation

With a barbecue scraper or similar tool, force blade tip in a thin part of shell underneath flesh, moving blade until muscle is freed from shell. Lift out flesh, remove intestine and wash flesh well. Slice off dark heel (sucker pad) or rub it off on a rough rock. Slice the flesh horizontally in two, wrap slices in muslin and pound well with the side of a meat mallet or cleaver until limp and velvety. Slices can be cut in thin strips or chopped, depending on cooking method.

Bearding Mussels

Using a stiff brush, scrub mussels well under running water, scraping shell with a knife to remove any marine growth. Tug beard toward pointed end to remove. Use whole as directed in recipe.

Opening Mussels

Put the cleaned Mussels in a bowl of warm, salted water. As they begin to open, insert point of knife between the two shells and slide it toward pointed end to sever the closing mechanism. Mussels can also be opened by heating briefly in microwave oven. Remove top shell if serving in the half shell, or leave in place if stuffing; remove Mussel entirely if only the meat is required.

Opening (Shucking) Oysters

Scrub the Oysters under running water to clean shells. Place Oyster, flat side up, on a board and press onto end opposite hinge using a cloth to protect hand. Insert tip of oyster knife next to hinge, push firmly against hinge and pry the shells apart, sliding the knife against the inside of the top shell to sever the muscle holding the shell together. Discard top shell, rinse Oyster in bottom shell lightly in a bowl of cold water to remove shell fragments and grit. With Oyster knife, loosen Oyster from bottom shell and turn it over for good presentation.

Opening Scallops

Place Scallop on board with flat shell up, insert the point of a strong paring knife between the shells, and run it across the underside of the top shell to sever the internal muscle. Pull shells apart. Slide knife under Scallop to free it. Lift out Scallop and pull off skirt and gut, leaving white Scallop flesh with coral attached. Remove any dark membrane adhering to Scallop flesh. Rinse well and drain. Wash and dry bottom shell to use as a receptacle for cooking and serving Scallops.

Clam, Cockle and Pipi Preparation

Place live Clams, Cockles or Pipis in a bucket of cold, salted water for 30-60 minutes so that sand and debris can be expelled by the shellfish. Lift out and use immediately when cooking in the shell is required.

If only the flesh is required, open the shellfish as for Mussels, rinse and remove flesh. Drain well and pack for freezer storage or use immediately for cooking.

Cephalopods

Cuttlefish Preparation

Cut the body cavity on the soft side, open out, remove and discard cuttlebone and gut. If ink sac is intact, it can be removed carefully and the ink extracted over a bowl to add to the dish being prepared. Cut off tentacles from head, just below eyes, remove beak, discard head.

Pull off skin from body and rinse well. Cut body in squares or strips. Squares can be 'honeycombed' by scoring in diamonds; these curl up during cooking. Rub skin off tentacles with a cloth dipped in salt. Rinse well and drain.

Octopus Preparation

Octopus is usually tenderised when purchased; if freshly caught, tenderise by holding by one tentacle and beat it thoroughly on a rock, about 40 strokes should be enough, gripping a different tentacle each few strokes. This has a better tenderising effect than beating with a mallet.

Cut off head/body section just below the eyes to remove tentacles. Cut out eyes and clean body cavity. Push beak up through centre of joined tentacles and cut off. Cut Octopus into pieces or leave both sections intact. Wash thoroughly, paying particular attention to tentacles as the suckers can contain sand.

To clean small, whole Octopus, cut up back of head/body and remove gut. Push up beak and cut out, cut out eyes, wash thoroughly.

Skin is difficult to remove from fresh Octopus. Skin can be left on for cooking; to remove, parboil for 5-10 minutes in a little water, then skin when cool enough to handle and proceed with recipe.

Squid Preparation

Pull off head and attached tentacles, the gut should also come away from the body (hood). Discard gut. Pull out quill-shaped bone from the hood cavity. Cut off section of head containing eyes and beak, discard. You will be left with tentacles joined together with a section of the head and the hood. Pull off fine purple skin to expose the white body. Skin may be rubbed off the tentacles if desired — use a cloth dipped in salt. Rinse well and drain.

Leave hood intact with flaps attached for stuffing; gently pull off flaps if slicing hood into rings; or slice hood and flaps into strips according to recipes. Chop tentacles or leave intact as required; intact tentacles from small Squid make a good garnish as they curl up into rosettes during cooking.

Other Seafood

Sea Urchin Preparation

Place the shell, with opening up, on a board. Press a knife blade across the top as if to cut the shell in four, and the shell will split in sections. Gently pull out the dark matter and discard. Using a long-handled teaspoon, loosen the 4 gonads or "tongues" from the base and remove gently. Do not touch with fingers as they will rupture, spoiling the flavour, texture and keeping qualities.

Place in a shallow dish and carefully remove any bits of shell. If not to be served immediately, stretch plastic wrap across the top of the dish, making sure it does not touch the roes, and store in the refrigerator for up to 2 days. Serve with a squeeze of lemon juice on buttered bread, or use as a sushi garnish.

Smoked Fish

Smoke-curing of fish, in conjunction with salting, is one of the earliest forms of food preservation. Today, because of the added benefit of refrigeration, less salt is generally used. Smoke-curing is a means of adding a distinctive and pleasant flavour as well as enhancing the keeping qualities. There are two methods of smoke-curing.

Cold-Smoked Fish

The fish is filleted or butterflied with backbone removed, soaked in brine and artificially coloured before smoking. Salmon and Sea Trout are dry-salted with additives such as sugar, pepper and herbs according to the curer's particular recipe. Smoke temperature is below 29C (85F), with the smoke source usually outside the smokehouse so that the smoke can cool before reaching the fish.

Store in refrigerator, wrapped well in clean white paper, and use within 10 days. An excellent alternative for smoked Salmon and Trout is to wrap in waxed or greaseproof paper then overwrap with foil to prevent drying. Avoid plastic wrap as the fish could sweat and spoil.

To Cook: Rinse fish and poach in milk, water or a mixture of both. Steam, grill or bake uncovered in a dish of water. Cook until flesh flakes and serve with a white sauce or melted butter, or flake and use in recipes. Smoked Salmon and Trout are sliced thinly and eaten raw with a squeeze of lemon juice, or use in recipes. Soak Kippers in water for 5 minutes, drain and dry then grill, basting with butter.

Hot-Smoked Fish

The fish is gutted and scaled, left whole or butterflied with backbone removed. It is lightly brined, then hot-smoked and cooked at temperatures between 80 and 90C (175 and 195F).

Wrap well in white paper and store in refrigerator for up to 2 weeks; if vacuum-packed when purchased, storage life in the refrigerator is considerably longer while package is intact. Be guided by "use by" date.

To Cook: Remove skin and bones and serve sliced for appetizers,

purée flesh and use in pates. Freshwater Trout can be heated whole in the oven. Place on a rack in a dish, with water added, cover dish with foil. Remove skin from each side and serve whole with a creamy sauce.

See page 119 for types of Cold and Hot Smoked Fish.

Fish Roes

Soft Roes

To store, place gently in a shallow bowl and cover with a clean, wet cloth; store in refrigerator for up to 2 days.

To Cook: Poach gently in salted water until just firm, drain, coat in seasoned flour and fry in butter until lightly browned. Can also be fried, with a flour coating, without the initial poaching. Serve with a squeeze of lemon juice.

Hard Roes

Mullet roe, removed from its membrane, is salted heavily to preserve it and is known as Tarama. It is used to make Taramosalata, a popular Greek dip. To store Smoked Fish Roe, wrap in waxed or greaseproof paper and overwrap with foil; put Tarama in a jar and seal. Store both in the refrigerator; they keep for some weeks.

To Serve: The Smoked Fish Roe is sliced thinly with membrane removed, and served on bread and butter with a squeeze of lemon juice. Tarama is puréed with soaked and squeezed white bread, a little onion, lemon juice and olive oil to make Taramosalata. Fresh Mullet hard roes are unsuitable for cooking.

Basic Cooking

Boiling Live Lobster, Crab, Bugs, Freshwater Crayfish and Marron

To dispatch Lobster and Crab painlessly, drown in freshwater or place in freezer long enough to stun it, but not long enough to freeze the flesh — about 30 minutes for each 500g (1 pound) body weight is sufficient. Freshwater Crayfish, Bugs and Marron will have to be placed in freezer. If plunged live into boiling water the flesh would toughen and the legs may fall off. Mud Crabs may need to be scrubbed before cooking.

Weigh Crustacean to calculate cooking time. Place in a large pan of cold salted water and bring quickly to simmering point. Add a tablespoon of brown sugar for extra flavour if desired. Simmer, do not boil, for 8 minutes per 500g (1 pound) weight; cook bugs until they turn red. Remove from pan when cooked. Serve hot, or cook rapidly in very cold water and refrigerate if serving cold.

Boiling Prawns

Place green (uncooked) Prawns in a

large pan of boiling salted water with a tablespoon of sugar or honey. Simmer until pink-red, about 3-5 minutes, taking care not to overcook. Drain immediately and place in cold water to cool. Drain, mix in a container with crushed ice and refrigerate until required.

Boiling Live Yabbies

To decrease or eliminate muddy taste, live Yabbies should be left in a large bucket of freshwater for several hours before cooking. Drain and place Yabbies in a plastic bag and freeze them long enough to stun them. Tip into a pan of boiling salted water and simmer for 5-10 minutes until they turn red. Remove with a slotted spoon and use hot or cool in cold water, chill until required. To ensure there is no muddy flavour, a few dillseeds, or the flower tops of fresh dill, may be added to cooking water.

Fried Parsley Garnish

Choose sound, compact parsley sprigs and allow 2-3 sprigs per serve. Wash, shake off excess moisture, gently pat dry with paper towels and wrap in a tea-towel. Place in refrigerator for an hour or so to dry and crisp the parsley.

After seafood is fried, plunge sprigs, a few at a time in hot oil and fry for about 3-5 seconds until crisp. Remove immediately and drain on crumpled kitchen paper. To handle sprigs quickly during frying, place in a frying basket or an all-metal sieve.

Fish Stock

INGREDIENTS

1kg (2lb) fish heads and bones
9 cups water
juice of 1 lemon
2 onions, sliced
1 bay leaf
4 sprigs parsley
1 sprig thyme
leafy top from 1 celery stalk
1 teaspoon salt

METHOD

Rinse the fish heads and bones and place in a large pan with remaining ingredients. Bring slowly to a simmer, skimming as required. Simmer, uncovered, for 20 minutes. Strain through a sieve placed over a large bowl, cool stock and skim. Use as required in recipes. Stock may be stored, covered, in refrigerator for up to 1 week, or store in freezer in 2-cup quantities.

Makes about 8 cups

Court Bouillon

INGREDIENTS

4 cups water
1 onion, sliced
1 carrot, sliced
1 celery stalk, chopped
1 lemon, sliced
4 parsley stems
1 sprig thyme
2 bay leaves
1 teaspoon salt
6 whole peppercorns tied in muslin
1 cup white wine

METHOD

Place all ingredients except peppercorns and wine in a large pan (not aluminium). Bring to the boil and simmer for 25 minutes, add peppercorns and wine and simmer for further 10 minutes. Remove peppercorns and bay leaves and use court bouillon as it is for poaching fish. Any liquid not used in a sauce for the poached fish, should be strained and used as a fish stock for soups and sauces.

White Sauce

INGREDIENTS

2 tablespoons butter
2 tablespoons flour
1 cup milk
salt and pepper (optional)

METHOD

Using medium heat, melt butter in a heavy-based saucepan, stir in flour and cook gently for 1-2 minutes until bubbling — do not allow roux to colour. Remove from heat and gradually stir in milk, stirring constantly. Return to medium heat and stir until thickened and bubbling. Let sauce boil gently on low heat for 1 minute. Add salt and pepper to taste if desired.

This makes a fairly thick white sauce; for a thicker sauce increase flour to 2½ tablespoons, leave other quantities as they are. For a thinner sauce to mask foods, add a little more milk during last stage of cooking. Use as required in recipes, doubling quantities if necessary.

Makes about 1¼ cups.

Shortcrust Pastry

INGREDIENTS

250g (8oz or 2 cups) plain flour
pinch salt
125g (4oz) firm butter or cooking margarine
3-4 tablespoons cold water

METHOD

Sift flour and salt into a mixing bowl. Cut butter into small pieces, add to flour and rub in with fingertips until mixture resembles fine breadcrumbs. Add cold water and mix with a round-bladed knife until a dough is formed, adding extra water if necessary. Alternatively, place flour, salt and cut-up butter in bowl of food processor, process to fine-crumb consistency, add water through feed tube until dough gathers onto blades. Turn dough out onto a lightly floured board and knead lightly until smooth. Wrap in plastic film and chill for at least 30 minutes before using as directed in recipes.

Sweet Shortcrust Pastry: As above, with the addition of 1 tablespoon castor sugar, 1 egg yolk and 1 teaspoon lemon juice. Reduce water to about 2 tablespoons. Finish as above and use for pastry flans for dessert dishes as directed in recipes.

Refer to glossary for blind baking.

A Shark catch ready for storage.

Seafood Storage Guide

Whether it be your own catch or what you have purchased, good seafood depends on good handling and good storage. We recommend you read this section carefully!

Good storage depends on proper handling from the time the seafood is obtained, either what you have caught yourself, or what you have purchased. Have a portable insulated container with ice or frozen ice bricks on hand for storing your "catch" for the trip home. The heat in a car, even for 30 minutes, would be sufficient to begin the process of spoilage. Lots of newspaper, wrapped around the seafood, is a good short-term insulator.

Live crustaceans and shellfish should be placed in a damp Hessian bag, or in a sealed bucket of freshwater or seawater. More details are given under individual species.

Fish

Whole Fish

Scale, gut, remove gills, rinse well and dry with paper towels before storage. Only very fresh fish should be stored.

Chilled Storage

Place on a plate and cover completely with plastic wrap, securing wrap underneath plate, or store in a sealed container. Store in refrigerator for up to 3 days.

Freezer Storage

Scales should be left on for added protection in freezer storage, but can be removed before storage to save time when fish is required for cooking. Sharp dorsal fins should be removed so that wrap is not punctured. Wrap fish closely in plastic film, place in freezer bag and extract air from bag using a freezer pump, or by pressing bag closely around fish and sealing quickly. Seal securely with freezer tape, label with date and fish type, and place flat in freezer until solid. Store oily fish for no more than 3 months; non-oily fish for up to 6 months.

Fish Fillets, Cutlets and Steaks

Fish must be very fresh. Wipe dry with paper towels.

Chilled Storage

Place prepared fish on a plate and cover with plastic wrap, securing wrap underneath plate. Store in refrigerator for up to 3 days.

Freezer Storage

Wrap each fillet, cutlet or steak individually in plastic wrap and place a number of the wrapped portions in a freezer bag. Extract air as for Whole Fish (above) and store as above, keeping package flat until fish is solid.

Crustaceans

Lobsters, Crabs, Bugs, Crayfish, Marron and Yabbies

Cooked crustaceans can be stored in refrigerator or freezer. Green (uncooked) crustaceans should be live when you take delivery of them; if dead (and uncooked), their flesh deteriorates very quickly. Keep in a damp Hessian bag in a cool place for up to 2 days, as this allows more oxygen than storing in a bucket of water. For basic cooking details, see page 315.

Chilled Storage

Cooked crustaceans should be rinsed of any mud or debris. Shake off excess moisture and store in a sealed container in the refrigerator for up to 3 days. Uncooked crustaceans should not be stored in the refrigerator, with the exception of Prawns (see separate details).

Freezer Storage

If live, freeze for 2-4 hours until dead, remove, scrub if necessary and dry well. Live saltwater crustaceans can be drowned in freshwater as an alternative. When dead, either place in a freezer container or wrap in heavy-gauge plastic and place in freezer bag. Sharp shells would puncture light plastic film or foil. Seal bag and store in freezer for up to 3 months.

Prawns

Green (uncooked) and cooked Prawns can be stored in refrigerator or freezer. Unless freshly caught by the user, green Prawns are usually dead when delivery is taken; check that they are firm, with a pleasant sea smell and no dark discolouration.

Chilled Storage

Put unshelled green Prawns in a bowl of iced water, cover and store in the refrigerator for up to 3 days. Cooked prawns are also better stored in the shell; place in a container, seal and refrigerate for up to 3 days.

Freezer Storage

Whether cooked or uncooked, leave in the shell, place in a freezer container and cover with cold water. Container should only be three-quarters filled with Prawns, and allow 2cm (¾ inch) head space when adding water. Seal and store in freezer for up to 3 months.

Molluscs

Abalone, Mussels and Oysters

If still in the shell, these should not be stored in the refrigerator as the cold will kill them. Store as follows:

Abalone
In a deep-sided container covered with a Hessian bag soaked in seawater. Store in a cool place for up to 5 days.

Mussels
In damp Hessian bag, in bucket of freshwater, saltwater or seawater, or in a bowl covered with a wet cloth. Store in a cool place for up to 3 days.

Oysters
In damp Hessian bag in a cool place for up to 1 week.

Chilled Storage

Place cleaned Abalone in an airtight container and store in the refrigerator for up to 3 days.

Uncooked Mussels should not be stored in the refrigerator. Cover Oysters on half shell with greaseproof paper and top with a wet cloth; store in refrigerator for up to 2 days, replacing wet cloth when necessary. Bottled Oysters in their liquid will keep for 7-10 days in refrigerator.

Freezer Storage

For cleaned Abalone and shelled Mussels, pack in freezer bags, extract air, seal and label. Store in freezer for up to 3 months. Remove Oysters from shell and place in icecube trays, adding a little diluted lemon juice over each lot of Oysters. When frozen, unmould and pack in freezer bags. Store for up to 3 months.

Clams, Cockles, Pipis and Scallops

These can stay alive in the refrigerator if carefully stored. Scallops are usually available already shelled; check that they have not been frozen if you plan to store them in the freezer.

Chilled Storage

Place the live shellfish in a colander and put this in a larger bowl. Cover top of shellfish with a wet cloth and store in refrigerator for up to 2 days, replacing wet cloth when necessary. Store fresh Scallop meat in an airtight container for up to 3 days.

Freezer Storage

All should be removed from their shells for freezer storage. Place in freezer containers in meal-size portions, seal, label and store for up to 3 months.

Cephalopods

Cuttlefish, Octopus and Squid

Should be stored raw. Prepare before storage according to directions on page 315.

Chilled Storage

Place on a plate and cover with plastic wrap, or put in a sealed container and store in refrigerator for up to 3 days.

Freezer Storage

Place in freezer bags in meal portions, expel air, seal and label. Store in freezer for up to 3 months.

Nature could freeze any catch caught at Cradle Mountain National Park, Tas.

Calorie Guide

*T*oday, people are becoming more aware of the dangers of being overweight or obese . . .

A healthy display of calories.

Obesity can lead to many serious conditions such as high blood pressure, heart conditions and gall bladder ailments. While it is not intended to make you paranoid about what you eat, this calorie (kilojoule) guide will assist you to reduce your calorie (kilojoule) intake by avoiding foods which are high in calories (kilojoules) and selecting those which are lower — usually high calorie (kilojoule) foods are rich in fats and sugar and should be avoided in the daily diet. If you indulge in some rich cake or pie, which often happens when attending a party, you can balance it out by selecting low calorie foods for the next day or two.

All Seafood, fruit and vegetable figures are for the raw product unless otherwise stated. Add extra calories (kilojoules) if the product is fried in shortening or has an accompanying sauce.

Included in this guide is a cross section of species as well as the average fish and shellfish figures.

Food	Calories	Kilojoules
Almonds, shelled, 30g	180	750
Apple, medium, 150g	79	33
Apricots, medium, 50g	16	65
Asparagus, approx. 5 spears	17	70
Avocado, ½ medium, 100g	190	805
Banana, 1 medium, 100g	58	245
Beef fillet, raw, 100g	124	520
Beer, 1 glass, 200mL	80	335
Berry pie, 1 serve	400	1674
Berries, fresh, black and blue, ½ cup	64	268
Black fish, 100g	102	425
Brandy, 30mL	66	275
Brazil nuts, 30g	191	800

Food	Calories	Kilojoules
Bread, regular white slice, 33g	80	335
regular brown slice, 33g	80	335
Bream, steamed, 100g	101	425
Butter, 1 teaspoon	35	145
Cake, cheese, 5cm (2 inch) slice	350	146
chocolate layer, 5cm (2 inch) slice	400	1674
Calamari, fried, 100g	280	1170
Cantaloupe (Rockmelon), 350g	48	205
Carrot, 100g	36	150
Cashew nuts, roasted, 30g	172	720
Caviar, 5g	13	55
Champagne, 120mL	91	380
Cheese, camembert, 30g	96	400
cheddar, 30g	120	505
cottage, plain, 30g	45	191
cream, 30g	103	435
parmesan, 30g	138	580
Chocolate, dairy milk, 50g	263	1100
Cider (strongbow) dry, 200mL	74	310
sweet, 200mL	97	405
Cod, 100g	76	320
Cream, 35% fat, ½ cup	456	1910
sour, ½ cup	416	1740
Custard apple, 100g	53	220
Dates, 5 pitted	85	360
Egg, 55g whole raw	78	325
boiled or poached	78	325
white only	16	65
yolk only	62	260
Fish average, 100g	100	420
Flathead, 100g	90	380
Flounder, 100g	79	330

Food	Calories	Kilojoules
French dressing, 1 tablespoon	77	320
Gelatine, 30g	110	460
Gemfish, 100g	130	550
Ghee, 1 tablespoon	180	755
Grapefruit, 150g	28	115
Grapefruit juice, fresh, 150mL	55	230
Grapes, 20 medium, 100g	63	260
Honey, 1 tablespoon, 30g	97	405
Jelly dessert, 100g	64	268
Jewfish, 100g	85	360
John Dory, 100g	90	380
Kingfish, 100g	95	399
Kiwifruit, 1 medium, 100g	42	180
Leather Jacket (Ocean), 100g	85	350
Lemon juice, fresh, 150mL	41	170
Ling, 100g	70	300
Lobster, flesh, 100g	85	360
Luderick (Blackfish), 100g	105	450
Lychee, 4 medium, 100g	40	205
Mackerel, 100g	188	785
Mandarin, 1 medium, 100g	29	120
Mango, 125g	53	220
Margarine, 1 teaspoon	35	145
Milk, whole, 200mL	138	560
skim, 200mL	66	275
Muffin, English, 1 whole	145	610
Mullet, whole, 100g	75	315
fillet, 100g	137	575
Mushrooms, button, 100g	24	100
Oatmeal, rolled oats, 100g dry	388	1625
Ocean Perch, 100g	83	350
Octopus, 100g	65	280
Oil, salad & cooking, 1 tablespoon	168	705
Olives, green pickled, 30g	38	160
Orange, 1 medium, 200g	60	250
Orange juice, fresh, 150mL	65	271
Oyster, 1 dozen medium, 120g	82	340
Passionfruit, 50g	10	40
Pasta, boiled 200g	228	995
Pastry, raw biscuit, 100g	520	2180
raw flaky, 100g	405	1695
raw puff, 100g	475	1985
Pawpaw, 200g	41	170
Peanut Butter, 1 tablespoon (21g)	125	525
Pear, 150g	73	305
Persimmon, 100g	46	190
Pineapple, 1 slice, 80g	21	85
Port, 60mL	94	395
Potato, boiled, 100g	80	335
Potatoes, french fried, 10 pieces	155	649
Prawn, cooked school, 100g flesh	95	400
cooked king, 100g flesh	100	410
Prunes, dried, 3-4 medium	76	320
Raisins, 2 tablespoons	84	350
Redfish, 100g	120	500
Rice, brown boiled, 175g	210	880
white boiled, 160g	171	715

Food	Calories	Kilojoules
Sea Bream (Morwong), 100g	85	360
Shark, average, 100g	110	460
Sherry, dry, 60mL	67	280
sweet, 60mL	88	365
Snapper, 100g flesh	90	380
Sole, 100g	79	330
Salmon, raw, 100g	175	740
baked, 100g	182	760
smoked, 100g	175	740
Scallops, 100g	80	335
Shellfish, average, 100g	85	355
Squid, 100g	75	320
Strawberries, 100g	36	150
Sugar, castor, 1 tablespoon (20g)	78	325
icing, 1 tablespoon (15g)	59	245
brown, 1 tablespoon (15g)	55	230
raw, 1 tablespoon (20g)	75	315
Teraglin, 100g	85	360
Tofu (soy bean curd), 100g	72	300
Trevally, 100g	105	450
Trout, Rainbow, 100g	195	815
smoked, 100g	107	450
Tuna, 100g	98	410
Walnuts, shelled, 30g	195	815
White sauce, ¼ cup	106	444
Whiting (sand), 100g	88	370
Wine, red, 120mL	82	345
dry white, 120mL	79	330
sweet white, 120mL	113	475
Yellowtail, 100g	130	540
Yoghurt, natural, 200g	110	465

Group fishing, a great way to keep fit.

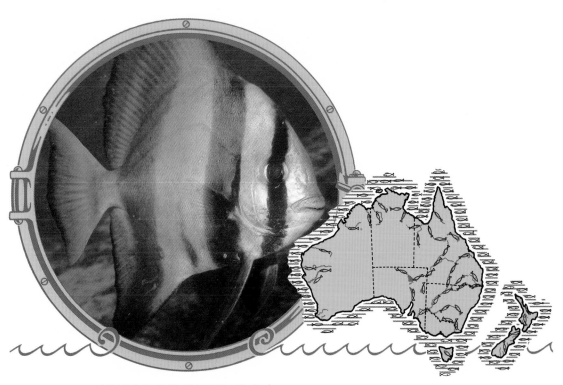

A Bat Fish, North West Island, New Zealand.

Glossary

Arrowroot
Starch used as a binder or thickener.

Aspic
A savoury jelly usually made with meat or fish stock and gelatine, chilled and used as a garnish and coating.

Bisque
A thick cream soup especially of puréed seafood or vegetables.

Blanch
To heat briefly in boiling water.

Bleed
To cause fish to lose blood as soon as it is caught. Cut the "throat" at the juncture of the gills and snap the head back. This improves the flavour of certain fish.

Blind Bake
Or bake blind. To line a pastry case with greased greaseproof paper and fill it with dried beans, rice, macaroni or special weights (ceramic or metal), so that shape it kept until pastry sets in the initial baking. The paper and weights are removed and the case returned to the oven to dry out before filling is added, or to complete cooking if a cooked pastry case is required. Dried beans, rice or macaroni should be stored in a container and used again for the same purpose.

Brackish
Slightly saltwater, such as near river mouths where the sea water mingles with the fresh.

Broil
See Grill.

Capsicum
Sweet green or red pepper, bell pepper.

Cardamom
The aromatic seeds of a tropical Asian plant, of the ginger family, used as a spice.

Castor Sugar
Fine, white granulated sugar used in baking in Australia, New Zealand and the U.K. North American granulated sugar is fine enough for this purpose.

Chowder
A thick soup or stew made of clams, fish or vegetables and seasonings.

Ciguatera
A toxin found in certain fish from coral reef waters. Smaller fish take in the toxin when feeding on organisms found on damaged coral. Larger fish feed on the smaller fish, and in turn the toxin is transferred. Most of the fish which may be implicated are not used for the table; however a few are, such as Groper, members of the Mackerel family and Coral Trout. It is just as well to prefer the smaller of these fish for the table, particularly if known to come from waters which harbour the organism in the coral.

Crouton
A small piece of fried or toasted bread, sometimes seasoned, used as a garnish for soups, salads and other dishes.

Copha
Also known as copha butter in Australia and New Zealand. It is a white vegetable shortening made from coconut oil. Where copha is not available, substitute coconut oil, or use a vegetable shortening for savoury foods.

Deep-fry
To fry in a quantity of oil or fat, sufficient to allow the food to float during frying, so that the coating becomes crisp and golden as the food it encloses is cooked.

Dredge
To sprinkle or coat with some powdered substance, especially flour.

Whisk
To beat with a wire balloon whisk either to mix ingredients quickly and thoroughly, or to incorporate air into a mixture.

Zest
The thin outer skin or peel of citrus fruits which contains the essential flavouring oils. Also called rind.

Endive
A plant often having a rosette of curly-edged leaves used in salads.

Flake
Refers to the texture of the flesh of fish when cooked; breaks into fine, medium or large flake when the flesh is broken apart with a fork.

Flambé
To pour liqueur over and ignite.

Ghee
Pure butter fat with no buttermilk residue or salt. It is a clear, golden oil when melted and can be heated to a higher temperature than butter. Clarified butter (melted butter with froth skimmed off and the clear oil poured from the sediment) can be substituted.

Green
A term used to indicate uncooked crustaceans.

Grill
To cook under a grill unit. In North America, the term 'broil' is used for this method of cooking, while 'grill' refers to cooking on the grill or grid of a barbecue.

Julienne
To cut into thin strips or small, matchlike pieces.

Liverwurst
A sausage made with a large percentage of liver, especially with pork liver and pork meat.

Marinade
A flavoured liquid into which food is placed for some time to give it more flavour and to tenderize it.

Marinate
To allow food to stand in a marinade.

Mask
To cover or coat cooked food evenly with a sauce, mayonnaise or jelly.

Melba toast
Slices of thin, crisp toast.

Meunière
Especially fish, dipped in flour, sautéed in butter and sprinkled with lemon juice and chopped parsley.

Oyster mushroom
An edible, brownish-grey to white mushroom, that grows in clusters on fallen trees and their stumps.

Parboil
To boil food for a short time or until partially cooked.

Pimiento
Red capsicum or sweet red (bell) pepper, either raw or skinned and packed in cans for use in cooking or as a garnish.

Plankton
Small animal and plant organisms that float or drift in the water, especially at or near the surface, on which many forms of sea life feed.

Poach
To cook gently in simmering liquid.

Prawn
Known elsewhere as 'Shrimp', especially in North America where 'Prawn' refers to a freshwater crustacean. King Prawn is Jumbo Shrimp.

Purée

A food especially vegetable or fruit, that has been put through a sieve, blender or the like.

Reduce

To evaporate liquid from, usually by boiling.

Ramekin

A small dish in which food can be cooked and served.

Roux

A mixture of butter and flour which forms the basis for most sauces.

Scald

Pour boiling water over items such as vegetable or fruit leaves in order to soften them sufficiently for use as a wrapping. Also to heat liquid to just below boiling point.

Shallot

A long green onion closely related to the spring onion, except that it is evenly slender and not bulbous at the end.

Green onion, scallion and spring onion are alternative names. Some of the green top should be used as well as the white section. While shallot is a popular term in Australia and New Zealand, it is not technically correct. A true shallot (or eschallot) is a small, brown-skinned onion shaped like a large garlic clove as it grows in clumps similarly to garlic.

Shallow-Fry

To fry in a quantity of oil or fat which allows food to be half immersed.

Simmer

To cook food in liquid just below boiling point. The bubbles should form slowly and just break the surface.

Silverbeet

A member of the beet family, also known as Swiss Chard elsewhere. It is often used in place of spinach; in fact it is often called spinach. However it is not related and the flavour

is quite different. Leaves should be removed from the white stalks, and the white rib cut out. Stalks and ribs can be used as a separate vegetable.

Skim

To remove fat or scum from the surface of liquid.

Spinach

Also known as English spinach. Leaves are long and slender and stalks are tender. Usually roots are attached, and these should be cut off in preparation. The leaves and tender stalks are both used and should be cooked together.

Steep

Pour hot or cold water over food, allowing it to stand to either soften it or to extract flavour and colour.

Toss

To stir or mix lightly until the ingredients are coated with the dressing (eg salad).

Tureen

A large, deep, covered dish for serving soup, stew and other foods.

Vandyke

The cutting of food such as citrus fruits, tomato, melon etc. with deep points for a decorative effect. Make a series of even, V-shaped cuts around the circumference of the fruit with a sharp-pointed knife, cutting into the centre. Pull the two halves apart carefully.

Waterbath

A roasting dish of warm or hot water in which a dish (or small dishes) containing prepared food is placed for oven cooking, so that the food cooks gently without the outside of the food drying out. The water should come half-way up the sides of the dish or dishes of food.

Hikers on the banks of the Tasman clear water stream near Mt Cook, New Zealand.

Weighing fish at Hamilton Marina, Qld.

Weights and Measures

M etric measurements are now used in Australia, but there are still many amongst us who relate better to the Imperial measures, that is the use of ounces and pounds. The tables on these pages will assist those who may still be confused.

Ingredients such as seafood and vegetables are often given in weights. However, a little more or less of grams or ounces will not affect the success of the recipe. Only structured recipes such as cakes, pastry, biscuits, breads and the like need accurate measurements. Australian standard 250ml cup, 20ml tablespoon and 5ml teaspoon have been used to test the recipes. The recipes will work just as well with the U.S. or Canadian 8oz cup or the

U.K. 300ml cup. Graded cup measures have been used in preference to tablespoon measures so that proportions will remain the same. Where tablespoon measures have been given, the smaller U.S. or U.K. tablespoon measure will not affect the recipe's success as these are not crucial measures. However, if accuracy is necessary for structured recipes, use 1 U.S. tablespoon (14.8mls) plus 1 teaspoon (5mls) for every Australian tablespoon (20mls).

Measures English and American

ENGLISH

All measurements similar to Australian with two exceptions; the English cup measures 10 fluid ounces (300ml), whereas the Australian cup measure is 8 fluid ounces (250ml). The English tablespoon measures 14.8ml against the Australian tablespoon of 20ml.

AMERICAN

The American reputed pint is 16 fluid ounces, a quart 32 fluid ounces, a gallon 128 fluid ounces. The Imperial measurement is 20 fluid ounces to the pint, 40 fluid ounces a quart and 160 fluid ounces one gallon. The American tablespoon is equal to 14.8ml, the teaspoon is 5ml. The cup measure is 8 fluid ounces (250ml) the same as Australia.

Cup Measurements

One cup is equal to the following weights.

	Metric	Imperial
Breadcrumbs, packet	125 g	4 oz
Breadcrumbs, soft	60 g	2 oz
Cheese, grated	125 g	4 oz
Coconut, desiccated	75 g	2½ oz
Flour	125 g	4 oz
Fruit, dried (mixed, sultanas etc)	125 g	4 oz
Honey, treacle, golden syrup	315 g	10 oz
Nuts, chopped	125 g	4 oz
Rice, cooked	155 g	5 oz
Rice, uncooked	185 g	6 oz
Shortening (butter, margarine)	250 g	8 oz
Sugar, brown	155 g	5 oz
Sugar, granulated or castor	250 g	8 oz
Sugar, sifted icing	155 g	5 oz

Dry Measures

All the measures are level, so when you have filled a cup or spoon, level it off with the edge of a knife. The following scale is the "cook's" equivalent, it is not an exact conversion of metric to imperial measurement.

METRIC	IMPERIAL
g = grams	oz = ounces
kg = kilograms	lb = pounds
15 g	½ oz
20 g	⅔ oz
30 g	1 oz
60 g	2 oz
90 g	3 oz
125 g	4 oz (¼ lb)
155 g	5 oz
185 g	6 oz
220 g	7 oz
250 g	8 oz (½ lb)
280 g	9 oz
315 g	10 oz
345 g	11 oz
375 g	12 oz (¾ lb)
410 g	13 oz
440 g	14 oz
470 g	15 oz
500 g (0.5 kg)	16 oz (1 lb)
750 g (0.75 kg)	24 oz (1½ lb)
1000 g (1 kg)	32 oz (2 lb)
1.5 kg	3 lb
2 kg	4 lb

Liquid Measures

Metric ml millilitres	Imperial fl oz	Cup & Spoon fluid ounce
5 ml	16 fl oz	1 teaspoon
20 ml	⅔ fl oz	1 tablespoon
30 ml	1 fl oz	1 tablespoon plus 2 teaspoons
60 ml	2 fl oz	¼ cup
85 ml	2½ fl oz	⅓ cup
100 ml	3 fl oz	
125 ml	4 fl oz	½ cup
150 ml	5 fl oz	(¼ pint) 1 gill
180 ml	6 fl oz	¾ cup
250 ml	8 fl oz	1 cup
300 ml	10 fl oz	(½ pint)
360 ml	12 fl oz	1½ cups
420 ml	14 fl oz	1¾ cups
500 ml	16 fl oz	2 cups
600 ml	20 fl oz	(1 pint) 2½ cups
1 litre	35 fl oz	(1¾ pints) 4 cups

Standard teaspoon measures in Australia, New Zealand, U.S.A., Canada and U.K. are 5 ml in capacity or 1/6 of a fluid ounce.

Oven Temperatures

The centigrade temperatures given here are not exact; they have been rounded off and give a guide only. Follow the manufacturer's temperature guide, relating it to oven description given in the recipe. Remember gas ovens are hottest at the top, electric ovens at the bottom and convection-fan forced ovens are usually even throughout. We have also included Regulo numbers for gas cookers which may assist.

	C	F	Regulo
Very Slow	120	250	1
Slow	150	300	2
Moderately slow	160	325	3
Moderate	180	350	4
Moderately hot	190/200	370/400	5/6
Hot	210/220	410/440	6/7
Very hot	230	450	8
Super hot	250/290	475/550	9/10

Loaf Pan Sizes

Metric	Imperial
23 x 12 cm	9 x 5 in
25 x 8 cm	10 x 3 in
28 x 18 cm	11 x 7 in

Length

In this book we have used both metric and imperial measurements. The measures have been rounded off to the easiest-to-use and most acceptable figures.

Metric	Imperial
mm = millimetres	in = inches
cm = centimetres	ft = feet
5 mm .5 cm	¼ in
10 mm 1.0 cm	½ in
20 mm 2.0 cm	¾ in
25 mm 2.5 cm	1 in
5 cm	2 in
8 cm	3 in
10 cm	4 in
12 cm	5 in
15 cm	6 in
18 cm	7 in
20 cm	8 in
23 cm	9 in
25 cm	10 in
28 cm	11 in
30 cm	12 in (1ft)

Cake Pan Sizes

(Measurements relate to diameter.)

Metric	Imperial
15 cm	6 in
18 cm	7 in
20 cm	8 in
23 cm	9 in

Goulburns' Big Marino Aerodrome, NSW.

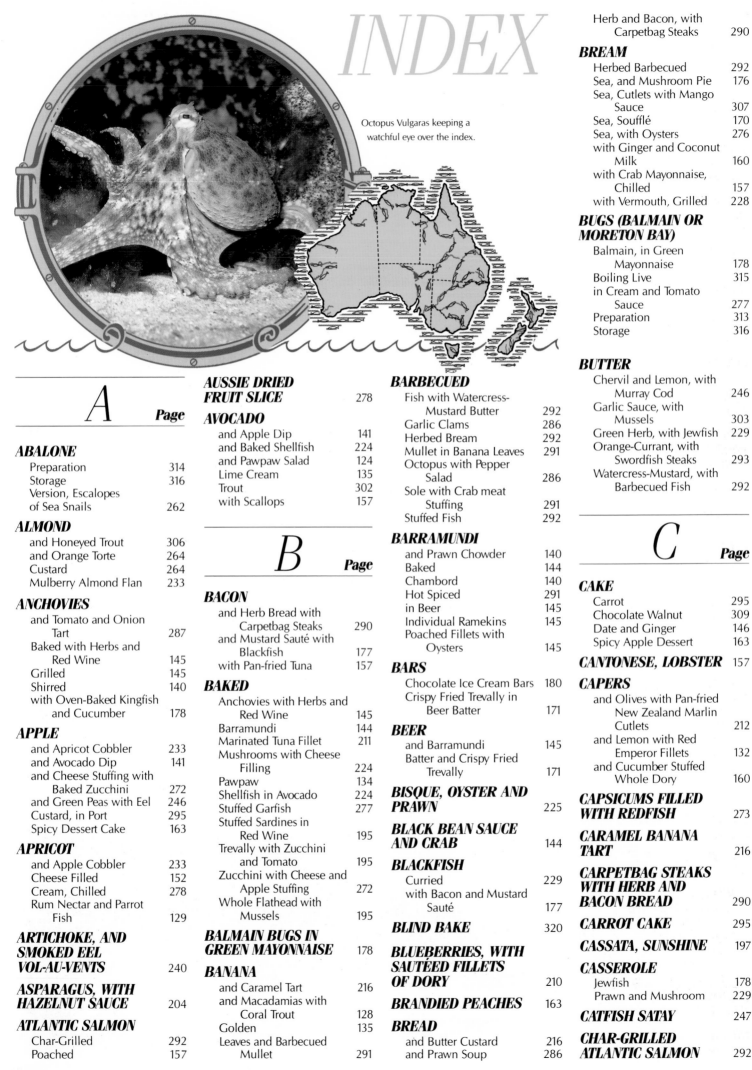

INDEX

Octopus Vulgaras keeping a watchful eye over the index.

D **Page**

Smooth corals in peaceful surrounds.

Ettamogah Pub, a great tourist attraction on the Sunshine Coast, Qld.

'Family fishing fun'.

Morning fog rises from reflections in the Victoria River, N.T.

'What a catch'.

Tourist boat, 'The Lady Stelfox' in a regal gorge at Launceston, Tas.

Pictorial Credits

Mike Cook's Fishworks, a seafood lover's paradise.

PHOTOGRAPHS SUPPLIED BY:
AUSTRALIAN PICTURE LIBRARY

Photographers:

David BALL	Noeline KELLY
Tsuneo NAKAMURA	Roger GARWOOD
ZEFA	Richard EASTWOOD
Fritz PRENZEL	Gary LEWIS
John BAKER	ORION
John CARNEMOLLA	Herb PARKIN
Doug & Ruby SPOWART	Aureo MARTELLI
Charles COPELAND	MIDDENWAY & JONES
Alan JONES	L & B HEMMINGS
Ron DORMAN	Robert BERTHOLD
Robert GREY	Lindon SCHICK
Owen HUGHES	Steve VIDLER
Dallas & John HEATON	Lesley DOWNIE
John MILES	N. QUINN

Pages include:

12-13, 18-19, 22, 23, 28 x 2, 29, 32-33, 35, 48-49, 51, 52-53, 57, 59, 63, 69, 64-65, 71, 73, 75, 81, 91, 92-93, 94, 95, 96-97, 105, 107, 109, 113, 115, 117, 120-121, 133, 142-143, 146, 154-155, 158-159, 160, 164-165, 166, 174-175, 177, 179, 182-183, 200, 208-209, 214-215, 216, 230, 234-235, 240, 244-245, 254-255, 260-261, 266-267, 268, 280-281, 284-285, 300-301, 310-311, 313, 314, 316, 317, 318, 319, 320, 321, 322, 323, 324, 325, 327, 329, 330-331, 333, 334.

A.M. PICTURE LIBRARY

Photographers:

Stuart Owen FOX	Richard WOLDENDORP
Mike SCOTLAND	Anjee CARR
Noeline KELLY	David BEAL
Leigh HEMMINGS	Robert BERTHOLD
Philip QUIRK	Ross ISAACS

Pages include:

4-5, 6-7, 14-15, 16-17, 26-27, 36-37, 39, 42, 44-45, 47, 62, 68-69, 72-73, 76-77, 86, 88-89, 90, 99, 111, 116, 116-117, 126-127, 166, 168-169, 186-187, 192-193, 202-203, 204, 218-219, 238-239, 250-251, 252, 282, 296-297.

AUSTRALASIAN MARINE

Photographer:

Neville COLEMAN

Pages include:
30, 119.

IMAGE BANK

Photographers:

Peter HENDRIE	Robbi NEWMAN
John CALLANAN	J. JANOCINSKI
Marc ROMANELLI	Michael COYNE
John BANAGAN	

Pages include:

10-11, 58, 104, 122, 220 x 2, 222-223, 270-271, 291, 298.

INDEPENDENT PHOTOGRAPHERS:

Hugh EDWARDS

Pages include:

Cover x 3, 2-3, 8-9, 25, 28, 37, 41, 43, 49, 56-57, 60-61, 67, 74 x 2, 79, 83, 84-85, 87, 97, 100-101, 102-103, 106, 110-111, 112, 114, 116, 122, 129, 138, 148-149, 150, 152, 180, 184, 188, 198-199, 224, 229, 231, 236, 247, 252, 264, 268, 278, 282, 284-285, 293, 298, 302, 312.

Jane LITTLE

Pages include:

24, 27, 31, 34, 38, 40-41, 45, 46, 50, 53, 54, 55, 61, 65, 70, 77, 78, 85, 86, 89, 103, 138, 140, 145, 170, 216, 233, 256.

AQUATIC PHOTOGRAPHICS:

Rudie H. KUITER

Pages include:

20-21, 24, 26, 30 x 2, 32, 34, 36, 38, 40, 42, 44, 46, 48, 50, 52, 58, 60, 64, 66, 68 x 2, 70, 72, 76, 78, 80 x 3, 82, 84, 88, 100, 102 x 2, 104, 108 x 3, 110, 112, 114, 226-227, 136-137.

AUSTRALIAN WILDLIFE PHOTOGRAPHY:

Gunther E. SCHMIDA

Pages include:

90, 94, 96, 98, 106.

Acknowledgements

The Publishers wish to thank their families and the many other people for making this book so successful:

Especially in production:

Gasgraphics TGC Pty. Ltd.
Unit D-105-117 Asquith St.
Auburn. NSW 2144.
Kathryn Munro
Patricia Schmelzenbert
Rachel Keen
Tina Clerk

Anthony Villani & Ass. Pty. Ltd.
29 Bellevue St.,
Surry Hills. NSW 2010.

Intertype Pty. Ltd.
61 Albion St.,
Surry Hills. NSW 2010.

Laser Typesetting
44A Foveaux St.,
Surry Hills. NSW 2010.

Mike Cook's Fishworks
544 Sydney Road,
Seaforth. NSW 2092.

Suppliers:

Arena's Fruit and Vegetable Shop – Mosman
Bond's Nursery – Terry Hills
Aquarium Livestock – Balgowlah
Sula Marina – Mona Vale
Australian Fly Fishermen – Rushcutters Bay
Brookvale Sand Company – Brookvale
Hudsons Timber – Brookvale
Country Floors – Willoughby
Waterford Wedgwood – Castle Hill

Noritake (Australia) – Botany
Villeroy and Boch (Australia) – Brookvale
Mikasa Tableware Pty. Ltd. – Edgecliff
Limoges (Australia) – Crows Nest
Primo Imports – Brookvale
The Lilac Bush – Mosman
Apply Hoare Antiques – Woollahra
Rousel Screen Printing Pty. Ltd. – Surry Hills